The Observer's Pocket Series

ASSOCIATION FOOTBALL

The Observer Books

A POCKET REFERENCE SERIES COVERING
A WIDE RANGE OF SUBJECTS

Natural History

BIRDS
BIRDS' EGGS
BUTTERFLIES
LARGER MOTHS
COMMON INSECTS
WILD ANIMALS
ZOO ANIMALS
WILD FLOWERS
GARDEN FLOWERS
FLOWERING TREES AND SHRUBS
HOUSE PLANTS
CACTI
TREES
GRASSES
FERNS
COMMON FUNGI
LICHENS
POND LIFE
FRESHWATER FISHES
SEA FISHES
SEA AND SEASHORE
GEOLOGY
ASTRONOMY
WEATHER
CATS
DOGS
HORSES AND PONIES

Transport

AIRCRAFT
AUTOMOBILES
COMMERCIAL VEHICLES
SHIPS
MANNED SPACEFLIGHT
UNMANNED SPACEFLIGHT
BRITISH STEAM LOCOMOTIVES

The Arts etc.

ARCHITECTURE
CATHEDRALS
CHURCHES
HERALDRY
FLAGS
PAINTING
MODERN ART
SCULPTURE
FURNITURE
POTTERY AND PORCELAIN
MUSIC
POSTAGE STAMPS
BRITISH AWARDS AND MEDALS

Sport

ASSOCIATION FOOTBALL
CRICKET

Cities

LONDON

The Observer's Book of
ASSOCIATION
FOOTBALL

ALBERT SEWELL

WITH 16 COLOUR PLATES AND
42 BLACK AND WHITE ILLUSTRATIONS

FREDERICK WARNE & CO LTD
FREDERICK WARNE & CO INC
LONDON   NEW YORK

© Frederick Warne & Co Ltd
London, England
1974

First Edition 1972
Second Edition 1974

Library of Congress
Catalog Card No.: 72–81144
ISBN 7232 1536 7

Filmset by Keyspools Ltd, Golborne, Lancs
Printed in Great Britain by
Tinling (1973) Limited, Prescot
Merseyside
1449.474

Contents

Foreword by Sir Alf Ramsey	7
The History of the Game	9
Guide to the 92 Football League Clubs in England and Wales	16
The Scottish League	108
Prominent European Clubs	120
World Stars of 1974–75	130
The World Cup	140
The European Championship	155
The European Cup	156
The European Cup-Winners' Cup	159
The U.E.F.A. Cup	162
The World Club Championship	165
Records Section:	
England's Complete Record in Full Internationals	166
Football League Champions and their Records	179
F.A. Cup Winners	181
Football League Cup Winners	186
Scottish League Champions	187
Scottish F.A. Cup Winners	188
Scottish League Cup Winners	191
The Field of Play	192

Acknowledgements

The author and publishers wish to thank the following for their kind permission to reproduce photographs: Syndication International, page 7, 130 (both), 131 (right), 132 (left), 133 (both), 134 (both), 135 (both), 136 (both), 137 (both), 138 (left), 139 (right) and Plate 13; Eric Batty page 131 (left), 132 (right), 138 (right), 139 (left); The Press Association Ltd, page 140 (left), 156 and Plates 3, 8, 10, 11, 12 and 14; The Associated Press Ltd, page 140 (right) and Plate 7; Hayters, Plate 15 (left and right), Sports Press Pictures, page 159; Topix, page 162; W. Pilkington, Plate 1; Colorsport, Plate 2; Arsenal Football Club, Plate 4; Sport and General Press Agency Ltd, Plate 5; Central Press Photos Ltd, Plate 6; Fox Photos Ltd, Plate 15 (centre); Sports Press Pictures, Plate 16.

Foreword
by Sir Alf Ramsey

For many years I have admired *The Observer's Pocket Series* because of the visual and technical detail which the books provide for those anxious to widen their knowledge. Yet I have sometimes thought it a pity that such a diverse and compact library of information did not embrace sport in its varying aspects.

Clearly, others held similar views and so I was naturally pleased that, in acknowledging the demand for an extension of their work into this field, the publishers should choose to kick off, so to speak, with Association Football.

The game, for me, has been a way of life since my formative years as a lad at school in Essex. Indeed, outside my home it is my constant companion.

Football is one of the truly international sports and its growth is reflected in the enormous appeal which the World Cup competitions now make among the 145 member countries which form the *Fédération Internationale de Football Association*.

Each era produces its own greatness, and comparisons between players of different periods are profitless exercises. Nevertheless, there has been a notable advance in the scientific development of football tactics during the past decade. The trained condition of players at top professional level has never been higher; their equipment, supervision and rewards are all first class and the modern footballers are now very much an integral part of the community.

I have been fortunate to know closely many of these players, more particularly, of course, those who have represented England since I was appointed team manager in

October 1962. Their qualities of loyalty, responsibility and, above all, self-control in testing circumstances, provide me with some of my most rewarding memories.

From time to time I read and hear criticism that some of the players selected for international duty are getting on in years. I would say that the age of a player is not important in itself. Far more important, to my mind, is his performance. Football at the highest reaches is a game which demands *experience*. You need only examine the most consistently successful teams in our own League competition to realize that.

I hope your interest will be stimulated by this *Observer Book of Association Football*, with its International, European and other splendidly informative sections, not least the club histories and well-tabulated records.

Most of all I commend its sensible size and illustrative format which is a hallmark of this particular series. It deserves to become the pocket companion of all those who enjoy and support this great game of ours.

The History of the Game

It is impossible to say exactly when football began, because its origins are lost, literally, in the mists of time. Some say men (and women) first began kicking 'an object' around as far back as the twelfth century. Perhaps they did, but it took a long time for the game to become organized.

The first real stirrings were in the middle of last century, when boys at established English public schools, and at universities such as Cambridge, began to play a form of soccer which at least bore some resemblance to our modern game. It is surprising that a game thought of mainly as a working man's pastime should have originated in the very bastions of the so-called privileged classes.

However, such was the popularity of football that it was not long before it appealed to a wider audience. The oldest Football League club was founded in 1862—26 years before the inauguration of the League itself—Notts County, who came into existence three years before their arch-rivals Nottingham Forest.

The following year, 1863, saw the formation of the Football Association—in a public house in central London. This was the world's first organized attempt at controlling the game at national level, and it was from the new body's title that As**soc**iation football, or **soc**cer, got its name.

Many people north of the Border believe that Scotland, not England, gave football to the world. With due respect to the Scots, who have contributed so much to the game, this is not so. The first Scottish club, the famous and once powerful Queen's Park, did not appear on the field until 1867, and the Scottish Football Association waited until 1873 for its inception.

One major difference between Notts County and Queen's Park was that while both started life as amateur organizations, the English club had turned professional by 1885. The Scots remained amateur, and today they alone among Britain's League clubs play strictly 'for fun'. Incidentally, it is an odd twist that they also play in Britain's biggest stadium, the 135,000-capacity Hampden Park in Glasgow.

Brazil, West Germany, Hungary may come and go. England and Scotland go on for ever in the International soccer sense, despite misguided attempts in the past to belittle the annual clash between these two. The first match was played in November 1872, in Glasgow, and resulted in a goalless draw (it was to be 98 years before the next similar result).

Irish soccer is one province in which that country's traditional luck usually deserts it. A small country to start with, Ireland suffers even more by having to supply players for two International sides—Northern Ireland and the Republic of Ireland. In February 1882, long before the partition, an all-Ireland side played England for the first time and crashed by the improbable score of 13–0 in Belfast. This is still a record for any British International match, and is not likely to be broken.

At this period, new developments in the game were coming thick and fast as its popularity spread rapidly. The official Home International Championship was first played for in the season 1883–84 and Scotland had a clean sweep, winning all three matches. In 1885 professionalism was legalized in English soccer, and a year later Arbroath carved their own slice of history by winning a Scottish Cup tie 36–0 against the luckless, and long-since defunct Bon Accord. This remains the highest score in any official senior football match in Britain. The present-day off-side law and the system of early-round elimination of weak teams both help to ensure that this kind of farce will never be seen again.

In October 1887, Preston North End made a brave effort to challenge Arbroath's feat when they annihilated Hyde 26–0 in an F.A. Cup match. Whether the Preston players had their eye on the record will never be known, but they certainly had no mercy on poor Hyde.

Soccer moved fast in the eighties. The Football League was formed in 1888 and for those who wonder why it should be honoured with the title *The* Football League, and not the English Football League, the answer is that it was the first such body in the world.

How many of today's soccer followers can reel off the names of those famous twelve clubs which formed the basis of what has become the world's greatest league competition? They were Accrington, Aston Villa, Blackburn Rovers, Bolton Wanderers, Burnley, Derby County, Everton, Notts County, Preston North End, Stoke City, West Bromwich Albion and Wolverhampton Wanderers. Of that number, only Accrington are not still members; they left the League in March 1962, after struggling through the years since the Second World War as Accrington Stanley, and are now to be found playing in the Lancashire Combination.

In 1970 two other founder members, Aston Villa and

Preston, were relegated to Division Three for the first time in their history. The following year Blackburn Rovers went down for the first time, along with Bolton, another of the famous originals. Such is the swing of fortune in soccer across the decades.

Modern fans think of Tottenham Hotspur in 1961 and Arsenal ten years later as the 'double clubs', i.e. those which have won both the League Championship and the F.A. Cup in the same season. But as long ago as 1888–89, the year in which the League began, Preston won the Cup without conceding a goal, and the Championship without losing a game. This was quite an achievement, even if competition was a lot less fierce in those days, and Aston Villa were the only other side before Tottenham, in 1960–61, to win both trophies in one season. They did it in the season 1896–97.

Floodlights are regarded as one of the wonders of modern soccer. But how many people realize that matches were being played under artificial light long before the end of last century? The first reference to a 'floodlit' game is found in records dated 1887, which tells of a game being played at Sheffield by *candlelight*! This is a difficult scene to imagine, but the players must have managed somehow.

As the nineteenth century drew to a close, the game continued to boom. Attendances rose each year, and while there was no sign yet of international competition against foreign opponents, the game was slowly being introduced abroad.

It is impossible to tell when football was first taught to other countries—to the Brazilians for example—but we do know that British sailors had a lot to do with it. The British Navies, Royal and Merchant, were at the height of their power and influence in the fifty years between 1875 and 1925, and it was during this half century that the game was taken round the world. Sailors on leave abroad often played football among themselves; local inhabitants watched with interest, learned quickly, and soon challenged the soccer 'missionaries' and sometimes beat them.

The first International match between England and a foreign country took place on 6 June 1908. England met Austria in Vienna and won handsomely 6–1. Two days later the teams met again at the same venue and this time the Austrians were beaten 11–1. England then went on to Budapest, and crushed Hungary 7–0, before moving finally to Prague and soundly defeating Bohemia (now Czechoslovakia) 4–0 to end a highly successful first professional tour abroad.

The following year the Austrians invited England back, no doubt hoping for revenge. This time they lost 8–1, so in three games in twelve months against the Austrians, all of them in Vienna, England piled up an aggregate of 25 goals and lost only three. However, and significantly in terms of the improvement in soccer standards abroad, when the teams next met, in May 1930—again in Vienna—there was a goalless draw, and when Austria first played here (at Chelsea in December 1932) England only just scraped home 4–3.

England should have been warned during the year between those two games, when the Scots crashed by a humiliating 5–0 in Vienna!

Despite that 1908 England tour, international football with overseas countries competing did not become established until the early thirties. The 1914–18 War had much to do with that, and throughout the twenties the total of matches played abroad by England was no more than fifteen.

It was not until the summer of 1950 that any British country played a team from the Americas. This was when England participated in the World Cup for the first time. They beat Chile 2–0 in their opening match of the final series in Brazil, but 29 June marked the blackest day in the entire playing history of British soccer. From Belo Horizonte came what must rate as the most fantastic scoreline in the international game: England 0, U.S.A. 1. It was a result which rocked the footballing world. Perhaps the least excited country was the United States itself, so little interest did they show in the game of Association Football.

To the North Americans soccer was, and to a large extent still is, a minority sport, and that freak result was as unlikely as, say England beating the U.S.A. at baseball. But it happened!

This match belongs, however, to soccer's comparatively modern history, and there is reason here to go back to the turn of the century. In the season 1898–99 a feat occurred which almost certainly will never be repeated in British soccer. Rangers, over the years Scotland's most successful club until the modern dominance of Celtic, took the Scottish League title in a canter. They won every one of the 18 games they played in the competition, and even allowing for the relatively low standard of Scottish club soccer, it was a tremendous achievement.

The overall standards of play in Scotland are certainly low. A look at past winners of the Scottish League Championship tells the tale. In 1932 Motherwell won the title for the first and only time. Apart from that year, the championship was shared between Rangers and Celtic from 1904, when it was won by Third Lanark, to 1948 when Hibernian took it. During those years the title went to Rangers no fewer than 20 times, and to Celtic 15. Indeed Motherwell's surprise victory in 1932 prevented what would otherwise have been a run of eight consecutive successes for Rangers.

Rangers' last Championship success in 1964 gave them a world record total of 34 League titles, but since 1965–66 every season has been monopolized by Celtic, and when they triumphed yet again in 1974, they brought Scotland a share in another world record—nine consecutive League Championships—previously held jointly by MTK Budapest, who won the Hungarian title from 1917–25 inclusive, and CDNA Sofia, when they were Champions of Bulgaria from 1954–62.

But if, in the past, Scottish football tended to stagnate because of the great strength of Rangers and Celtic, the game elsewhere grew in power. The development that was to make soccer a world game came in 1904, when F.I.F.A.—the Federation of International Football Associations—was founded in Paris. Seven countries—France, Belgium, Holland, Switzerland, Spain, Denmark and Sweden—were the original members. Today there are 145 members of the world body.

Amateur soccer, or rather a twentieth century version of the original amateur game, came along in 1907 when the Amateur F.A. was formed and the following year Britain put a team in the Olympic Games and won the final at London's White City, beating Denmark 2–0.

The 1914–18 War inevitably caused a major disruption in sport, and football suffered along with the rest. Unlike the 1939–45 War, when unofficial soccer continued as a means of giving the population something else to think about, there was virtually nothing organized. But when the war ended the game soon got back into its stride. A look at the 1920s tells us that. . . . *In 1923* Wembley staged its first Cup Final, with an attendance of 126,000, many of whom stormed the gates and broke in. *In 1926* Huddersfield Town won the League Championship for the third successive year, the first team to do so, and a feat as yet emulated only by Arsenal in 1933–34–35. Huddersfield were also runners-up 1927, and again in 1928, the greatest period in their history.

In 1927 Cardiff City beat Arsenal 1–0 at Wembley and

became the first, and only, side to take the F.A. Cup out of England. This feat is still reckoned to be the most outstanding in Welsh soccer, which has always had to take second place in popularity to rugby. *In 1929* England lost for the first time on foreign soil, Spain triumphing 4–3 in Madrid, and the following year the World Cup was launched.

Uruguay beat Argentina 4–2 in the Final, and South America was on the world soccer map. And so into the thirties.

The record individual number of goals in any British senior League or Cup match was set in April 1936 when Joe Payne, Luton Town centre-forward, scored ten in his club's 12–0 win against Bristol Rovers in a Division 3 match.

A year later the largest crowd ever to watch a match in Britain squeezed into Hampden Park for the Scotland–England International. The official attendance was 149,547, and unless a new stadium is built it is a British record which will never be broken. Still in Scotland, Celtic's Jimmy McGrory retired in 1938 after scoring an all-time record 550 goals in first-class soccer. This was a record for Britain; overseas players have scored more—Brazil's Pele has topped the 1000 mark.

If Scottish club soccer was often overshadowed on the field by its English counterpart, the largest crowds were to be found north of the Border. Manchester United and Arsenal set up the still-existing record for an English League match— 82,950. That was on 17 January 1948, at Maine Road (United were still using Manchester City's ground while their own at Old Trafford was being restored after bomb damage during the War). In March of the same year Rangers and Hibernian met in the Scottish Cup semi-final at Hampden Park in front of 143,570. Then, in the Final, nearly a quarter of a million fans saw the two matches Rangers needed to beat Greenock Morton. Those were the days of the great crowds, after years when people had been starved of top-class competitive football.

Coming more up to date—although that depends to a large extent on the age of the reader—in 1953 Stanley Mortensen scored a hat-trick in the Coronation Year F.A. Cup Final against Bolton Wanderers. He was the first man to achieve such a feat, but even his success was overshadowed by that of his partner, Stanley (now Sir Stanley) Matthews.

Bolton, led by Nat Lofthouse, were 3–1 ahead well into the second half. It seemed all over for Blackpool, and for the great

Matthews who had never won a Cup-winners' medal, and was playing in what was to be his last Final. Then the two Stanleys broke loose. Matthews mesmerized a Bolton side playing one short after injury—there were no substitutes then—and Blackpool triumphed 4–3.

It was a sad ending for Bolton, who have never been quite the same since, but a fairy-tale finish for Blackpool and Stanley Matthews in one of the great all-time F.A. Cup Finals.

The 'Matthews Final' could be regarded as almost the end of an era in British football. Six months later, at Wembley in November 1953, came the 6–3 slaughter of England by Hungary—those magnificent Magyars—which led to a vast re-thinking on the game's tactics and economics.

A new competitive dimension was brought to the game in 1955 with the launching of the European Cup, and both in that and the two other big European tournaments—the Cup-Winners' Cup and Fairs Cup (now the U.E.F.A. Cup) British clubs have figured prominently among the honours, as will be seen from reference to the European section of this book.

One of the most important factors in the revolution within British football was the removal of the maximum wage in 1961. This ensured that our stars did not need to go to Italy to earn salaries commensurate with their skills, as world-class players like John Charles, Denis Law, Jimmy Greaves and others had been disposed to do.

The long-overdue acceptance of substitutes in League football was at last approved in 1965. A year later came the greatest achievement of all for British soccer, with England's triumph at Wembley as host nation in the World Cup. In Mexico in 1970 the world crown was taken by Brazil for the third time. And so to West Germany for the 1974 series in which the presence of countries such as Australia, Haiti and Zaire put larger question marks than ever against the qualification system—especially when the list of non-qualifiers included such countries as Hungary, Russia, Spain . . . and England.

Guide to the 92 Football League Clubs in England and Wales

as at the end of the 1973–74 season

Aldershot

Recreation Ground,
High St., Aldershot.
Aldershot 20211

Shirts: Red, Blue Trim
Shorts: White
Stockings: Red, Blue Tops

The years of the Second World War provided Aldershot with the most colourful teams in their history. Many of the game's best names were on military service in the garrison town and appeared as guests for the club. Among them were Frank Swift, Tommy Lawton, Matt Busby, Denis Compton, and the full England half-back line of that era, Cliff Britton, Stan Cullis and Joe Mercer.

In more settled times Aldershot rarely achieved much of distinction until, by attaining fourth place in Division Four in season 1972–73, they won promotion for the first time. Before that, their most successful season was in 1969–70 when they were sixth in Division Four. That was the season, too, when they attracted their record attendance to the Recreation Ground, 19,138 watching their fourth round F.A. Cup replay against Carlisle.

Another notable Cup triumph occurred in 1963–64 when they defeated Aston Villa, then a Division One team, 2–1 after a goalless draw at Villa Park. Aldershot can claim a share of at least one record—that of the quickest goal. Albert Mundy scored six seconds after the kick-off at Hartlepool on 25 October 1958.

Record attendance: 19,138 v. Carlisle (F.A. Cup), January 1970
Modern Capacity: 20,000.
Entered Football League: 1932—Div. 3 (South).
Biggest win: 8–1 v. Gateshead (Div. 4), September 1958.
Heaviest defeat: 0–9 v. Bristol City (Div. 3 South), December 1946.
Highest final League position: 4th in Div. 4, 1972–73.
Best in F.A. Cup: 5th, Round, 1932–33.
Best in Football League Cup: 2nd Round, 1960–61, 1962–63, 1963–64, 1965–66, 1966–67, 1970–71, 1971–72.
Pitch measurements: $117\frac{1}{2} \times 76$ yd.
Highest League Scorer in Single Season: Ron Fogg—24 in 1963–64 (Div. 4).
Transfers—
  Highest fee paid: £13,500—Joe Jopling (from Leicester), March 1974.
  Highest fee received: £50,000—Joe Jopling (to Leicester), September 1970.

Arsenal

Arsenal Stadium,
Highbury, London, N5.
01–226–0304

Shirts: Red, White Sleeves
Shorts: White
Stockings: Red, with Thin White Band

By performing the League Championship–F.A. Cup double in 1971, Arsenal not only caught up with their illustrious past—they exceeded it. They became the first club to win the Championship eight times, and the 'double' was signalled by Bertie Mee being voted 'Manager of the Year' and captain Frank McLintock winning the 'Footballer of the Year' award.

Arsenal have been constant members of Division One since 1919, and their greatest era until the seventies occurred during the 1930's when they 'came to power' under the managership of Herbert Chapman. They were League Champions in 1931, 1933, 1934, 1935, and 1938, and won the F.A. Cup in 1930 and 1936.

After the war they won the First Division title in 1948 and 1953, and the F.A. Cup again in 1950. But then came a long period of non-success from which the way back to former glory followed two losing appearances in the Football League Cup Final.

In the 1970 Fairs Cup they achieved their first European prize; a year later they completed the double and, in a bid to add to their laurels, in December 1971 Arsenal paid a new British record transfer fee of £220,000 for Alan Ball, from Everton.

League Champions: 1930–31, 1932–33, 1933–34, 1934–35, 1937–38, 1947–48, 1952–53, 1970–71.
F.A. Cup Winners: 1929–30, 1935–36, 1949–50, 1970–71.
European Fairs Cup Winners: 1969–70.
The Double (League and F.A. Cup Winners): 1970–71.
Record attendance: 73,295 v. Sunderland (League), March 1935.
Modern Capacity: 63,000.
Entered Football League: 1893—Div. 2.
Biggest win: 12–0 v. Loughborough T. (Div. 2), March 1900.
Heaviest defeat: 0–8 v. Loughborough T. (Div. 2), December 1896.
Best in Football League Cup: Runners-up 1967–68, 1968–69.
Pitch measurements: 110 × 71 yd.
Highest League Scorer in Single Season: Ted Drake—43 in 1934–35 (Div. 1).
Transfers—
  Highest fee paid: £220,000—Alan Ball (from Everton), December 1971.
  Highest fee received: £140,000—John Roberts (to Birmingham), October 1972.

17

Aston Villa

Villa Park,
Trinity Road,
Birmingham B6 6HE.
021–327–6604

Shirts: Claret, Light Blue Collar and Sleeves
Shorts: White
Stockings: White

The deeds of few clubs are written as deeply into the game's history as those of Aston Villa. They were among the 12 founder members of the Football League in 1888; they were Champions 6 times between 1894 and 1910, and in 1897 they achieved the 'double' of League title and F.A. Cup, a feat previously performed by Preston N.E. in 1888–89 and which Tottenham Hotspur (1960–61) and Arsenal (1970–71) have since equalled. When they finished runners-up to Arsenal in 1930–31, they scored 128 League goals, which remains a record for a First Division club. Villa hold the F.A. Cup record of 7 wins and in addition won the Football League Cup in 1961, its inaugural year.

Certainly, those lads of the Aston Villa Wesleyan Church could never have realized in 1874 what glories the club they formed would achieve! It would need many pages to record Villa's great players: Charlie Wallace, Harold Halse, Harry Hampton, Clem Stephenson and Joe Bache (the 1913 Cup Final attack); Sam Hardy, Frank Barson, Andy Ducat, Frank Moss, 'Pongo' Waring, Billy Walker, Jimmy Hagan, Alex Massie, Trevor Ford, Peter McParland. These are but a few.

League Champions: 1893–94, 1895–96, 1896–97, 1898–99, 1899–1900, 1909–10.
Division 2 Champions: 1937–38, 1959–60.
Division 3 Champions: 1971–72.
F.A. Cup Winners: 1886–87, 1894–95, 1896–97, 1904–05, 1912–13, 1919–20, 1956–57.
League Cup Winners: 1960–61.
The Double (League and F.A. Cup Winners): 1896–97.
Record attendance: 76,588 v. Derby County (F.A. Cup), March 1946.
Modern Capacity: 64,000.
Entered Football League: 1888—Div. 1.
Biggest win: 13–0 v. Wednesbury Old Athletic (F.A. Cup), 1886–87.
Heaviest defeat: 1–8 v. Blackburn R. (F.A. Cup), 1888–89.
Pitch measurements: 115 × 75 yd.
Highest League Scorer in Single Season: T. ('Pongo') Waring—49 in 1930–31 (Div. 1).
Transfers—
  Highest fee paid: £100,000—Bruce Rioch (from Luton), July 1969.
  Highest fee received: £200,000—Bruce Rioch (to Derby), February 1974.

Barnsley

Oakwell Ground,
Grove Street, Barnsley.
Barnsley 84113

Shirts: Red
Shorts: White
Stockings: Red

Ever since their formation, Barnsley have known the extremes of fortune. Often, it must be said, the emphasis has been on the struggle to make ends meet. Yet there have been great occasions such as winning the F.A. Cup as a Second Division side in 1912 after herculean efforts against West Bromwich Albion. The teams met first at the old Crystal Palace in a goalless draw, and Barnsley snatched victory by the only goal during extra time in the replay at Bramall Lane, Sheffield. This was deserved compensation for their 2—0 defeat by Newcastle, in the Final two years earlier, when a second match was also required to decide the outcome.

One of their biggest disappointments was missing promotion to Division One in 1922 on goal average. Three times Barnsley were Third Division North Champions: in 1933—34, when they scored 118 goals; in 1938—39, when they won 30 and drew 7 of their 42 League games; and in 1954—55.

Like other clubs living in the shadows of better-known neighbours, Barnsley have discovered many stars, among them Eric Brook and Fred Tilson, who together played in Manchester City's 1934 F.A. Cup-winning team; George Hunt, Wilf Copping, Dick Spence, Danny Blanchflower and Tommy Taylor, who lost his life in the Munich air disaster involving Manchester United in February, 1958.

F.A. Cup Winners: 1911—12.
Division 3 (North) Champions: 1933—34, 1938—39, 1954—55.
Record attendance: 42,056 v. Stoke (F.A. Cup), February 1935.
Modern Capacity: 38,500.
Entered Football League: 1898—Div. 2.
Biggest win: 9—0 v. Loughborough T. (Div. 2), January 1899 and 9—0 v. Accrington Stanley (Div. 3 North), February 1934.
Heaviest defeat: 0—9 v. Notts County (Div. 2), November 1927.
Best in Football League Cup: 3rd Round, 1962—63.
Pitch measurements: 110×74 yd.
Highest League Scorer in Single Season: Cecil McCormack —33 in 1950—51 (Div. 2).
Transfers—
  Highest fee paid: £20,000 (joint fee)—Frank Sharp and Leslie Lea (from Cardiff), August 1970.
  Highest fee received: £40,000—Stewart Barraclough (to Newcastle), July 1970.

Birmingham City

St Andrew's,
Birmingham, B9 4NH.
021–772–0101/2689

Shirts: Royal Blue, Broad White Stripe on Front
Shorts: White
Stockings: Royal Blue

Although the League Championship, F.A. Cup and European prizes still elude them, Birmingham City have seldom been short of class players in one or more key positions. Their speciality has been goalkeepers of international calibre, among them Dan Tremelling, Harry Hibbs, Gil Merrick and Jim Herriot.

As Small Heath, the club were founder members of Division Two in 1892. They stepped into Division One in 1894, but slipped back two years later. Promotion came once more in 1901, but this time they lasted only one season. They climbed again in 1903; the name Small Heath was dropped in favour of Birmingham in 1905, and a year later they moved to their present St Andrew's home from Muntz Street.

Since the last war, as Birmingham City, they have been F.A. Cup Finalists (1956), Fairs Cup Finalists twice (1960, 1961), League Cup Winners (1963) and promoted three times to the First Division—in 1948, 1955 and 1972. In February 1974, facing the threat of relegation again, City transferred 22-year-old striker Bob Latchford to Everton to set a new British record equivalent of £350,000 (for details see foot of page).

Division 2 Champions: 1892–93, 1920–21, 1947–48, 1954–55.
League Cup Winners: 1962–63.
Record attendance: 66,844 v. Everton (F.A. Cup), Feb. 1939.
Modern Capacity: 52,500.
Entered Football League: 1892—Div. 2.
Biggest win: 12–0 v. Walsall Town Swifts (Div. 2), December 1892 and 12–0 v. Doncaster Rovers (Div. 2), April 1903.
Heaviest defeat: 1–9 v. Sheffield Wednesday (Div. 1), December 1930.
Best in F.A. Cup: Final, 1930–31, 1955–56.
Pitch measurements: 115 × 74 yd.
Highest League Scorer in Single Season: Joe Bradford—29 in 1927–28 (Div. 1).
Transfers—
  Highest fee paid: £180,000—Howard Kendall (from Everton), February 1974.
  Highest fee received: £350,000 equivalent (British record)—Bob Latchford (to Everton—£80,000 cash plus Howard Kendall, valued £180,000, and Archie Styles, valued £90,000), February 1974.

Blackburn Rovers

Ewood Park,
Blackburn, BB2 4JF.
Blackburn 55432/3

Shirts: Blue and White Halves
Shorts: White
Stockings: White with Blue Rings

The F.A. Cup was almost the exclusive property of Blackburn Rovers during the latter part of the last century. They won the trophy in three successive years, 1884–86, and again in 1890 and 1891, then had to wait 37 years to win it for the sixth time by beating Huddersfield 3–1 at Wembley in 1928.

Rovers were original members of the Football League in 1888 and carried off the First Division Championship in 1912 and 1914. They remained continuously in the top flight of League clubs until 1936. Since then, however, they have had varying spells in the Second Division and their fortunes slumped to a new low in 1970–71 when, together with Bolton Wanderers, another Lancashire club steeped in tradition, they dropped into Division Three.

Many chroniclers of the game—and certainly those old enough to remember—maintain that Bob Crompton was the finest full-back of any era. In the early part of the century he was capped 41 times for England and played for Rovers for 23 years.

Since the 1939–45 war Rovers most-capped players, both for England, have been winger Bryan Douglas (36 Internationals) and half-back Ronnie Clayton (35), who holds the Blackburn record of 580 League appearances.

League Champions: 1911–12, 1913–14.
Second Division Champions: 1938–39.
F.A. Cup Winners: 1883–84, 1884–85, 1885–86, 1889–90, 1890–91, 1927–28.
Record attendance: 61,783 v. Bolton (F.A. Cup), March 1929.
Modern Capacity: 52,000.
Entered Football League: 1888—Div. 1.
Biggest win: 11–0 v. Rossendale United (F.A. Cup), 1884–85.
Heaviest defeat: 0–8 v. Arsenal (Div. 1), February 1933.
Best in Football League Cup: Semi-final 1961–62.
Pitch measurements: 116 × 72 yd.
Highest League Scorer in Single Season: Ted Harper—43 in 1925–26 (Div. 1).
Transfers—
  Highest fee paid: £60,000—Jimmy Kerr (from Bury), May 1970.
  Highest fee received: £95,000—Mike England (to Tottenham), August 1966.

Blackpool

Bloomfield Road,
Blackpool, FY1 6JJ.
Blackpool 46118

Shirts: Tangerine
Shorts: White
Stockings: Tangerine

Their appearances at Wembley in the years immediately after the Second World War will remain treasured memories for all associated with the Blackpool club. They went down 4–2 to Manchester United in the 1948 F.A. Cup Final, which has a place among Wembley's finest games; then they lost 2–0 to Newcastle in 1951 and finally came their memorable 4–3 triumph over Bolton in 1953. That was the match in which Stanley Matthews inspired his team-mates to snatch victory.

Stanley Mortensen, who achieved a hat-trick in the Bolton final, scored nearly 200 League goals for the club he later managed. Another notable personality of that era was the captain, Harry Johnston, who received the 'Footballer of the Year' award in 1951—of which Matthews was the first holder in 1948.

Blackpool came closest to taking the First Division title in 1956 when they finished runners-up. They continued as a power through the fifties when much of the credit was due to their astute manager Joe Smith, the former England and Bolton inside forward who served from 1935 to 1958.

After being relegated in 1967, they bounced back again in 1970, but their comeback lasted only one season as they finished bottom of Division One—a sad ending to the Blackpool career of one of their finest ever players, Jimmy Armfield, who made more than 550 League appearances for the club and was capped 43 times at full-back for England.

F.A. Cup Winners: 1952–53.
Second Division Champions: 1929–30.
Record attendance: 39,118 v. Man. Utd. (League), April 1952.
Modern Capacity: 38,000.
Entered Football League: 1896—Div. 2.
Biggest win: 8–4 v. Charlton Ath. (Div. 1), September 1952.
Heaviest defeat: 1–10 v. Huddersfield Town (Div. 1), December 1930.
Best in Football League Cup: Semi-final 1961–62.
Pitch measurements: 111 × 73 yd.
Highest League Scorer in Single Season: Jimmy Hampson —45 in 1929–30 (Div. 2).
Transfers—
  Highest fee paid: £60,000—Alan Suddick (from Newcastle), December 1966.
  Highest fee received: £150,000—Tony Green (to Newcastle), October 1971.

Bolton Wanderers

Burnden Park,
Bolton, BL3 2QR.
Bolton 21101

Shirts: White
Shorts: Navy Blue
Stockings: White

Three times between 1923—the first Wembley F.A. Cup Final—and 1929, Bolton Wanderers won the game's most coveted domestic trophy. They did so without conceding a single goal at Wembley, and those were indeed golden years for one of the founder members of the Football League.

Five Wanderers players took part in each of those successful Finals—against West Ham in 1923 (2–0), Manchester City 1926 (1–0) and Portsmouth 1929 (2–0). They were Pym in goal, Haworth, Nuttall, Seddon and Butler. Bolton won the Cup again in 1958 and were losing finalists in 1894, 1904 and 1953.

Curiously, for all their Cup-fighting prowess and many years in Division One, Bolton have never won the League Championship. Relegated in 1964, they sank into Division Three for the first time in 1971, but two years later began the climb back as Third Division Champions.

No one ever typified the fighting spirit of Wanderers better than centre-forward Nat Lofthouse, the club's most-capped player. He played 33 times for England and, between 1946–61, scored 255 League goals—the club record.

Tragedy struck Burnden Park on 9 March 1946, when crush barriers broke at an F.A. Cup-tie between Bolton and Stoke City. Thirty-three people were killed and more than four hundred injured in the worst football disaster ever known in England.

F.A. Cup Winners: 1922–23, 1925–26, 1928–29, 1957–58.
Second Division Champions: 1908–09.
Third Division Champions: 1972–73.
Record attendance: 69,912 v. Manchester City (F.A. Cup), February 1933.
Modern Capacity: 60,000.
Entered Football League: 1888—Div. 1.
Biggest win: 13–0 v. Sheffield United (F.A. Cup), February 1890.
Heaviest defeat: 0–7 v. Manchester City (Div. 1), March 1936.
Best in Football League Cup: 4th Round, 1960–61, 1971–72.
Pitch measurements: $112\frac{1}{2} \times 76$ yd.
Highest League Scorer in Single Season: Joe Smith—38 in 1920–21 (Div. 1).
Transfers—
  Highest fee paid: £70,000—Terry Wharton (from Wolves), October 1967.
  Highest fee received: £80,000—Wyn Davies (to Newcastle), October 1966.

A.F.C. Bournemouth

Dean Court,
Bournemouth.
Bournemouth 35381

Shirts: Red and Black Stripes
Shorts: Black
Stockings: Black, with Red and White Tops

No era has been more exciting or rewarding for Bournemouth than the early seventies. Their promotion from the Fourth Division in 1971 was followed by three more good seasons, in each of which they challenged for a Second Division place.

Centre-forward Ted MacDougall broke several Bournemouth goal-scoring records, among them most goals in a season, previously held by Ron Eyre with 32 in season 1928–29. During the successful 1970–71 season MacDougall was the Football League's highest scorer with 42, and the following season scored nine goals in a match—a new F.A. Cup record—when Bournemouth beat Margate 11–0 in the first round, their record victory.

But eventually the club was unable to hold him any more than opposing defences could, and in September 1972 manager John Bond reluctantly sold his shooting star to Manchester United for £220,000.

The club was originally known simply as Boscombe, but when elected to the Third Division (South) in 1923, Bournemouth was incorporated in the title. In 1972 they 'went Continental' by changing their name to A.F.C. Bournemouth.

Record attendance: 28,799 v. Manchester United (F.A. Cup), March 1957.
Modern Capacity: 24,000.
Entered Football League: 1923—Div. 3 (South).
Biggest win: 11–0 v. Margate (F.A. Cup), November 1971.
Heaviest defeat: 1–8 v. Bradford City (Div. 3), January 1970.
Highest final League position: 2nd in Div. 3 South, 1947–48.
Best in F.A. Cup: 6th Round 1956–57.
Best in Football League Cup: 4th Round 1961–62, 1963–64.
Pitch measurements: 115 × 75 yd.
Highest League Scorer in Single Season: Ted MacDougall —42 in 1970–71 (Div. 4).
Transfers—
  Highest fee paid: £70,000 Brian Clark (from Cardiff), October 1972.
Highest fee received: £220,000—Ted MacDougall (to Manchester United), September 1972.

Bradford City

Valley Parade,
Bradford, BD8 7DY.
Bradford 26565

Shirts: Amber
Shorts: Amber
Stockings: Amber

Bradford City have been striving hard to keep first-class Association football alive in the area since neighbours Bradford Park Avenue lost their membership of the Football League in 1970.

Yet most of City's glories belong to the past. They were in Division One between 1908 and 1922, and became the first holders of the present F.A. Cup in 1911 when they defeated Newcastle United 1–0 at Old Trafford, after a goalless draw at the old Crystal Palace. During seasons 1910–11 and 1911–12, Bradford City played 12 consecutive F.A. Cup ties without conceding a goal.

When they won the Third Division North title in season 1928–29, City scored 128 goals and obtained 63 points, by far their best statistics in League football.

Not surprisingly in an area noted for the handling game, Bradford City F.C. developed in 1903 from a Rugby club—Manningham. Since then a number of fine players have worn City's colours, among them Sam Barkas, Alf Quantrill, Tommy Cairns, Arthur Whitehurst (who scored seven goals v. Tranmere in 1929), Willie Watson and Trevor Hockey.

F.A. Cup Winners: 1910–11.
Division 2 Champions: 1907–08.
Division 3 (North) Champions: 1928–29.
Record attendance: 39,146 v. Burnley (F.A. Cup), March 1911.
Modern Capacity: 24,000.
Entered Football League: 1903—Div. 2.
Biggest win: 11–1 v. Rotherham (Div. 3 North), August 1928.
Heaviest defeat: 1–9 v. Colchester Utd. (Div. 4), December 1961.
Best in Football League Cup: 5th Round 1964–65.
Pitch measurements: 112 × 71 yd.
Highest League Scorer in Single Season: David Layne—34 in 1961–62 (Div. 4).
Transfers—
  Highest fee paid: £10,000—Ken Leek (from Northampton), November 1965; £10,000—Gerry Ingram (from Preston), February 1972; £10,000—John Napier (from Brighton), October 1972.
  Highest fee received: £23,000—Bruce Bannister (to Bristol Rovers), November 1971.

Brentford

Griffin Park,
Braemar Road,
Brentford, Middlesex.
01-560-2021

Shirts: Red and White Stripes
Shorts: Black, White Striped Seams
Stockings: Black, Red and White Hooped Tops.

Formed in 1888, when by one vote they decided against setting up as a Rugby club, Brentford turned professional in 1900, and after successes in the Southern League became founder members of the Third Division in 1920. Under the progressive management of Harry Curtis they began a long period of success which took them into Division One in 1935.

Among their achievements was to win all 21 home League matches in the Third Division (South) in season 1929-30 but, curiously, they failed to win promotion that year, finishing runners-up. In 1932-33 they took the title and added the Second Division crown two seasons later.

After the Second World War, Brentford slipped from First to Fourth Division. In January 1967 they were near to going out of existence, but they resisted a take-over bid by Queen's Park Rangers, and by November 1971 they had cleared a debt of £104,000. The struggle has continued on the field, for promotion to Division Three in 1972 lasted only one season.

Division 2 Champions: 1934-35.
Division 3 (South) Champions: 1932-33.
Division 4 Champions: 1962-63.
Record attendance: 39,626 v. Preston N.E. (F.A. Cup), March 1938.
Modern Capacity: 38,000.
Entered Football League: 1920 — Div. 3.
Biggest win: 9-0 v. Wrexham (Div. 3), October 1963.
Heaviest defeat: 0-7 v. Swansea (Div. 3 South), November 1924 and 0-7 v. Walsall (Div. 3 South), January 1957.
Best in F.A. Cup: 6th Round 1937-38, 1945-46, 1948-49.
Best in Football League Cup: 3rd Round 1960-61, 1968-69.
Pitch measurements: 114 × 75 yd.
Highest League Scorer in Single Season: Jack Holiday — 36 in 1932-33 (Div. 3 South).
Transfers—
  Highest fee paid: £17,500 — John Dick (from West Ham), September 1962.
  Highest fee received: £50,000 — Stewart Houston (to Manchester United), December 1973.

Brighton and Hove Albion

Goldstone Ground,
Old Shoreham Road,
Hove 4,
Sussex, BN3 7DE.
Brighton 739535

Shirts: Blue and White Stripes
Shorts: White
Stockings: White, Blue Trimmed Top

Relegated from the Second Division in 1973 and situated near the foot of the Third six months later, Brighton sought a big-name manager to improve their image. They appointed Brian Clough on November 1, less than three weeks after his resignation at Derby, where he had won Second and First Division Championships. Clough's arrival sent interest booming at Brighton, but they went out of the F.A. Cup in the first round, beaten 4–0 in a home replay by amateurs Walton and Hersham, and three days later suffered further humiliation before their own supporters, crashing 8–2 to Third Division leaders Bristol Rovers—the heaviest home defeat in Brighton's history.

Cup competitions have produced other memorable occasions for the club. In 1932 the Football Association made Brighton play through all the early qualifying rounds because application for exemption had been overlooked. And in a first round proper tie in November 1965, they recorded their biggest victory—a 10–1 beating of Wisbech.

Division 3 (South) Champions: 1957–58.
Division 4 Champions: 1964–65.
Record attendance: 36,747 v. Fulham (League), December 1958.
Modern Capacity: 38,000.
Entered Football League: 1920—Div. 3.
Biggest win: 10–1 v. Wisbech (F.A. Cup), November 1965.
Heaviest defeat: 0–9 v. Middlesbrough (League), August 1958.
Best in F.A. Cup: 5th Round 1929–30, 1932–33, 1945–46, 1959–60.
Best in Football League Cup: 4th Round 1966–67.
Pitch measurements: 112 × 75 yd.
Highest League Scorer in Single Season: A. Vallance—30 in 1929–30 (Div. 3 South).
Transfers—
  Highest fee paid: £70,000 (combined deal)—Ron Welch & Harry Wilson (both from Burnley), December 1973.
  Highest fee received: £15,000—Bill Curry (to Derby), September 1960; £15,000—Kit Napier (to Blackburn), August 1972.

Bristol City

Ashton Gate,
Bristol, BS3 2EJ.
Bristol 664093/665428

Shirts: Red, White Trim
Shorts: White
Stockings: Red and White

Nothing they have achieved since can compare with Bristol City's performances before the First World War. In their first season in Division One, in 1906–07, they finished runners-up to Newcastle, and two years later reached the F.A. Cup Final for the only time in their history. Playing in that match at the old Crystal Palace which Manchester United won 1–0 was Billy Wedlock, probably the greatest of all City's servants. He was only five feet four, but as a centre-half he represented England for six successive seasons.

Since those heady early years Bristol City have never been able to regain First Division status, which they surrendered in 1911. They have alternated between Divisions Two and Three during the past 60 years with seasons of occasional brilliance, such as 1954–55 when they strode away with the old Third Division (South) title. They obtained 70 points—nine more than the second club.

But the City team of 1974 gave Bristol reasons to dwell more on the present than the past, knocking out F.A. Cup favourites and runaway First Division leaders Leeds 1–0 in a fifth round replay at Elland Road after a 1–1 draw. Reaching the last eight for the first time in 53 years, they then lost by the only goal to Liverpool on another full-house occasion at Ashton Gate.

Divison 2 Champions: 1905–06.
Division 3 (South) Champions: 1922–23, 1926–27, 1954–55.
Record attendance: 43,335 v. Preston N.E. (F.A. Cup), February 1935.
Modern Capacity: 40,500.
Entered Football League: 1901—Div. 2.
Biggest win: 11–0 v. Chichester (F.A. Cup), November 1960.
Heaviest defeat: 0–9 v. Coventry City (League), April 1934.
Best in F.A. Cup: Final 1908–09.
Best in Football League Cup: Semi-final 1970–71.
Pitch measurements: 115 × 78 yd.
Highest League Scorer in Single Season: Don Clark—36 in 1946–47 (Div. 3 South).
Transfers—
  Highest fee paid: £70,000—Bobby Gould (from West Bromwich Albion), December 1972.
  Highest fee received: £100,000—Chris Garland (to Chelsea), September 1971.

Bristol Rovers

Bristol Stadium,
Eastville,
Bristol BS5 6NN.
Bristol 558620

Shirts: Blue and White Quarters
Shorts: White
Stockings: Blue and White

Although twice in the 1950s Bristol Rovers finished sixth in Division Two, most of their existence has been spent in Third Division company, but season 1973–74 raised hopes of a shining new era at Eastville. From kick-off day in August, Rovers were unbeaten in 27 League games until February 1, a sequence stretched to 32 by five matches without defeat at the end of the previous season.

On the strength of such a run, which was highlighted by the free scoring of Alan Warboys and Bruce Bannister, Rovers set up a long lead in the Third Division. The 8–2 win at Brighton on December 1 was the biggest victory in their history, and with City doing great deeds in the F.A. Cup, Bristol became a region of intense football interest in 1973–74.

Rovers have always had a reputation for developing their own players, and Ronnie Dix, Phil Taylor, Roy Bentley and Larry Lloyd are just a few who have achieved distinction elsewhere.

Unlike their neighbours, Bristol City, the Rovers have never reached the Final of the F.A. Cup. The furthest they have gone is the sixth round, in 1951 and 1958—the year in which they knocked out Burnley, then a First Division side.

Division 3 (South) Champions: 1952–53.
Record attendance: 38,472 v. Preston N.E. (F.A. Cup), January 1960.
Modern Capacity: 40,000.
Entered Football League. 1920—Div. 3.
Biggest win: 8–2 v. Brighton (Div. 3), December 1973.
Heaviest defeat: 0–12 v. Luton Town (Div. 3 South), April 1936.
Best in F.A. Cup: 6th Round 1950–51, 1957–58.
Best in Football League Cup: 5th Round 1970–71, 1971–72.
Pitch measurements: 112 × 76 yd.
Highest League Scorer in Single Season: Geoff Bradford—33 in 1952–53 (Div. 3 South).
Transfers—
  Highest fee paid: £35,000—Alan Warboys (from Sheffield Utd), March 1973.
  Highest fee received: £55,000—Phil Roberts (to Portsmouth), May 1973.

Burnley

Turf Moor,
Burnley.
Burnley 27777

Shirts: Claret, Blue Collar and Cuffs.
Shorts: White
Stockings: White, Claret and Blue Hooped Turnover

Creatively managed by Jimmy Adamson, one of Turf Moor's outstanding post-war defenders, Burnley returned to First Division football in 1973 after two seasons' absence. They did so as Second Division Champions—six of the side were ever-present in that triumph—and their style suggested a lasting return to top company.

Burnley, one of the League's founder clubs in 1888, shattered all records in season 1920–21, by playing 30 consecutive matches without defeat. This memorable League record from 6 September to 25 March read: played 30, won 21, drawn 9, goals 68–17, points 51. Thus Burnley won the First Division title for the first time in their history, and their record unbeaten sequence was not surpassed until 1969–70 when Leeds played 34 matches before losing.

Another successful period for Burnley, who have astutely operated the transfer market to survive in the shadow of the two glamour clubs of Manchester, occurred in the early 1960s. They won the League Championship for the second time in 1960, and two years later finished runners-up both in Division One and in the F.A. Cup.

League Champions: 1920–21, 1959–60.
Division 2 Champions: 1897–98, 1972–73.
F.A. Cup Winners: 1913–14.
Record attendance: 54,775 v. Huddersfield Town (F.A. Cup), February 1924.
Modern Capacity: 39,000.
Entered Football League: 1888—Div. 1.
Biggest League win: 9–0 v. Darwen (Div. 1), January 1892; 9–0 v. Crystal Palace (F.A. Cup), 1908–09; 9–0 v. New Brighton (F.A. Cup), January 1957.
Heaviest League defeat: 0–10 v. Aston Villa (Div. 1), August 1925 and 0–10 v. Sheffield United (Div. 1), January 1929.
Best in Football League Cup: Semi-final 1960–61, 1968–69.
Pitch measurements: $115\frac{1}{2} \times 73$ yd.
Highest League Scorer in Single Season: George Beel—35 in 1927–28 (Div. 1).
Transfers—
  Highest fee paid: £60,000—Paul Fletcher (from Bolton), March 1971.
  Highest fee received: £190,000—Ralph Coates (to Tottenham), May 1971.

Bury

Gigg Lane,
Bury, BL9 9HR.
061-764-4881/2

Shirts: White
Shorts: Royal Blue
Stockings: Royal Blue

Bury, nicknamed 'The Shakers', have certainly stirred the football world in their time, starting from season 1894-95, when they won the Second Division championship in their first year as League members. Five years later they defeated Southampton 4-0 in the F.A. Cup Final at the old Crystal Palace, and in 1903 they caused an even bigger stir by winning the trophy again without conceding a single goal in any of their ties. They trounced Derby County on the same ground by six goals to nil—which remains the biggest winning margin in the Final.

Bury stayed in the First Division for seventeen seasons; they dropped to the Second Division in 1912 and regained higher status in 1924, but this time they survived for only five seasons. Since then they have achieved occasional periods of glory such as winning the Division Three title in 1960-61 by a margin of six points. They reached the semi-final of the Football League Cup in season 1962-63 before losing 4-3 on aggregate to Birmingham City, the eventual winners of the trophy. Bury showed their tenacity as Cup fighters in 1955 when they played Stoke City for a record 9 hours 22 minutes, in five meetings in the F.A. Cup third round before Stoke won 3-2 at Old Trafford. But in recent times 'The Shakers' have themselves been shaken as they slipped back to the Third Division in 1967 and in 1971 to the Fourth.

F.A. Cup Winners: 1899-1900, 1902-03.
Division 2 Champions: 1894-95.
Division 3 Champions: 1960-61.
Record attendance: 35,000 v. Bolton Wanderers (F.A. Cup), January 1960.
Modern Capacity: 35,000.
Entered Football League: 1894—Div. 2.
Biggest win: 12-1 v. Stockton (F.A. Cup), 1896-97.
Heaviest defeat: 0-10 v. Blackburn Rovers (F.A. Cup), 1887-88.
Best in Football League Cup: Semi-final 1962-63.
Pitch measurements: 116 × 80 yd.
Highest League Scorer in Single Season: Norman Bullock —31 in 1925-26 (Div. 1).
Transfers—
  Highest fee paid: £25,000—Alf Arrowsmith (from Liverpool), December 1968.
  Highest fee received: £60,000—Alec Lindsay (to Liverpool), March 1969.

Cambridge United

The Abbey Stadium,
534 Newmarket Road,
Cambridge.
Teversham 2170

Shirts: Amber, Black
　　　　Collar and Cuffs
Shorts: Black
Stockings: Amber

From the moment they turned professional in 1946, Cambridge United rapidly established a reputation as a progressive-thinking club while playing in the Cambridgeshire, Eastern Counties and Southern Leagues. They won the Southern League Championship in successive years, 1968–69 and 1969–70, and by then their credentials had so impressed Football League clubs that at the annual meeting, in June 1970, they were elected to the Fourth Division in place of Bradford Park Avenue.

Understandably the switch to higher class football produced many fresh challenges for Cambridge and the first season in the League was very much one of trial and error. United finished 20th, only one place clear of the re-election zone, but in 1972 they improved to tenth and a year later third place in the final table took them up to Division Three. They dropped again to the Fourth, however, in 1974.

One of the highlights of their inaugural year as a Football League club was a fixture with Chelsea, in May 1970, which attracted a crowd of 14,000. The match was Chelsea's 'thank you' for signing Ian Hutchinson, who had joined them from Cambridge in July 1968, and this is the only instance of an existing official attendance record for a League club being set at a friendly game.

Record attendance: 14,000 v. Chelsea (Friendly), May 1970.
Modern Capacity: 14,000.
Entered Football League: 1970—Div. 4.
Biggest League win: 6–0 v. Darlington (Div. 4), September 1971.
Heaviest defeat: 0–6 v. Aldershot (Div. 4), April 1974.
Highest Final League Position: 3rd in Div. 4, 1972–73.
Best in F.A. Cup: 3rd Round 1973–74.
Best in Football League Cup: 2nd Round 1973–74.
Pitch measurements: 112 × 75 yd.
Highest League Scorer in Single Season: Brian Greenhalgh —19 in 1971–72 (Div. 4).
Transfers—
　Highest fee paid: £30,000—Bobby Shinton (from Walsall), March 1974.
　Highest fee received: £40,000—Brian Greenhalgh (to Bournemouth), February 1974.

Cardiff City

Ninian Park,
Cardiff, CF1 8SX.
Cardiff 28501 & 33230

Shirts: Blue, White Trim
Shorts: White
Stockings: Blue

The most memorable event in Cardiff City's history occurred in 1927, when they became the first non-English club to win the F.A. Cup. That year they beat Arsenal 1–0 at Wembley and the drama of the occasion was heightened by the fact that the Arsenal goalkeeper, Dan Lewis, whose error allowed Cardiff to triumph, was himself a Welshman.

Three years earlier another mistake—this time by a City player—cost Cardiff the First Division Championship. They needed two points from their final match against Birmingham, but missed a penalty late in the game and could only draw.

In the Cardiff goal, during First Division days of the 1920s, was Tom Farquharson their longest-serving player. He made nearly 450 League appearances between 1922 and 1935.

Cardiff's star waned, however, and the club slipped into the Second Division in 1929 and the Third (South) two seasons later, but re-emerged as Southern Section Champions in 1947. Since the last war they have had two spells totalling seven years in the First Division, from 1952–57 and 1960–62.

As regular Welsh Cup winners, Cardiff (founded in 1899) have made eight appearances in the European Cup-Winners' Cup and become one of Britain's most travelled clubs. In 1967–68 they reached the semi-finals.

F.A. Cup Winners: 1926–27.
Division 3 (South) Champions: 1946–47.
Record attendance: 61,566 Wales v. England (International), October 1961.
Modern Capacity: 60,000.
Entered Football League: 1920—Div. 2.
Biggest win: 9–2 v. Thames (Div. 3 South), February 1932.
Heaviest defeat: 2–11 v. Sheffield United (Div. 1), January 1926.
Best in Football League Cup: Semi-final 1965–66.
Pitch measurements: 112 × 76 yd.
Highest League Scorer in Single Season: Stan Richards—31 in 1946–47 (Div. 3 South).
Transfers—
  Highest fee paid: £60,000—Willie Anderson (from Aston Villa), February 1973.
  Highest fee received: £110,000—John Toshack (to Liverpool), November 1970.

Carlisle United

Brunton Park,
Carlisle, CA1 1LL
Carlisle 26237

Shirts: Blue with Broad White Stripe, Red Piping
Shorts: White
Stockings: Red

Carlisle United's progress was unspectacular following their formation in 1903. In 1928 they were elected to Division Three (North) in place of Durham City and finished eighth in their first campaign. But they had to seek re-election in 1934—35.

They were third in 1951, but when Division Four was formed from the bottom 12 clubs of each section of the Third in 1958, Carlisle were among them.

They gained promotion in 1962, dropped straight back the following season, but immediately went up again, with Hugh McIlmoyle scoring 39 out of a grand total of 113 League goals.

Carlisle, situated so close to the Border that at one time there was speculation about their joining the Scottish League, swept on into Division Two in 1965, just twelve months after leaving the Fourth Division. In 1967 they finished only one place from the First Division, and in 1974 they at last brought top-division football to their North-west outpost by finishing third in Div. 2 —a wonderful achievement for a club of their size.

Division 3 Champions: 1964—65.
Record attendance: 27,500 v. Birmingham City (F.A. Cup), January 1957, and 27,500 v. Middlesbrough (F.A. Cup), February 1970.
Modern Capacity: 30,000.
Entered Football League: 1928—Div. 3 (North).
Biggest win: 8—0 v. Hartlepool (Div. 3 North), September 1928, and 8—0 v. Scunthorpe Utd (Div. 3 North), December 1952.
Heaviest League defeat: 1—11 v. Hull City (Div. 3 North), January 1939.
Best in F.A. Cup: 5th Round 1963—64, 1969—70.
Best in Football League Cup: Semi-final 1969—70.
Pitch measurements: 117 × 78 yd.
Highest League Scorer in Single Season: Jimmy McConnell —42 in 1928—29 (Div. 3 North).
Transfers—
  Highest fee paid: £35,000—Ken Wilson (from Dumbarton), September 1972; £35,000—Mick Barry (from Huddersfield), May 1973.
  Highest fee received: £110,000—Stan Bowles (to Queen's Park Rangers), September 1972.

Charlton Athletic

The Valley,
Floyd Road, Charlton,
London, SE7 8AW.
01-858-3711/2

Shirts: Red, White Trim
Shorts: White, Red Stripe
Stockings: Red

Charlton Athletic was a name to conjure with between 1935 and 1947 when the London club distinguished themselves in League and Cup. They came within touching distance of a memorable League hat-trick after winning the Division Three (South) Championship in 1935. The following season they gained promotion to Division One, and twelve months later they were runners-up for the Championship itself. Beaten in extra time in the F.A. Cup Final of 1946 by Derby. Charlton returned to Wembley the following season and won the Cup by beating Burnley 1-0 after extra time.

But after the glories of the forties came the slump with Charlton falling into Division Two in 1957 and then, in 1972, further down to Division Three, which they had left in 1935.

Among Charlton's best-known players were Sam Bartram, who kept goal for them in 583 League games from 1934-56, and South Africans John Hewie (capped 19 times by Scotland at full-back) and Stuart Leary, who holds the club scoring record with 153 goals between 1953-62.

In December 1957 Charlton staged one of the most amazing recoveries in football history. With 20 minutes left in a Second Division match at home to Huddersfield, they were losing 5-1 and reduced to ten men—yet finished winners by 7-6, with Johnny Summers scoring five of the goals.

F.A. Cup Winners: 1946-47.
Division 3 (South) Champions: 1928-29, 1934-35.
Record attendance: 75,031 v. Aston Villa (F.A. Cup), February 1938.
Modern Capacity: 67,000.
Entered Football League: 1921—Div. 3 (South).
Biggest win: 8-1 v. Middlesbrough (Div. 1), September 1953.
Heaviest defeat: 1-11 v. Aston Villa (Div. 2), November 1959.
Best in Football League Cup: 4th Round 1962-63, 1964-65.
Pitch measurements: 114 × 73 yd.
Highest League Scorer in Single Season: Ralph Allen—32 in 1934-35 (Div. 3 South).
Transfers—
  Highest fee paid: £50,000—Eamonn Rogers (from Blackburn), October 1971.
  Highest fee received: £80,000—Len Glover (to Leicester), November 1967; £80,000—Paul Went (to Fulham), July 1972.

Chelsea

Stamford Bridge Grounds,
Fulham Road,
London, SW6 1HS.
01-385-5545/6

Shirts: Royal Blue
Shorts: Royal Blue, White Seam
Stockings: White

For the first fifty years of their existence Chelsea did not win a single prize. Then they celebrated their golden jubilee by taking the League Championship of 1954-55 under the managership of Ted Drake. Under his successor, Tommy Docherty, they won the League Cup in 1964-65 and, guided by Dave Sexton, they collected two more trophies in successive seasons.

In 1970 Chelsea at last lifted the F.A. Cup, dramatically beating Leeds 2-1 in extra time at Old Trafford in the first replayed Final since 1912. That victory qualified them for the Cup-Winners' Cup, and led them a year later to their first European prize, Real Madrid being beaten in the replayed Final in Athens. In 1972 they reached their third successive Final—this time in the League Cup—but Stoke beat them 2-1, so Chelsea have still to win a peacetime trophy at Wembley.

No other club ever gained election to the Football League without taking part in any competition or so much as a friendly match, as Chelsea did in 1905. Apart from season 1962-63, they have been permanent members of the First Division since 1930.

Having established a place among the élite, Chelsea embarked on a multi-million pound ground reorganization that promised, by the late 1970s, to put Stamford Bridge among Europe's finest homes of football.

League Champions: 1954-55.
F.A. Cup Winners: 1969-70.
League Cup Winners: 1964-65.
Winners of European Cup-Winners' Cup: 1970-71.
Record attendance: 82,905 v. Arsenal (League), October 1935.
Modern Capacity: 55,000
Entered Football League: 1905—Div. 2.
Biggest win: 13-0 v. Jeunesse Hautcharage, Luxembourg (European Cup-Winners' Cup), September 1971.
Heaviest defeat: 1-8 v. Wolves (Div. 1), September 1953.
Pitch measurements: $114 \times 71\frac{1}{2}$ yd.
Highest League Scorer in Single Season: Jimmy Greaves—41 in 1960-61 (Div. 1).
Transfers—
  Highest fee paid: £170,000—Steve Kember (from Crystal Palace), September 1971.
  Highest fee received: £275,000—Peter Osgood (to Southampton), March 1974.

Chester

The Stadium,
Sealand Road,
Chester, CH1 4LW.
Chester 21048

Shirts: Royal Blue and
 White Stripes
Shorts: White
Stockings: Royal Blue

For Chester F.C., proximity to those two great Merseyside clubs, Everton and Liverpool, has always meant severe competition for players and supporters. The club was formed in 1884—four years before the Football League began—but did not gain election to the old Third Division North until 1931. The early seasons were full of promise. The team finished third in their début year, fourth the following season, third in 1934–35, were runners-up in 1935–36, and third in 1936–37.

A number of International players, among them Tommy Lawton and Don Welsh, assisted the club while on military service during the Second World War. On the resumption of peacetime League football in 1946–47, Chester filled third place once more, but since then a succession of managers, including Frank Brown, Louis Page and John Harris, have not been able to bring the Cheshire club much success.

In the F.A. Cup, Chester have never gone beyond the fourth round, but for a brief period in the winter of 1952 they attracted attention in the competition by holding First Division Chelsea to a 2–2 draw in the third round at Stamford Bridge. A record crowd of 20,500 saw Chester lose the replay 3–2.

Record attendance: 20,500 v. Chelsea (F.A. Cup), January 1952.
Modern Capacity: 20,000.
Entered Football League: 1931—Div. 3 (North).
Biggest win: 12–0 v. York City (Div. 3 North), February 1936.
Heaviest defeat: 2–11 v. Oldham Athletic (Div. 3 North), January 1952.
Highest final League position: 2nd in Div. 3 (North), 1935–36.
Best in F.A. Cup: 4th Round 1932–33, 1936–37, 1938–39, 1946–47, 1947–48, 1969–70.
Best in Football League Cup: 3rd Round 1962–63, 1964–65.
Pitch measurements: 114 × 75 yd.
Highest League Scorer in Single Season: Dick Yates—36 in 1946–47 (Div. 3 North).
Transfers—
  Highest fee paid: £11,000—Jimmy Redfern (from Bolton), July 1973.
  Highest fee received: £110,000—Paul Futcher (to Luton), May 1974.

Chesterfield

Recreation Ground,
Chesterfield, S40 4SX
Chesterfield 2318

Shirts: Royal Blue, White Trim
Shorts: White
Stockings: Royal Blue, White Tops

Membership of Chesterfield F.C. in their formation year of 1866 cost a couple of shillings or ten new pence. Exactly 100 years later the club's most distinguished product, Gordon Banks, kept goal for England in their World Cup Final victory over West Germany at Wembley. Banks, later of Leicester City and Stoke City, has always acknowledged the value of those early days with Chesterfield. He is one of two outstanding goalkeepers developed post-war by the club. The other was Ray Middleton, who became a Justice of the Peace following his work for local youth organizations. Other well-known players in the town of the Crooked Spire have included members of the Milburn family, 'Legs' Linacre, Tommy Capel and Gordon Dale.

Chesterfield played in Division Two between 1899 and 1909 but then dropped out of the League until 1921, when they re-entered as members of Division Three (North), a section which they won in 1931 and 1936.

They have spent two separate periods in Division Two since those early days, and in 1947 finished fourth—the highest final placing they have attained in the Football League. More recently they have alternated between the Third and Fourth Divisions, but last season (1973-74) they were among the principal contenders for a place in Division Two, which they left in 1951.

Division 3 (North) Champions: 1930-31, 1935-36.
Division 4 Champions: 1969-70.
Record attendance: 30,968 v. Newcastle (League), April 1939.
Modern Capacity: 28,500.
Entered Football League: 1899—Div. 2.
Biggest win: 10-0 v. Glossop N.E. (Div. 2), January 1903.
Heaviest defeat: 1-9 v. Port Vale (Div. 2), September 1932.
Best in F.A. Cup: 5th Round 1932-33, 1937-38, 1949-50.
Best in Football League Cup: 4th Round 1964-65.
Pitch measurements: 114 x 73 yd.
Highest League Scorer in Single Season: Jimmy Cookson —44 in 1925-26 (Div. 3 North).
Transfers—
  Highest fee paid: £15,000—Frank Barlow (from Sheffield United), July 1972.
  Highest fee received: £60,000—Jim Brown (to Sheffield United), March 1974.

Colchester United

Layer Road Ground,
Colchester CO2 7JJ.
Colchester 74042

Shirts: Blue and White Stripes
Shorts: Blue
Stockings: White

Colchester United first made an impact on soccer in England in 1948, when they achieved a series of astonishing F.A. Cup giant-killing acts. While still members of the Southern League, they knocked out Huddersfield Town and Bradford (who had previously defeated Arsenal) before finally falling at Blackpool in the fifth round. Their manager then was Ted Fenton, who later guided West Ham back to the First Division.

Not surprisingly after such impressive evidence of their talents, Colchester were elected to the Football League in 1950. And 21 years later, in the fifth round of season 1970–71, they celebrated their 'coming of age' with another incredible Cup triumph. This time they defeated Leeds United 3–2 at Layer Road, and by now even Wembley seemed a possibility for manager Dick Graham's team of Fourth Division enthusiasts, but in the quarter-finals Colchester were drawn away to Everton and beaten 5–0.

Three times in the Sixties Colchester lost their place in Division Three, but they returned again at the end of season 1973–74 on the strength of magnificent home form and the individual scoring power of 24-goal Bobby Svarc.

Record attendance: 19,072 v. Reading (F.A. Cup), November 1948.
Modern Capacity: 16,000.
Entered Football League: 1950—Div. 3 (South).
Biggest win: 9–1 v. Bradford City (Div. 4), December 1961.
Heaviest defeat: 0–7 v. Leyton Orient (Div. 3 South), January 1952; 0–7 v. Reading (Div. 3 South), September 1957.
Highest final League position: 2nd in Div. 4, 1961–62.
Best in F.A. Cup: 6th Round 1970–71.
Best in Football League Cup: 4th Round 1963–64.
Pitch measurements: 110 × 74 yd.
Highest League Scorer in Single Season: Bobby Hunt—37 in 1961–62 (Div. 4).
Transfers—
  Highest fee paid: £15,000—Dave Simmons (from Aston Villa), December 1970.
  Highest fee received: £15,000—Bobby Hunt (to Northampton), March 1964; £15,000—Duncan Forbes (to Norwich), September 1968.

Coventry City

Highfield Road Ground,
Coventry.
Coventry 57171

Shirts: Sky Blue, Black Trim
Shorts: Black
Stockings: Sky Blue

The rise of Coventry City from the obscurity of the Fourth Division in 1959, to the glamour of the First Division eight years later, is one of the success stories of modern soccer.

From the old Southern League, they gained admission to the Football League in 1919 and just avoided relegation from the Second Division in their first season. They dropped down to the Third Division in 1925 and took eleven seasons to get back into the Second, finishing 1935–36 as Third Division South Champions.

Coventry slipped again in 1952 and became founder members of the Fourth Division in 1958. After only one season in the Fourth, however, the new-look City gained promotion to the Third and began the thrilling climb that took them into the First Division in 1967. Thus they became the only club to have played in six divisions of the Football League (3N, 3S, 4, 3, 2, 1).

That ebullient manager, Jimmy Hill, led the Sky Blue Revolution of the sixties, and having reached the First Division for the first time, City had to survive a two-season threat of relegation before they could breathe more comfortably in the top section.

Divison 2 Champions: 1966–67.
Division 3 (South) Champions: 1935–36.
Division 3 Champions: 1963–64.
Record attendance: 51,455 v. Wolves (League), April 1967.
Modern Capacity: 52,000.
Entered Football League: 1919—Div. 2.
Biggest win: 9–0 v. Bristol City (Div. 3 South), April 1934.
Heaviest defeat: 2–10 v. Norwich City (Div. 3 South), March 1930.
Best in F.A. Cup: 6th Round 1962–63, 1972–73 (also reached the last eight in old 4th Round 1909–10).
Best in Football League Cup: 5th Round 1964–65, 1970–71, 1973–74.
Pitch measurements: 110 x 72 yd.
Highest League Scorer in Single Season: Clarrie Bourton—49 in 1931–32 (Div. 3 South).
Transfers—
  Highest fee paid: £150,000—David Cross (from Norwich), November 1973.
  Highest fee received: £200,000—Jeff Blockley (to Arsenal), October 1972.

Crewe Alexandra

Gresty Road,
Crewe.
Crewe 3014

Shirts: Red
Shorts: White
Stockings: Black, Red and White Tops

The club owes its origins to the game of cricket. In 1876 a local cricket team decided to form a football section, and only 12 years later, while still amateurs, Crewe Alexandra—derived from the name of the town and the hotel they used—had reached the semi-final of the F.A. Cup.

They turned professional in 1893, the year after becoming a founder member of Division Two of the Football League. Unhappily, they were not re-elected in 1896 and remained in comparative obscurity until after the First World War when they re-entered the League in Division Three (North) in 1921.

Since then the story of Crewe has almost always been one of hard struggle. Promotion from Division Four in 1962–63, when they were third, and again in 1967–68 (fourth) provided brief periods of reward, and another was the club's remarkable 2–1 F.A. Cup third round win at Chelsea in January 1961.

The most melancholy period in Crewe's long history occurred during 1956–57 when they played a record 30 consecutive League matches without a win. One of the finest players produced by Crewe was Frank Blunstone, who moved to Chelsea as a boy winger in February 1953 and went on to gain five full caps for England.

Record attendance: 20,000 v. Tottenham (F.A. Cup), January 1960.
Modern Capacity: 16,000.
Entered Football League: 1892—Div. 2.
Biggest win: 8–0 v. Rotherham Utd (Div. 3 North), October 1932.
Heaviest defeat: 2–13 v. Tottenham (F.A. Cup), February 1960.
Highest final League position: 3rd in Div. 4, 1962–63.
Best in F.A. Cup: Semi-final 1887–88.
Best in Football League Cup: 3rd Round 1960–61.
Pitch measurements: 112 × 75 yd.
Highest League Scorer in Single Season: Terry Harkin—35 in 1964–65 (Div. 4).
Transfers—
  Highest fee paid: £5000—Gordon Wallace (from Liverpool), October 1967.
  Highest fee received: £20,000—John Mahoney (to Stoke), March 1967.

Crystal Palace

Selhurst Park,
London, SE25 6PU.
01-653-2223

Shirts: Royal Blue and
   Red Stripes
Shorts: Royal Blue
Stockings: Royal Blue,
   Red and White
   Turnover

The progress of Crystal Palace to First Division status became more than a dream from April 1966, when they appointed Bert Head as manager. He joined them from Bury, but first made his mark in football management at Swindon, where he built a star-studded team from nothing, and by 1969 Palace completed the astonishing climb from Fourth Division to First in only eight years.

Selhurst Park was redeveloped to match the club's proudly-won status, but despite enormous spending in the transfer market Palace were always struggling to stay in top company. In March 1973 the flamboyant Malcolm Allison was appointed manager, but he could not save the club from relegation that season or the next, when Palace's sad decline continued with a further fall to Division Three.

Palace were elected to the Football League in 1920 and celebrated by finishing at the top of the Third Division, but that was the only notable landmark in their history until 1961, when they climbed out of the Fourth Division and began the rise to the top.

Division 3 Champions: 1920–21.
Record attendance: 49,498 v. Chelsea (League), December 1969.
Modern Capacity: 52,000.
Entered Football League: 1920—Div. 3.
Biggest win: 9–0 v. Barrow (Div. 4), October 1959.
Heaviest defeat: 4–11 v. Manchester City (F.A. Cup), February 1926.
Best in F.A. Cup: 6th Round 1964–65 (also reached last eight in old 4th Round 1906–07).
Best in Football League Cup: 5th Round 1968–69, 1970–71.
Pitch measurements: 110 × 75 yd.
Highest League Scorer in Single Season: Peter Simpson—46 in 1930–31 (Div. 3 South).
Transfers—
   Highest fee paid: £140,000—Don Rogers (from Swindon), October 1972.
   Highest fee received: £170,000—Steve Kember (to Chelsea), September 1971.

Darlington

Feethams Ground,
Darlington.
Darlington 65097/67712

Shirts: White
Shorts: White
Stockings: White

Eighty pounds would not buy a complete set of team kit today. Yet in season 1924—25 Darlington won the Third Division North title with a team assembled for just that modest sum. They finished five points ahead of the next two clubs, Nelson and New Brighton, neither of whom are now members of the Football League. Unfortunately they survived only two seasons before being relegated.

Darlington are one of the comparatively few League clubs to have used only one ground—the Feethams—since their formation in 1883. In their early years they played in the Northern League and became professional in 1908, when they joined the North-Eastern League. The club was reformed after the First World War, and in 1921 became one of the original members of the old Division Three North.

They remained there until Division Four was created in 1958, and in season 1965—66 they delighted their supporters by finishing runners-up with the same number of points (59) as the champions, Doncaster Rovers. A year later, however, they were relegated. Darlington's best-known players have included centre-forward David Brown (74 League goals in 97 matches from 1923—26) and Ken Furphy, who has gone on to manage Workington, Watford, Blackburn and Sheffield United.

Division 3 (North) Champions: 1924—25.
Record attendance: 21,023 v. Bolton Wanderers (League Cup), November 1960.
Modern Capacity: 21,000.
Entered Football League: 1921—Div. 3 (North).
Biggest win: 13—1 v. Scarborough (F.A. Cup), 1886.
Heaviest defeat: 0—10 v. Doncaster (Div. 4), January 1964.
Best in F.A. Cup: 5th Round 1957—58.
Best in Football League Cup: 5th Round 1967—68.
Pitch measurements: 110 × 74 yd.
Highest League Scorer in Single Season: David Brown—39 in 1924—25 (Div. 3 North).
Transfers—
  Highest fee paid: £7000—Frank McMahon (from Lincoln), March 1973.
  Highest fee received: £17,000—Bryan Conlon (to Millwall), November 1967.

Derby County

Baseball Ground,
Shaftesbury Crescent,
Derby, DE3 8NB.
Derby 40105

Shirts: White
Shorts: Dark Blue
Stockings: White

The revival of Derby County began with the appointment of Brian Clough, former Middlesbrough and England centre-forward, in May 1967. Under his inspiring managership (and, on the field, rallied by the captaincy and playing skill of Dave Mackay) Derby roared back into the First Division two years later.

In season 1971–72 they became League Champions for the first time, but in October 1973 Clough sensationally quit the club, and the task of restoring calm after a major upheaval fell upon Mackay, who left Nottingham Forest to return to Derby.

Why do Derby County—one of the original 12 Football League clubs in 1888—have a home with the unlikely name of the Baseball Ground? In 1895 a wealthy businessman, Sir Francis Ley, formed a baseball club in the town and built a fine ground, but the American game did not catch on. After a few months, the baseball club was disbanded, and County moved in. Previously they had played at the Derby racecourse ground.

In 1946 Derby, with world-class inside-forwards in Raich Carter and Peter Doherty, won their first major trophy, beating Charlton 4–1 in extra time in the F.A. Cup Final. But between 1953 and 1955 they slumped from First to Third Division North.

League Champions: 1971–72
Division 2 Champions: 1911–12, 1914–15, 1968–69.
Division 3 (North) Champions: 1956–57.
F.A. Cup Winners: 1945–46.
Record attendance: 41,826 v. Tottenham (League), September 1969.
Modern Capacity: 42,000.
Entered Football League: 1888—Div. 1.
Biggest win: 9–0 v. Wolves (Div. 1), January 1891; 9–0 v. Sheffield Wednesday (Div. 1), January 1899.
Heaviest defeat: 2–11 v. Everton (F.A. Cup), 1889–90.
Best in Football League Cup: Semi-final 1967–68.
Pitch measurements: 110 × 71 yd.
Highest League Scorer in Single Season: Jack Bowers—37 in 1930–31 (Div. 1); Ray Straw—37 in 1956–57 (Div. 3 North).
Transfers—
  Highest fee paid: £250,000—David Nish (from Leicester), August 1972.
  Highest fee received: £90,000—John Robson (to Aston Villa), December 1972.

Doncaster Rovers

Belle Vue Ground,
Doncaster, DN4 5HT.
Doncaster 55281

Shirts: White with Two Red Hoops and Trim
Shorts: Red
Stockings: White

Doncaster Rovers' past is crowded with players of distinction: the Keetley brothers, Frank, Harold, Joe and Tom (who still holds the club record for the most League goals—178); Fred Emery, later manager; Sam Cowan who won England caps with Manchester City; Jack Lambert, Arsenal's centre-forward in the 1930 and 1932 F.A. Cup Finals; Peter Doherty, rated by many as the most skilful inside-forward of his era; Clarrie Jordan (42 League goals in 1946–47); Manchester United and Northern Ireland goalkeeper Harry Gregg; England Under-23 forward Alick Jeffrey, with 36 goals, was the League's top scorer in 1964–65.

The Belle Vue ground, opposite Doncaster racecourse, is at 118½ by 79 yards the largest pitch in the League and no more notable performances have been achieved on it than in 1946–47. That season Rovers won the old Third Division North title with the astonishing total of 72 points from 42 League matches, including 37 from away games. Not surprisingly, that points tally has remained a League record.

The highlights last season (1973–74) were a 0–0 draw by Rovers, then 92nd in the Football League, away to Champions Liverpool in the F.A. Cup third round and a crowd of 22,499 at Doncaster for the replay which Liverpool won 2–0.

Division 3 (North) Champions: 1934–35, 1946–47, 1949–50.
Division 4 Champions: 1965–66, 1968–69.
Record attendance: 37,149 v. Hull (League), October 1948.
Modern Capacity: 40,000.
Entered Football League: 1901—Div. 2.
Biggest win: 10–0 v. Darlington (Div. 4), January 1964.
Heaviest defeat: 0–12 v. Small Heath (Div. 2), April 1903.
Best in F.A. Cup: 5th Round 1951–52, 1953–54, 1954–55, 1955–56.
Best in Football League Cup: 3rd Round 1960–61, 1964–65, 1966–67.
Pitch measurements: 118½ × 79 yd.
Highest League Scorer in Single Season: Clarrie Jordan—42 in 1946–47 (Div. 3 North).
Transfers—
  Highest fee paid: £10,000—John Flowers (from Stoke), July 1966.
  Highest fee received: £70,000—Mike Elwiss (to Preston), February 1974.

Everton

Goodison Park,
Liverpool, L4 4EL,
051-525-5263/4

Shirts: Royal Blue, White Trim
Shorts: White
Stockings: White

In 1888 Everton became one of the original members of the Football League and were Division ·One champions in 1890—91. Fifteen years later they won the F.A. Cup for the first time. Everton stayed in the First Division for 42 years until 1930, then spent only one season in the Second before returning to win the First Division twice more (1932 and 1939) before the Second World War. By a fractional goal average, the club went down again in 1951, and it took them three years to get back.

Twice during Harry Catterick's managership, in 1963 and 1970, Everton won the Championship, making seven League titles in all for the Goodison Park club, and in 1966 they took the F.A. Cup for the third time. But in May 1973, after three moderate seasons, Everton appointed a new manager—Billy Bingham, their former Irish International right-winger.

Everton broke all British transfer records in February 1974 when, in a part-exchange deal with Birmingham City, they paid the equivalent of £350,000 for striker Bob Latchford (for details see foot of page).

League Champions: 1890—91, 1914—15, 1927—28, 1931—32, 1938—39, 1962—63, 1969—70.
Division 2 Champions: 1930—31.
F.A. Cup Winners: 1905—06, 1932—33, 1965—66.
Record attendance: 78,299 v. Liverpool (League), September 1948.
Modern Capacity: 56,000.
Entered Football League: 1888—Div. 1.
Biggest win: 11—2 v. Derby County (F.A. Cup), 1889—90.
Heaviest defeat: 4—10 v. Tottenham (Div. 1), October 1958.
Best in Football League Cup: 5th Round 1960—61.
Pitch measurements: 112 × 75 yd.
Highest League Scorer in Single Season: Bill ('Dixie') Dean—60 in 1927—28 (Div. 1).
Transfers—
  Highest fee paid: £350,000 equivalent (British record)—Bob Latchford (from Birmingham City—£80,000 cash plus Howard Kendall, valued £180,000, and Archie Styles, valued £90,000), February 1974.
  Highest fee received: £220,000—Alan Ball (to Arsenal), December 1971.

Exeter City

St James's Park,
Exeter, EX4 6PX.
0392—54073

Shirts: Red and White Stripes
Shorts: Red
Stockings: Red, White Tops

No one would suggest that life has been easy for the City club which has never journeyed above the Third Division. Nevertheless, a number of distinguished players began their careers at St James's Park. They include left-winger Cliff Bastin, who became an England international and collected F.A. Cup-winning and First Division Championship medals with Arsenal before he was 20; Dick Pym, Bolton's goalkeeper in three successful Cup Finals at Wembley in the 1920s; and the modern Fourth Division hero of Exeter's schoolboys was Fred Binney, City's leading scorer in seasons 1971—72, 1972—73 and 1973—74, but then transferred to Brighton.

Who among Exeter's older supporters will forget the wonderful Cup run in 1931? After fighting through to the competition proper, they beat First Division Derby 3—2 at Exeter; next they won 2—1 at Bury and then, in front of their own followers again, defeated Leeds United 3—1. That victory put Exeter in the last eight for the only time, and when the 'Grecians' held Sunderland 1—1 at Roker Park, it seemed they were heading for the semi-finals. But before a record crowd of nearly 21,000 the replay was lost by four goals to two.

Record attendance: 20,984 v. Sunderland (F.A. Cup), March 1931.
Modern Capacity: 18,500.
Entered Football League: 1920—Div. 3.
Biggest win: 8—1 v. Coventry City (Div. 3 South), December 1926; 8—1 v. Aldershot (Div. 3 South), May 1935.
Heaviest defeat: 0—9 v. Notts County (Div. 3 South), October 1948; 0—9 v. Northampton (Div. 3 South), April 1958.
Highest final League position: Runners-up Division 3 (South) 1932—33.
Best in F.A. Cup: 6th Round 1930—31.
Best in Football League Cup: 4th Round 1973—74.
Pitch measurements: 115 × 75 yd.
Highest League Scorer in Single Season: Fred Whitlow—34 in 1932—33 (Div. 3 South).
Transfers—
  Highest fee paid: (£15,000 (combined fee)—John Templeman and Lammie Robertson (from Brighton), May 1974.
  Highest fee received: £40,000 equivalent (£25,000 plus two players in exchange)—Fred Binney (to Brighton), May 1974.

Fulham

Craven Cottage,
Stevenage Road,
Fulham, London. SW6.
01–736–5621/7035

Shirts: White
Shorts: Black
Stockings: White

Although this Thames-side club has fielded many outstanding players, among them the former England captain Johnny Haynes and George Cohen, one of England's 1966 World Cup-winning team, it has never won the League Championship or, in fact, reached an F.A. Cup Final.

Twice Fulham have experienced brief spells of First Division football, but after losing top status for the second time in 1968, they dropped straight into the Third Division which they had left in 1932. They returned to Division Two as runners-up in 1971.

From 1928 to 1932, Fulham were in the Third Division but then returned to the Second with centre-forward Frank Newton scoring 41 of their 111 goals that season. Although F.A. Cup semi-finalists three more times, Fulham have still to reach Wembley, despite the assistance of such players as Ronnie Rooke, Arthur Rowley, Bedford Jezzard, Tony Macedo, Roy Bentley, Johnny Haynes, George Cohen, Jimmy Hill and Alan Mullery.

In March 1974 they paid £25,000 to sign yet another big name—Bobby Moore, former England captain, from West Ham at the end of his record 108-cap International career.

Division 2 Champions: 1948–49.
Division 3 (South) Champions: 1931–32.
Record attendance: 49,335 v. Millwall (League), October 1938.
Modern Capacity: 45,000.
Entered Football League: 1907—Div. 2.
Biggest win: 10–1 v. Ipswich (Div. 1), December 1963.
Heaviest defeat: 0–9 v. Wolves (Div. 1), September 1959.
Best in F.A. Cup: Semi-final 1907–08, 1935–36, 1957–58, 1961–62.
Best in Football League Cup: 5th Round 1967–68, 1970–71.
Pitch measurements: 110 × 75 yd.
Highest League Scorer in Single Season: Frank Newton—41 in 1931–32 (Div. 3 South).
Transfers—
  Highest fee paid: £80,000—Paul Went (from Charlton), July 1972.
  Highest fee received: £154,000—Paul Went (to Portsmouth), December 1973.

LEAGUE CLUBS: COLOUR GUIDE

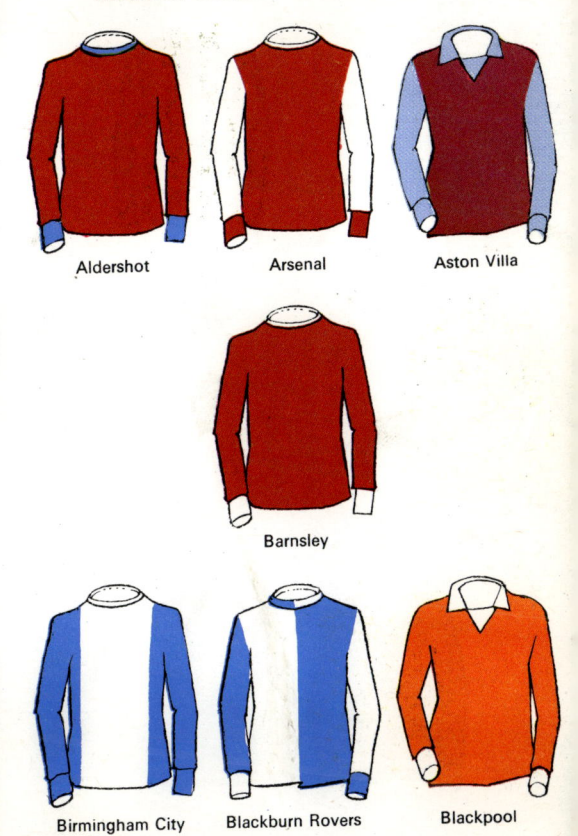

Aldershot

Arsenal

Aston Villa

Barnsley

Birmingham City

Blackburn Rovers

Blackpool

LEAGUE CLUBS: COLOUR GUIDE

Bolton Wanderers

A.F.C. Bournemouth

Bradford City

Brentford

Brighton & Hove Albion

Bristol City

Bristol Rovers

LEAGUE CLUBS: COLOUR GUIDE

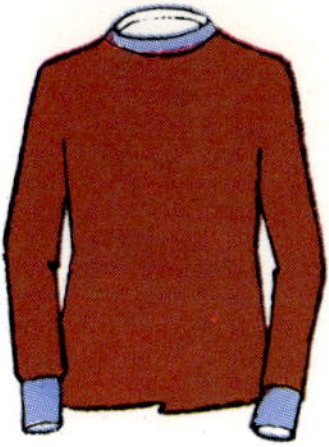

Burnley

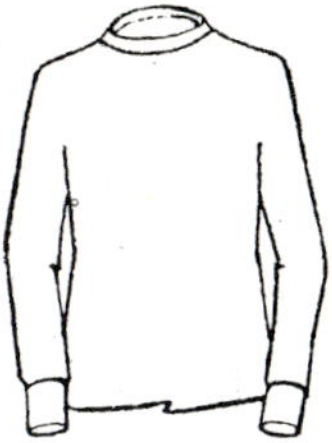

Bury

Cambridge United

Cardiff City

Carlisle United

Charlton Athletic

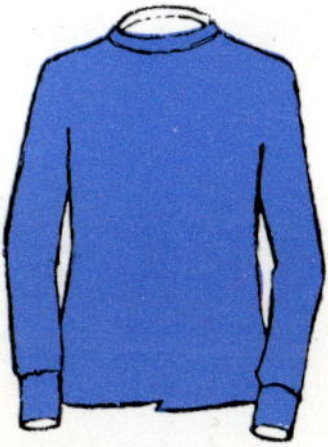

Chelsea

Chester

LEAGUE CLUBS: COLOUR GUIDE

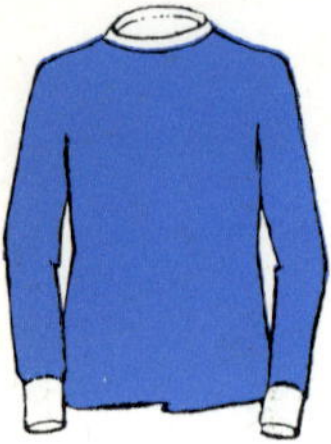

Chesterfield  | Colchester United 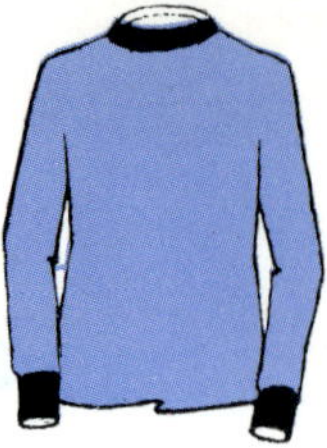 | Coventry City

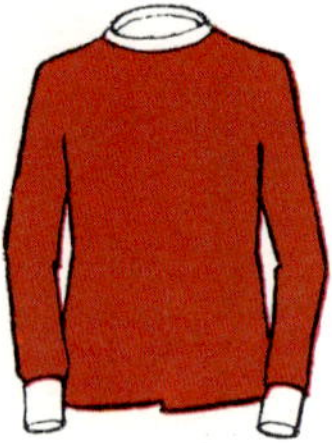

Crewe Alexandra  | Crystal Palace

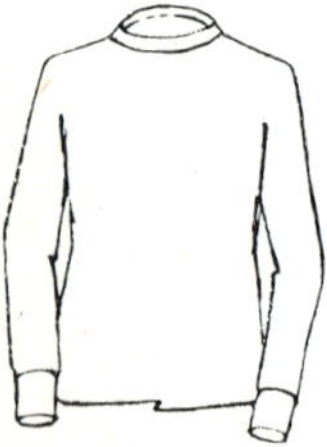

Darlington 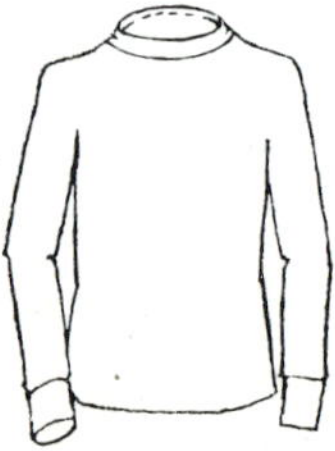 | Derby County  | Doncaster Rovers

LEAGUE CLUBS: COLOUR GUIDE

Everton

Exeter City

Fulham

Gillingham

Grimsby Town

Halifax Town

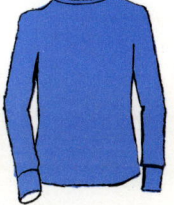

Hartlepool

Hereford

LEAGUE CLUBS: COLOUR GUIDE

Huddersfield Town

Hull City

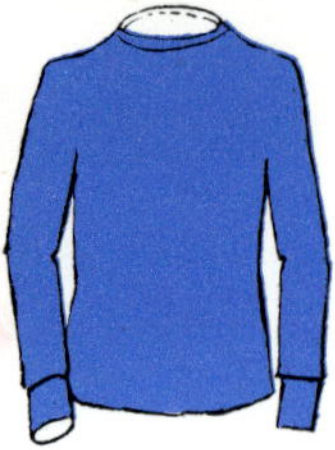

Ipswich Town

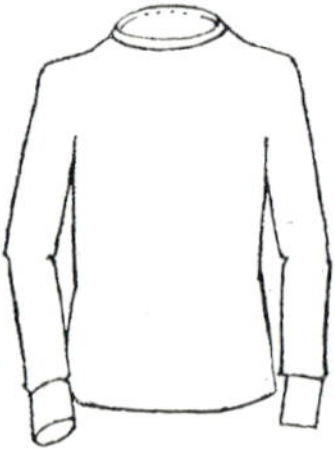

Leeds United

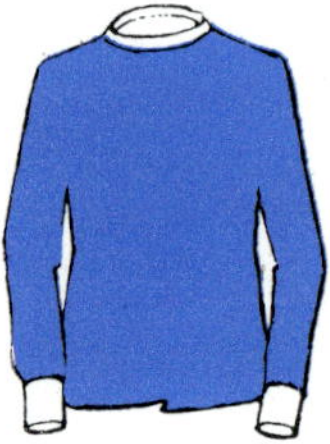

Leicester City

Lincoln City

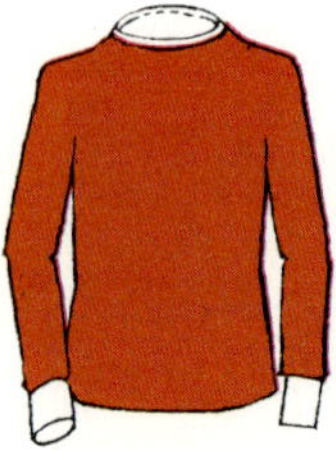

Liverpool

Luton Town

LEAGUE CLUBS: COLOUR GUIDE

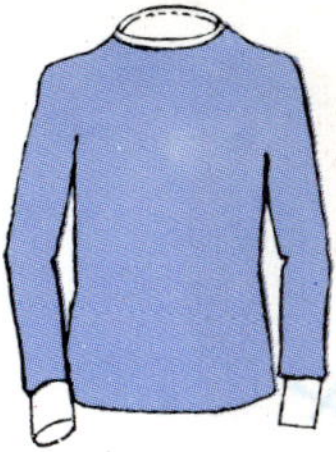

| Manchester City | Manchester United | Mansfield Town |

| Middlesbrough | Millwall |

| Newcastle United | Newport County | Northampton Town |

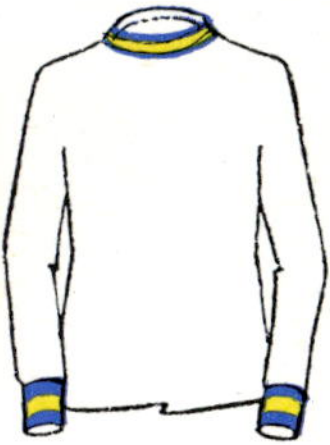

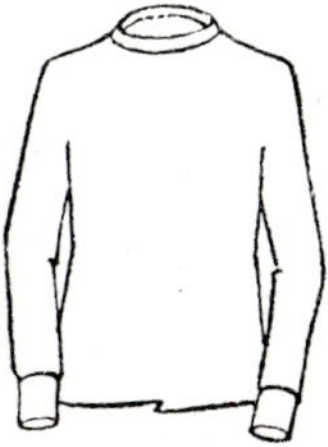

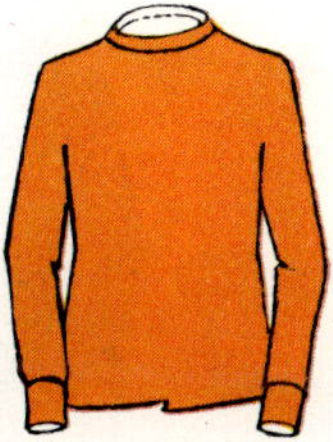

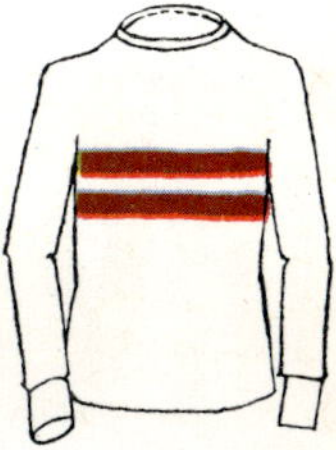

LEAGUE CLUBS: COLOUR GUIDE

Norwich City

Nottingham Forest

Notts County

Oldham Athletic

Orient

Oxford United

Peterborough United

LEAGUE CLUBS: COLOUR GUIDE

Plymouth Argyle

Portsmouth

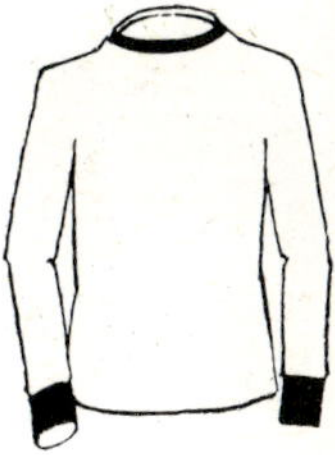

Port Vale

Preston North End

Queen's Park Rangers

Reading

Rochdale

Rotherham United

LEAGUE CLUBS: COLOUR GUIDE

Scunthorpe United    Sheffield United    Sheffield Wednesday

Shrewsbury Town    Southampton

Southend United    Southport    Stockport County

LEAGUE CLUBS: COLOUR GUIDE

Stoke City

Sunderland

Swansea City

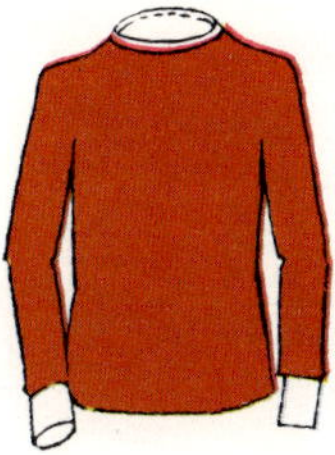

Swindon Town

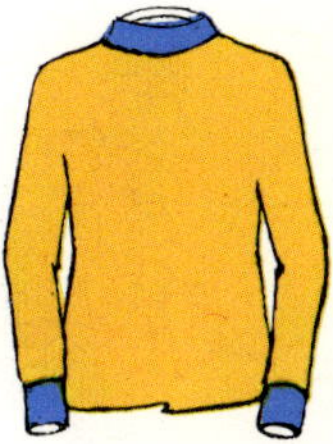

Torquay United

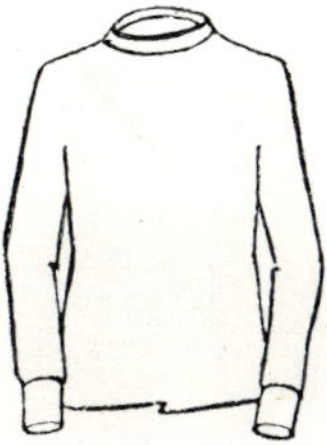

Tottenham Hotspur

Tranmere Rovers

INTERNATIONAL SHIRTS

England

Scotland

Wales

Northern Ireland

Republic of Ireland

COLOURS OF SOME WELL-KNOWN SCOTTISH CLUBS

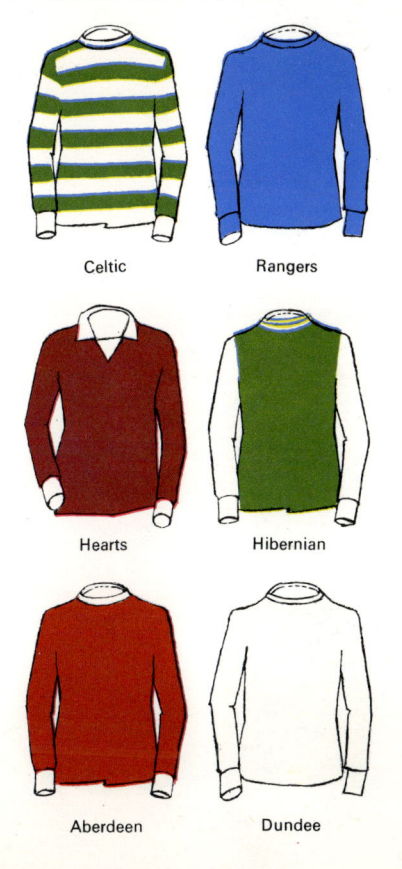

Celtic

Rangers

Hearts

Hibernian

Aberdeen

Dundee

GOALKEEPERS' COLOURS

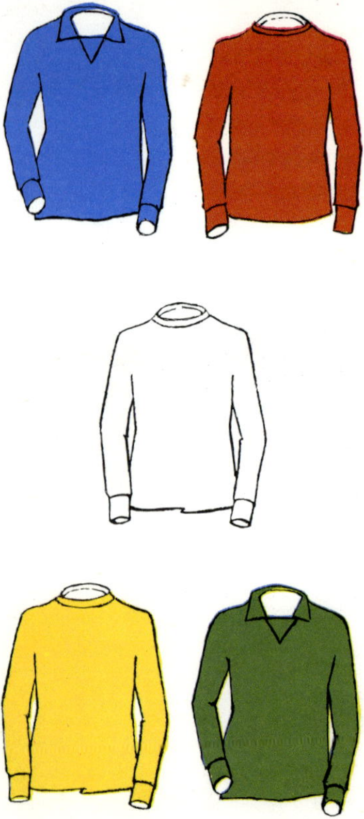

Internationals only

LEAGUE CLUBS: COLOUR GUIDE

Walsall

Watford

West Bromwich Albion

West Ham United

Wolverhampton Wanderers

Workington

Wrexham

York City

INTERNATIONAL BADGES

England

Scotland

Wales

Northern Ireland

Republic of Ireland

Gillingham

Priestfield Stadium,
Gillingham, Kent.
Medway 51854

Shirts: Blue
Shorts: Blue
Stockings: Blue

When Gillingham were voted out of the Football League in 1938 and replaced by Ipswich Town, their existence as a senior club seemed to be over. But after the war, under an energetic and far-seeing management, they became a force in the Southern League. When, in 1950, the Football League decided to increase membership from 88 to 92 clubs, by extending each Third Division section (North and South) from 22 to 24 teams, 'The Gills' were readmitted.

The club started life as New Brompton Excelsior, changing their name to Gillingham in 1913. The subsequent playing years until they left the League provided little of distinction. In fact, the club had to wait until season 1963—64 for their first major success—the Championship of the Fourth Division. They lost only nine of their 46 matches and beat Carlisle United to the title on goal average, each club obtaining 60 points.

Gillingham were relegated in 1971, but returned to the Third Division this year (1974) as last season's highest-scoring team with 90 goals. Their sharpshooter was Brian Yeo, whose 31 League goals equalled the club record set 19 years earlier by Ernie Morgan.

Division 4 Champions: 1963—64.
Record attendance: 23,002 v. Queen's Park Rangers (F.A. Cup), January 1948.
Modern Capacity: 22,000.
Entered Football League: 1920—Div. 3.
Biggest win: 10—1 v. Gorleston (F.A. Cup), November 1957.
Heaviest defeat: 2—9 v. Nottingham Forest (Div. 3 South), November 1950.
Best in F.A. Cup: 5th Round 1969—70.
Best in Football League Cup: 4th Round 1963—64.
Pitch measurements: 114 × 75 yd.
Highest League Scorer in Single Season: Ernie Morgan—31 in 1954—55 (Div. 3 South); Brian Yeo—31 in 1973—74 (Div. 4).
Transfers—
  Highest fee paid: £8000—Rodney Green (from Bradford City), July 1964.
  Highest fee received: £50,000—David Peach (to Southampton), January 1974.

Grimsby Town

Blundell Park,
Cleethorpes, Lincs.
Cleethorpes 61420/61803

Shirts: Black and White Stripes
Shorts: Black
Stockings: Red

In the period between the two wars Grimsby Town, whose ground is situated in the town of Cleethorpes, played in four sections of the Football League—the Third Division and Third North, as well as the First and Second Divisions.

They were still in Division One immediately after the Second World War, but finished bottom in 1948, and after ups and downs between Divisions Two and Four, they found themselves having to seek re-election through finishing 91st on the League ladder in season 1968–69. Three years later they were Fourth Division champions.

The club was founded as Grimsby Pelham in 1878, but after a year dropped the name Pelham. They won the Division Two Championship in 1901 and again in 1934. Two years later they lost to Arsenal by the only goal in the semi-final of the F.A. Cup. They again reached the last four in 1939, this time crashing 5–0 to Wolverhampton Wanderers.

Grimsby have produced many first-class forwards, none better than Ernest (Pat) Glover, who scored 42 League goals in 1933–34, and Jackie Bestall, the finest creator of attacks in the club's history.

Division 2 Champions: 1900–01, 1933–34.
Division 3 (North) Champions: 1925–26, 1955–56.
Division 4 Champions: 1971–72.
Record attendance: 31,650 v. Wolves (F.A. Cup), February 1937.
Modern Capacity: 28,000.
Entered Football League: 1892–Div. 2.
Biggest win: 9–2 v. Darwen (Div. 2), April 1899.
Heaviest defeat: 1–9 v. Arsenal (Div. 1), January 1931.
Best in F.A. Cup: Semi-final 1935–36, 1938–39.
Best in Football League Cup: 5th Round 1965–66.
Pitch measurements: 111 × 74 yd.
Highest League Scorer in Single Season: Pat Glover—42 in 1933–34 (Div. 2).
Transfers—
  Highest fee paid: £20,000—Phil Hubbard (from Norwich), October 1972.
  Highest fee received: £20,000—Doug Collins (to Burnley), September 1968.

Halifax Town

Shay Ground,
Halifax HX1 2YS.
Halifax 53423

Shirts: Blue, Tangerine Trim
Shorts: Blue
Stockings: Blue, Tangerine Tops

The seasons of reward have been strictly limited for Halifax Town since their early days in the Yorkshire Combination and Midland League. So there was understandable excitement in 1971 when the club made a sustained bid to bring Second Division football to The Shay for the first time. In the end, they had to be content with third place behind Preston and Fulham.

Two seasons earlier the Town side had won their way into the Third Division as runners-up to Doncaster Rovers after an unbroken sequence as members of the Third Division (North) and then the Fourth Division. In those bleak days Halifax had to seek re-election seven times, and it says much for their perseverance that they were repeatedly voted back.

The Shay bulged at its sides one February day in 1953, when nearly 37,000 turned up to watch Tottenham Hotspur in the F.A. Cup fifth round. Halifax had made the most of their luck in being drawn at home in every tie, and after dealing with Ashton and Southport, they put out First Division 'giants' Cardiff and Stoke. But for all the urgings of their record crowd they went down 3–0 to Spurs.

Record attendance: 36,885 v. Tottenham (F.A. Cup), February 1953.
Modern Capacity: 38,000.
Entered Football League: 1921—Div. 3 (North).
Biggest win: 7–0 v. Bishop Auckland (F.A. Cup), January 1967.
Heaviest defeat: 0–13 v. Stockport County (Div. 3 North), January 1934.
Highest final League position: Runners-up Div. 3 (North) 1934–35; runners-up Div. 4 1968–69.
Best in F.A. Cup: 5th Round 1932–33, 1952–53.
Best in Football League Cup: 4th Round 1963–64.
Pitch measurements: 110 × 70 yd.
Highest League Scorer in Single Season: Albert Valentine —34 in 1934–35 (Div. 3 North).
Transfers—
  Highest fee paid: £14,000—Fred Kemp (from Blackpool), January 1972.
  Highest fee received: £45,000—Alan Waddle (to Liverpool), June 1973.

Hartlepool

Victoria Ground,
Clarence Road,
Hartlepool.
Hartlepool 2584/3492

Shirts: Blue
Shorts: White
Stockings: Blue and White Hoops

Overshadowed throughout their existence by their powerful north-eastern neighbours, Newcastle and Sunderland, the Hartlepool club have known more of life's struggles than success. Indeed, they have had to apply ten times for re-election.

They joined the old Division Three North on its formation in 1921, and stayed in this section until they moved into the newly created Fourth Division in 1958. They did finish runners-up in 1956—57, but in those days only one club gained promotion from each Third Division section. They scored 90 goals in their 46 matches that season, and on that form they were unlucky to miss a higher grade.

They had to wait another 11 years, until 1968, before they experienced promotion. Then they took third place in Division Four behind Luton and Barnsley. Unfortunately, at the end of the following season they were relegated. In April 1959, they briefly commanded attention by thrashing Barrow 10—1; three years later they lost by the same margin to Wrexham.

One of Hartlepool's longest-serving managers was Fred Westgarth in the after-war years, and the club also launched Brian Clough on a managerial career that developed so successfully with Derby County.

Record attendance: 17,420 v. Manchester United (F.A. Cup), January 1957.
Modern Capacity: 18,000.
Entered Football League: 1921—Div. 3 (North).
Biggest win: 10—1 v. Barrow (Div. 4), April 1959.
Heaviest defeat: 1—10 v. Wrexham (Div. 4), May 1962.
Highest final League position: Runners-up Div. 3 (North) 1956—57.
Best in F.A. Cup: 4th Round 1954—55.
Best in Football League Cup: 2nd Round 1965—66, 1967—68, 1969—70, 1972—73.
Pitch measurements: 113 × 76 yd.
Highest League Scorer in Single Season: Bill Robinson—28 in 1927—28 (Div. 3 North).
Transfers—
  Highest fee paid: £10,000—Ambrose Fogarty (from Sunderland), November 1963.
  Highest fee received: £15,000—Bill Green (to Carlisle), July 1973.

Hereford United

Edgar Street,
Hereford.
Hereford 4037

Shirts: White, Black Trim
Shorts: Black
Stockings: White, Black Hooped Tops

After striving for years for Football League membership, Southern League Hereford United so captured the public imagination with spectacular deeds in the 1971–72 F.A. Cup that, four months later, they were voted into the Fourth Division, displacing Barrow by 29–20 votes.

By knocking Newcastle United (six times winners of the F.A. Cup) out 2–1 in the third round after drawing 2–2 at St James's Park, Hereford became the first non-League club to dismiss First Division opponents since Yeovil in 1949. The romantic story continued on their entry to the Football League, for their first season ended with promotion as Fourth Division runners-up.

From player-manager Colin Addison (absent from October onwards with a broken leg) and his team, this was the complete answer to anyone who doubted whether rurally-situated Hereford could make their mark in League football on a population of 300,000 in and around the cathedral city on the banks of the River Wye.

They gained promotion with the season's highest Fourth Division average—9000, compared with 5000 during good times in the Southern League.

Record attendance: 18,114 v. Sheffield Wednesday (F.A. Cup), January 1958.
Modern capacity: 20,000.
Entered Football League: 1972—Div. 4.
Biggest win: 11–0 v. Thynnes (F.A. Cup), September 1947.
Heaviest defeat: 2–9 v. Yeovil Town (S. League), September 1955.
Highest final League position: 2nd in Div. 4, 1972–73.
Best in F.A. Cup: 4th Round 1971–72.
Best in Football League Cup: 1st Round 1972–73, 1973–74.
Pitch measurements: 111 x 80 yd.
Highest League Scorer in Single Season: Brian Owen—11 in 1972–73 (Div. 4).
Transfers—
  Highest fee paid: £11,000—Dudley Tyler (from West Ham), November 1973.
  Highest fee received: £25,000—Dudley Tyler (to West Ham), May 1972.

Huddersfield Town

Leeds Road,
Huddersfield, HD1 6PE.
Huddersfield 20335/6

Shirts: Royal Blue and White Stripes
Shorts: White
Stockings: White

In the mid-twenties Huddersfield reigned supreme as First Division Champions for three successive years (1924—25—26), the finest era in their history. Yet not many years earlier the club had struggled through periods of financial crisis.

The appointment of Herbert Chapman as manager (1922—25) heralded the club's dominant period. In that great team of the twenties which Chapman created were the captain Clem Stephenson, who had played for Aston Villa, winger Billy Smith, who made nearly 500 appearances in 15 years, full-backs Roy Goodall and Sam Wadsworth.

Having won the F.A. Cup for the first time in 1922, Town went on to their Championship treble, the first in League history.

They stayed in Division One until 1952, then won back their place first time. In 1956 they dropped again and spent 14 years in the Second Division. Their return as Div. 2 champions was but a fleeting revival, for by 1973 this club of once-great achievement and tradition had tumbled for the first time into the Third Division.

League Champions: 1923—24, 1924—25, 1925—26.
Division 2 Champions: 1969—70.
F.A. Cup Winners: 1921—22.
Record attendance: 67,037 v. Arsenal (F.A. Cup), February 1932.
Modern Capacity: 52,000.
Entered Football League: 1910—Div. 2.
Biggest win: 10—1 v. Blackpool (Div. 1), December 1930.
Heaviest defeat: 0—8 v. Middlesbrough (Div. 1), September 1950.
Best in Football League Cup: Semi-final 1967—68.
Pitch measurements: 116 × 76 yd.
Highest League Scorer in Single Season: Sam Taylor—35 in 1919—20 (Div. 2); George Brown—35 in 1925—26 (Div. 1).
Transfers—
   Highest fee paid: £70,000—Alan Gowling (from Manchester United), June 1972.
   Highest fee received: £100,000—Trevor Cherry (to Leeds), June 1972.

Hull City

Boothferry Park,
Hull, HU4 6EU.
0482–52195/7

Shirts: Amber, Black Trim
Shorts: Black
Stockings: Black, Amber Ringed Tops

Hull City were formed as an amateur club in 1904 and gained admission to the Second Division in 1905. Four times up to 1960 they dropped into the Third Division, then regained their status in the higher grade in 1966, scoring 31 victories and 109 goals in winning the Third Division title that year.

They came closest to promotion to Division One in 1910 when Oldham Athletic pipped them for second place by ·286 of a goal. During the Second World War Hull's ground in Anlaby Road was hit by enemy bombs, and in 1946 the club was reformed and acquired their present impressive home, Boothferry Park, which has its own railway station.

The list of City's post-war managers includes Frank Buckley, Raich Carter, Cliff Britton and Terry Neill, and since 1966 they have been firmly established members of the Second Division.

Hull have often been impressive F.A. Cup fighters. They were semi-finalists in 1930 [despite being on their way down to the Third Division (North)], and as a Second Division side in 1921 sprang a sensation in the third round by beating Burnley 3–0.

That season Burnley won the First Division title and, their defeat by Hull apart, played 30 matches between September and March without being beaten.

Division 3 (North) Champions: 1932–33, 1948–49.
Division 3 Champions: 1965–66.
Record attendance: 55,019 v. Man. Utd. (F.A. Cup), Feb. 1949.
Modern Capacity: 42,000.
Entered Football League: 1905—Div. 2.
Biggest win: 11–1 v. Carlisle (Div. 3 North), January 1939.
Heaviest defeat: 0–8 v. Wolves (Div. 2), November 1911.
Best in F.A. Cup: Semi-final 1929–30.
Best in Football League Cup: 4th Round 1973–74.
Pitch measurements: 113 × 73 yd.
Highest League Scorer in Single Season: Bill McNaughton —39 in 1932–33 (Div. 3 North).

Transfers—
 Highest fee paid: £60,000—Ken Knighton (from Blackburn), March 1971; £60,000—Dennis Burnett (from Millwall), October 1973.
 Highest fee received: £200,000 equivalent (£170,000 plus a player)—Stuart Pearson (to Man. United), May 1974.

Ipswich Town

Portman Road,
Ipswich, IP1 2DA.
Ipswich 51306/57107

Shirts: Royal Blue
Shorts: White
Stockings: Royal Blue

Football fame came to Ipswich in 1962 when they won the League Championship in their first season in Division One. Under Alf Ramsey the club had a remarkable rise.

Ramsey took over as manager in August 1955, after Town had gone down to the Third Division. Two years later they were back in the Second Division. They won promotion to the First as Champions after four more seasons, and a year later surprised the whole soccer world by winning the League Championship.

After their shock Championship triumph in 1962, with Ray Crawford (33) and Ted Phillips (28) scoring 61 of their 93 goals, Ipswich slipped down to the Second Division in 1964 and it took them four seasons to fight their way back.

Crawford holds the aggregate goal record (203) for Ipswich and Phillips, who also played a great part in their meteoric rise to fame, set a new club record for the most goals in a season— 41 in the Third Division South, 1956–57.

By finishing fourth in the 1972–73 League Championship, Ipswich regained a place in Europe, in which last season's U.E.F.A. Cup victories over Real Madrid and Lazio confirmed the extent of the Suffolk club's revival under the managership of Bobby Robson.

League Champions: 1961–62.
Division 2 Champions: 1960–61, 1967–68.
Division 3 (South) Champions: 1953–54, 1956–57.
Record attendance: 34,636 v. Arsenal (League), March 1973.
Modern Capacity: 35,000.
Entered Football League: 1938—Div. 3 (South).
Biggest win: 10–0 v. Floriana, Malta (European Cup), September, 1962.
Heaviest defeat: 1–10 v. Fulham (Div. 1), December 1963.
Best in F.A. Cup: 5th Round 1953–54, 1958–59, 1966–67, 1970–71.
Best in Football League Cup: 5th Round 1965–66.
Pitch measurements: 112 × 75 yd.
Highest League Scorer in Single Season: Ted Phillips—41 in 1956–57 (Div. 3 South).
Transfers—
  Highest fee paid: £125,000—David Johnson (from Everton), October 1972.
  Highest fee received: £88,000—Danny Hegan (to W.B.A.), May 1969.

Leeds United

Elland Road,
Leeds, LS11 0ES.
Leeds 716031

Shirts: White
Shorts: White
Stockings: White

Since the late sixties, Leeds have established a reputation as one of the most consistent and powerful clubs in Europe. Yet in 1962 they finished only two places away from Third Division football, at which point player-manager Don Revie took over as the full-time boss and rebuilt the team.

During the past ten years Leeds have won seven major prizes: Second Division (1964), League Cup (1968), two League Championships (1969, 1974), the Fairs Cup twice (1968,1971) and the F.A. Cup (1972). Over the same period they were runners-up ten times in domestic and European competitions.

In 1969 they set a new First Division points record (67) and under Revie they have become a major all-international force led by two outstanding captains, Jack Charlton—who retired in 1973 with the club record of 629 League appearances spread over 20 years' service—and Billy Bremner.

Three times Leeds have been close to completing the League Championship–F.A. Cup double (1965, 1970, 1972). Though the Cup was at last won in 1972, this competition has provided United's biggest upsets, with odd-goal defeats from Fourth Division Colchester (1971), Second Division Sunderland (in the 1973 Final) and another Second Division side, Bristol City, in 1974.

League Champions: 1968–69, 1973–74.
Division 2 Champions: 1923–24, 1963–64.
F.A. Cup Winners: 1971–72.
League Cup Winners: 1967–68.
European Fairs Cup Winners: 1967–68, 1970–71.
Record attendance: 57,892 v. Sunderland (F.A. Cup), March 1967.
Modern Capacity: 48,000.
Entered Football League: 1905—Div. 2 (as Leeds City).
Biggest win: 10–0 v. Lyn Oslo (European Cup), September 1969.
Heaviest defeat: 1–8 v. Stoke City (Div. 1), August 1934.
Pitch measurements: 115 × 76 yd.
Highest League Scorer in Single Season: John Charles—42 in 1953–54 (Div. 2).
Transfers—
  Highest fee paid: £165,000—Allan Clarke (from Leicester), June 1969.
  Highest fee received: £100,000—Gary Sprake (to Birmingham), October 1973.

Leicester City

Filbert Street Ground,
Leicester.
Leicester 57111/2

Shirts: Blue, White Trim
Shorts: White
Stockings: White

A dozen old boys of Wyggeston School paid ninepence each to buy a football and start a soccer team in 1884. They called themselves Leicester Fosse. At first they used the Leicester rugby ground, but in 1889 moved to Filbert Street and five years later they were elected to the Second Division.

The name was changed from Fosse to City in 1919. By then they were a well-established Second Division club. They have won the Division Two championship five times—they got their first taste of First Division football in 1925. However, until the sixties, Leicester did not figure often in the football honours list. They have played in the F.A. Cup Final four times—thrice in the sixties—and never won it. City's highest final position in the Championship was second, a point behind Sheffield Wednesday, in 1929.

In 1964 they did win the League Cup and were its runners-up in the following season. City returned to the First Division in 1971 under the managership of Frank O'Farrell, since succeeded by Jimmy Bloomfield.

Two Arthurs have been principal goalscoring heroes of Leicester. Arthur Chandler achieved a total of 262 between 1923 and 1935—his feat of scoring in 16 consecutive matches in season 1924–25 (Div. Two) remains a British record—and Arthur Rowley scored 44 League goals in the 1956–57 season to help them to the Second Division title.

Division 2 Champions: 1924–25, 1936–37, 1953–54, 1956–57, 1970–71.
League Cup Winners: 1963–64.
Record attendance: 47,298 v. Tottenham (F.A. Cup), February 1928.
Modern Capacity: 42,000.
Entered Football League: 1894—Div. 2 (as Leicester Fosse).
Biggest win: 10–0 v. Portsmouth (Div. 1), October 1928.
Heaviest defeat: 0–12 v. Nottingham F. (Div. 1), April 1909.
Best in F.A. Cup: Runners-up 1948–49, 1960–61, 1962–63, 1968–69.
Pitch measurements: 112 × 75 yd.
Highest League Scorer in Single Season: Arthur Rowley—44 in 1956–57 (Div. 2).
Transfers—
  Highest fee paid: £150,000—Allan Clarke (from Fulham), June 1968.
  Highest fee received: £250,000—David Nish (to Derby), August 1972.

Lincoln City

Sincil Bank,
Lincoln LN5 8LD.
Lincoln 21912/21298

Shirts: Red and White Stripes
Shorts: Black
Stockings: Red, White Top

Lincoln City have experienced sharply contrasting fortunes since becoming founder members of Division Two in 1892. Twice they were voted out of the section after finishing at the foot of the table—in 1908 and 1911. Three times they have won the Championship of the old Division Three North, and five times they have had to apply for re-election to Division Four.

Andy Graver, who had two spells with the club, scored 144 League goals for Lincoln through the 1950s and another successful centre-forward was Jim Hutchinson whose 32 goals in 1947–48 made him leading marksman in the Third Division that season. For rapid scoring, no one in League history has bettered Tom Keetley's six goals in 21 minutes against Halifax (Div. Three North) at Lincoln in January 1932.

Lincoln's most impressive season of all was in 1951–52, the last time they won honours. As Third North Champions they were the highest-scoring Football League side that season with 121 goals. Graver, later transferred to Leicester and then bought back again—each time at a still-existing record fee for Lincoln—scored 37 of them, including six in the club's biggest ever win of 11–1 against Crewe Alexandra.

Division 3 (North) Champions: 1931–32, 1947–48, 1951–52.
Record attendance: 23,196 v. Derby County (League Cup), November 1967.
Modern Capacity: 25,000.
Entered Football League: 1892—Div. 2.
Biggest win: 11–1 v. Crewe Alexandra (Div. 3 North), September 1951.
Heaviest defeat: 3–11 v. Manchester City (Div. 2), March 1895.
Best in F.A. Cup: 4th Round 1953–54, 1960–61.
Best in Football League Cup: 4th Round 1967–68.
Pitch measurements: 110 × 75 yd.
Highest League Scorer in Single Season: Alan Hall—42 in 1931–32 (Div. 3 North).
Transfers—
  Highest fee paid: £15,000—Andy Graver (from Leicester), June 1955.
  Highest fee received: £29,500—Andy Graver (to Leicester), December 1954.

Liverpool

Anfield Road,
Liverpool L4 0TH.
051–263–2361

Shirts: Red, White Trim
Shorts: Red
Stockings: Red

For football fanaticism there is no place quite like Merseyside, where the game is almost a religion, with Anfield the worshipping shrine for half the city's soccer devotees. It is hard to realize that as recently as 1962 Liverpool were in the Second Division.

Twice in three seasons (1963–66) they were crowned League Champions, and in the year between they won the F.A. Cup for the first time. For sheer consistency Bill Shankly's team have rivalled Leeds United over the past decade, and by winning the Championship in season 1972–73—when also taking the U.E.F.A. Cup—Liverpool equalled Arsenal's record of eight First Division titles. They added the F.A. Cup to their honours list in 1974.

Liverpool's start in League football augured well for a successful future. They took the Second Division title in their first season (1893–94), going unbeaten through the 28-match programme, and altogether they have won twelve Championships. Yet if it had not been for Everton, Liverpool might never have graced the football world. Everton had been playing at Anfield when, around 1892, the owner decided to put up the rent. Rather than pay the extra money, Everton moved to Goodison Park, but a few of their members stayed at Anfield . . . and formed Liverpool.

League Champions: 1900–01, 1905–06, 1921–22, 1922–23, 1946–47, 1963–64, 1965–66, 1972–73.
Division 2 Champions: 1893–94, 1895–96, 1904–05, 1961–62.
F.A. Cup Winners: 1964–65, 1973–74.
U.E.F.A. Cup Winners: 1972–73
Record attendance: 61,905 v. Wolves (F.A. Cup), February 1952.
Modern Capacity: 56,000.
Entered Football League: 1893—Div. 2.
Biggest win: 10–0 v. Dundalk (Fairs Cup), September 1969.
Heaviest defeat: 1–9 v. Birmingham (Div. 2), December 1954.
Best in Football League Cup: 5th Round 1972–73, 1973–74.
Pitch measurements: 110 × 75 yd.
Highest League Scorer in Single Season: Roger Hunt—41 in 1961–62 (Div. 2).
Transfers—
  Highest fee paid: £110,000—John Toshack (from Cardiff), November 1970; £110,000—Peter Cormack (from Nottingham Forest), July 1972.
  Highest fee received: £80,000—Tony Hateley (to Coventry), September 1968.

Luton Town

70–72 Kenilworth Road,
Luton LU1 1 DH.
0582–23151

Shirts: Orange with Black and White Stripe
Shorts: Navy Blue
Stockings: Orange

Luton Town established more than a club record with the sale of centre-forward Malcolm Macdonald to Newcastle United for £185,000 in May 1971. That fee made him the highest-priced player to leave the Second Division, and Macdonald's personal contribution in two seasons at Luton had been 58 goals.

Thirty-four years before the Macdonald era, Luton had another headline-making centre-forward in Joe Payne, their top scorer, with 55 goals, when they gained promotion to Division Two in 1937. The previous season Payne, who later joined Chelsea, scored *ten* goals as emergency centre-forward in Luton's 12–0 win over Bristol Rovers. It is an individual scoring record that has never been equalled in League or F.A. Cup football.

In 1955 Luton moved up to Division One after a triple tie on points, their superior goal average allowing them, and not Rotherham, to be promoted with Birmingham. Four years later they reached the F.A. Cup Final for the first time, losing 2–1 to Nottingham Forest. But in 1960 Luton were relegated (with Leeds) and continued to drop—to Division Three in 1963 and to the Fourth in 1965. The way back began with promotion to the Third Division in 1968; two years later Luton were welcomed back to Division Two, from which, as runners-up, they returned to the First Division in 1974.

Division 3 (South) Champions: 1936–37.
Division 4 Champions: 1967–68.
Record attendance: 30,069 v. Blackpool (F.A. Cup), March 1959.
Modern Capacity: 31,000.
Entered Football League: 1897—Div. 2.
Biggest win: 12–0 v. Bristol Rovers (Div. 3 South), April 1936.
Heaviest defeat: 1–9 v. Swindon Town (Div. 3 South), August 1921.
Best in F.A. Cup: Runners-up 1958–59.
Best in Football League Cup: 4th Round 1962–63, 1973–74.
Pitch measurements: 112 × 72 yd.
Highest League Scorer in Single Season: Joe Payne—55 in 1936–37 (Div. 3 South).
Transfers—
  Highest fee paid: £110,000—Paul Futcher (from Chester), May 1974.
  Highest fee received: £185,000—Malcolm Macdonald (to Newcastle), May 1971.

Manchester City

Maine Road,
Moss Side,
Manchester, MI4 7WM.
061–226–1191/2

Shirts: Sky Blue, White Trim
Shorts: White
Stockings: Sky Blue, Maroon and White Ringed Tops

Following their return from the Second Division as recently as 1966, Manchester City became one of Britain's most formidable sides under the dual influence of Joe Mercer as manager and Malcolm Allison, coach. In three seasons they won four of the game's top prizes—the League Championship trophy in 1968, the F.A. Cup in 1969 and, in 1970, the League Cup and Cup-Winners' Cup.

In the early 1930s City overshadowed United in Manchester's battle for soccer prestige and in 1937 they won their first League Championship. The following season they were relegated in unique circumstances—as the First Division top scorers with 80 goals. After the war the success pendulum swung Old Trafford way, until City made Mercer their manager at the age of 50, in July 1965.

Space permits mention of only a few of the club's great-name players of the past such as Billy Meredith, Jimmy McMullan, Eric Brook, Sam Cowan, Jackie Bray, Peter Doherty, Matt Busby, and two of the finest goalkeepers the game has seen, Frank Swift and German-born Bert Trautmann.

League Champions: 1936–37, 1967–68.
Division 2 Champions: 1898–99, 1902–03, 1909–10, 1927–28, 1946–47, 1965–66.
F.A. Cup Winners: 1903–04, 1933–34, 1955–56, 1968–69.
League Cup Winners: 1969–70.
Winners of European Cup-Winners' Cup: 1969–70.
Record attendance: 84,569 v. Stoke (F.A. Cup), March 1934.
Modern Capacity: 52,000
Entered Football League: 1892—Div. 2 (as Ardwick).
Biggest win: 11–3 v. Lincoln City (Div. 2), March 1895.
Heaviest defeat: 1–9 v. Everton (Div. 1), September 1906.
Pitch measurements: 117 × 79 yd.
Highest League Scorer in Single Season: Tom Johnson—38 in 1928–29 (Div. 1).
Transfers—
  Highest fee paid: £275,000—Dennis Tueart (from Sunderland), March 1974.
  Highest fee received: £125,000—Tony Towers (to Sunderland), March 1974.

Manchester United

Old Trafford,
Manchester M16 ORA.
061-872-1661/2

Shirts: Red, White Trim
Shorts: White
Stockings: Black, Red Top

Manchester United's is a history of two clubs, not one. The first died on 6 February 1958, when the aircraft bringing them home from a European Cup-tie crashed in snow on take-off from Munich. Eight players were among the 23 who lost their lives in the worst ever disaster to hit a British club.

The life of manager Matt Busby was also in the balance, and by the time he was able to return to Old Trafford, a new Manchester United team had been born. Less than three months later they played Bolton in the most emotion-charged F.A. Cup Final of all. In 1963 they returned to Wembley and won the Cup for the third time, they became League Champions again in 1965 and 1967 and, at Wembley a year later, on 29 May 1968, they defeated Benfica 4–1, after extra time, to become England's first holders of the European Cup.

Since Sir Matt became a director, United have employed three managers. Scotland's Tommy Docherty, appointed in December 1972, spent massively to survive relegation that season, which ended with Bobby Charlton's retirement after 606 League games for the club. But in 1973–74, United faced an even grimmer struggle—and lost the First Division place they had held since 1938.

League Champions: 1907–08, 1910–11, 1951–52, 1955–56, 1956–57, 1964–65, 1966–67.
Division 2 Champions: 1935–36.
F.A. Cup Winners: 1908–09, 1947–48, 1962–63.
European Cup Winners: 1967–68.
Record attendance: 76,962—Wolves v. Grimsby (F.A. Cup Semi-final), March 1939. (Record crowd for a League match in England is 82,950 for Man. United v. Arsenal, January 1948 —played on Man. City's ground).
Modern Capacity: 61,000.
Entered Football League: 1892—Div. 1 (as Newton Heath).
Biggest win: 10–0 v. Anderlecht, Belgium (European Cup), September 1956.
Heaviest defeat: 0–7 v. Aston Villa (Div. 1), December 1930.
Best in Football League Cup: Semi-final 1969–70, 1970–71.
Pitch measurements: 116 × 76 yd.
Highest League Scorer in Single Season: Dennis Viollet— 32 in 1959–60 (Div. 1).
Transfers—Highest fee paid: £200,000—Ian Moore (from Nott'm Forest), March 1972; £200,000—Lou Macari (from Celtic), January 1973. **Highest fee received:** £170,000— Ted MacDougall (to West Ham), February 1973.

Mansfield Town

Field Mill Ground,
Quarry Lane,
Mansfield.
Mansfield 23567

Shirts: White, Blue and Amber Neck and Cuffs
Shorts: Royal Blue, Amber Seam
Stockings: White, Blue and Amber Top

The name of Mansfield Town was on many people's lips one February night in 1969—and no wonder. The Third Division club had just astounded the football world by beating West Ham United—who included three World Cup players, Bobby Moore, Geoff Hurst and Martin Peters—3-0 in the F.A. Cup fifth round.

Forty years earlier in 1929 Mansfield, then a non-League club, produced an equally remarkable Cup result by winning 1-0 away to Second Division Wolves in the third round.

Such days of spectacular deeds help to compensate followers of smaller clubs for seasons of comparatively unexciting activity. Since winning the Midland League in 1924, 1925 and 1929, Mansfield have rarely attracted national acclaim.

Entering the League (Division Three South) in 1931, they have never reached the Second Division, missing it by one place in 1951 and 1965.

Roy Goodall, Freddie Steele, Charlie Mitten, Sam Weaver, Raich Carter and Tommy Cummings are among illustrious names who as managers of Mansfield have tried, with varying degrees of success since the last war, to bring a higher standard of football to Field Mill. The attempt continues.

Record attendance: 24,467 v. Nott'm F. (F.A. Cup), Jan. 1953.
Modern Capacity: 22,000.
Entered Football League: 1931—Div. 3 (South).
Biggest win: 9-2 v. Rotherham (Div. 3 North), December 1932; 9-2 v. Hounslow Town (F.A. Cup), November 1962.
Heaviest defeat: 1-8 v. Walsall (Div. 3 North), January 1933.
Highest final League position: Runners-up Div. 3 (North) 1950-51.
Best in F.A. Cup: 6th Round 1968-69.
Best in Football League Cup: 3rd Round 1964-65, 1965-66.
Pitch measurements: 115 × 72 yd.
Highest League Scorer in Single Season: Ted Harston—55 in 1936-37 (Div. 3 North).
Transfers—
  Highest fee paid: £10,000—Bill Williams (from W.B.A.), January 1966; £10,000—Sam Ellis (from Sheffield Wed.), March 1972.
  Highest fee received: £50,000—Malcolm Partridge (to Leicester), September 1970; £50,000—Stuart Boam (to Middlesbrough), May 1971.

Middlesbrough

Ayresome Park,
Middlesbrough,
Teesside, TS1 4P.B.
Middlesbrough 89659/85996

Shirts: Red, with White Chest Band
Shorts: Red, White Seam
Stockings: White, Red Tops

Former Leeds and England centre-half Jack Charlton's first season as a manager ended triumphantly in 1974 with Middlesbrough returning to the First Division after an interval of 20 years. Charlton instilled Leeds-type efficiency into 'Boro's play, and they led the field from the start to give the North-east a second successive year of conquest following Sunderland's F.A. Cup success in 1973.

Middlesbrough, the only League club to have won the Amateur Cup (1895, 1898), joined the Second Division in 1899 and were promoted three years later. Ayresome Park has been their home since 1903.

They caused a sensation in 1905, when they paid Sunderland the game's first transfer fee of £1000 for Alf Common, and not long afterwards Steve Bloomer, another famous name in soccer history, joined 'Boro' from Derby.

During their earlier years, Middlesbrough set several records. Two came in 1926–27 when, after the change in the offside law, they scored what is still the Division Two record of 122 goals, of which local-born centre-forward George Camsell contributed 59, another unbeaten record for the same division. In 1927–28, Middlesbrough and Tottenham obtained a less enviable record—the highest points totals (37 and 38) for teams relegated from the First Division.

Division 2 Champions: 1926–27, 1928–29, 1973–74.
F.A. Amateur Cup Winners: 1894–95, 1897–98.
Record attendance: 53,596 v. Newcastle Utd (League), December 1949.
Modern Capacity: 42,500.
Entered Football League: 1899—Div. 2.
Biggest win: 10–3 v. Sheffield Utd (Div. 1), November 1933.
Heaviest defeat: 0–9 v. Blackburn (Div. 2), November 1954.
Best in F.A. Cup: 6th Round 1935–36, 1946–47, 1969–70.
Best in Football League Cup: 3rd Round 1961–62, 1965–66, 1967–68, 1970–71, 1972–73, 1973–74.
Pitch measurements: 115 × 75 yd.
Highest League Scorer in Single Season: George Camsell —59 in 1926–27 (Div. 2).
Transfers—
   Highest fee paid: £60,000—John Craggs (from Newcastle), August 1971.
   Highest fee received: £57,000—Geoff Butler (to Chelsea), September 1967.

Millwall

The Den, Coldblow Lane,
New Cross,
London, SE14 5RH.
01-639-3143/4

Shirts: White
Shorts: White
Stockings: White

Between 1964 and 1967 Millwall established a League record that will not easily be beaten. They played 59 consecutive home matches without defeat, a sequence that started in the Fourth Division on 24 August 1964 and ended in a Second Division match against Plymouth Argyle on 14 January 1967. A much earlier Millwall record was their aggregate of 127 goals in the winning of the Third Division (South) Championship of 1927–28.

The club was formed in 1885 as Millwall Rovers and was among the original members of the Third Division in 1920. In 1937 they became the first Third Division club to reach the F.A. Cup semi-finals, beating First Division opponents Chelsea, Derby County and Manchester City at The Den, before falling 2–1 to Sunderland at the last hurdle before Wembley.

A year later Millwall were back in Division Two, but after the war their fortunes slumped and they dropped from Second Division to Third and then through the trapdoor to the Fourth. Their present spell in the Second Division dates from 1966.

In May 1970 Millwall received their highest fee when they transferred forward Keith Weller to Chelsea for £100,000, and that figure was exceeded in January 1973, when they collected £115,000 from the transfer of Derek Possee to Crystal Palace.

Division 3 (South) Champions: 1927–28, 1937–38.
Division 4 Champions: 1961–62.
Record attendance: 48,672 v. Derby County (F.A. Cup), February 1937.
Modern Capacity: 40,000.
Entered Football League: 1920—Div. 3.
Biggest win: 9–1 v. Torquay Utd (Div. 3 South), August 1927; 9–1 v. Coventry City (Div. 3 South), November 1927.
Heaviest defeat: 1–9 v. Aston Villa (F.A. Cup), January 1946.
Best in F.A. Cup: Semi-final 1899–1900, 1902–03, 1936–37.
Best in Football League Cup: 5th Round 1973–74.
Pitch measurements: 110 × 72½ yd.
Highest League Scorer in Single Season: Dick Parker—37 in 1926–27 (Div. 3 South).
Transfers—
  Highest fee paid: £45,000—Alf Wood (from Shrewsbury), May 1972.
  Highest fee received: £115,000—Derek Possee (to Crystal Palace), January 1973.

Newcastle United

St. James' Park
Newcastle-upon-Tyne
NE1 4ST.
0632—28361/2

Shirts: Black and White Stripes
Shorts: Black, White Seam
Stockings: Black and White Hoops

Blaydon Races, the Geordie folk-song, rang out in the unlikely surroundings of Budapest in June 1969. The occasion: Newcastle's 3–2 second-leg victory over the Hungarian side Ujpest Dozsa giving them the Fairs' Cup 6–2 on aggregate at their first attempt in Europe.

Tyneside fans also sang with great gusto at Wembley, in 1951 and 1952, when their club became the first this century to take the F.A. Cup in successive seasons. In 1955 they won it again, for the sixth time, but their 100 per cent Wembley record ended in 1974, when United lost 3–0 to Liverpool in their record eleventh F.A. Cup Final.

Newcastle's most renowned player appeared in the 1920s. Hughie Gallacher helped them to their fourth League Championship in 1926–27, when he set up the club record with 36 goals.

After the Second World War Tyneside roared to the sharp-shooting of 'Wor Jackie' Milburn, who scored 178 League goals (the club aggregate record) from 1946–57. Together with fullback Bob Cowell and left-winger Bobby Mitchell, he played in the Cup-winning teams of 1951, 1952 and 1955, but Newcastle fans did not see the goalscoring like of Milburn again until the start of season 1971–72, with the £185,000 signing of Malcolm Macdonald from Luton.

League Champions: 1904–05, 1906–07, 1908–09, 1926–27.
Division 2 Champions: 1964–65.
F.A. Cup Winners: 1909–10, 1923–24, 1931–32, 1950–51, 1951–52, 1954–55.
European Fairs Cup Winners: 1968–69.
Record attendance: 68,386 v. Chelsea (League). Sept. 1930.
Modern Capacity: 56,000.
Entered Football League: 1893—Div. 2.
Biggest win: 13–0 v. Newport County (Div. 2), October 1946.
Heaviest defeat: 0–9 v. Burton Wanderers (Div. 2), April 1895.
Best in Football League Cup: 3rd Round 1963–64, 1968–69, 1971–72, 1972–73, 1973–74.
Pitch measurements: 110×75 yd.
Highest League Scorer in Single Season: Hughie Gallacher —36 in 1926–27 (Div. 1).
Transfers—
  Highest fee paid: £185,000—Malcolm Macdonald (from Luton), May 1971.
  Highest fee received: £120,000—Bryan Robson (to West Ham), February 1971.

Newport County

Somerton Park,
Newport, Mon.
Newport 71543/71271

Shirts: Tangerine
Shorts: Black
Stockings: Tangerine

Older supporters of Newport County still wonder what the club might have achieved but for the outbreak of the Second World War. Their speculation is understandable for in 1938–39, the last full League season before hostilities, Newport won the Division Three South Championship in confident style.

But when, after a seven-year wait, League football resumed in 1946–47, they faced the Second Division with a reshaped team and were promptly relegated. They finished bottom with only 23 points from the 42 fixtures, and conceded 133 goals. At Newcastle, on 5 October 1946, County crashed 13–0, which equalled what is still the heaviest Football League defeat (Stockport County 13, Halifax Town 0 in Div. 3 North on 6 January 1934).

These statistics gave Newport all the wrong reasons by which to remember their only season in the Second Division, and since then life for them has been an almost continuous struggle for survival in a Rugby Union stronghold.

For clubs such as Newport who are constantly beset by financial problems, a run in the F.A. Cup can be a boon. Unfortunately, such occasions have been rare, though in 1949 Newport reached the fifth round before losing, a little unluckily, 3–2 at Portsmouth. On the way they overcame Leeds United and Huddersfield Town, and that remains their farthest progress in the F.A. Cup.

Division 3 (South) Champions: 1938–39.
Record attendance: 24,268 v. Cardiff City (League), October 1937.
Modern Capacity: 20,000.
Entered Football League: 1920—Div. 3.
Biggest win: 10–0 v. Merthyr Town (Div. 3 South), April 1930.
Heaviest defeat: 0–13 v. Newcastle Utd (Div. 2), October 1946.
Best in F.A. Cup: 5th Round 1948–49.
Best in Football League Cup: 3rd Round 1962–63.
Pitch measurements: 110 × 75 yd.
Highest League Scorer in Single Season: Tudor Martin—34 in 1929–30 (Div. 3 South).
Transfers—
  Highest fee paid: £10,000—Brian Godfrey (from Bristol Rovers), June 1973.
  Highest fee received: £10,000—Ollie Burton (to Norwich), February 1961.

Northampton Town

County Ground,
Abington Avenue,
Northampton, NN1 4PS.
Northampton 31553

Shirts: White with Two Claret Bands
Shorts: Claret
Stockings: Claret and White

Northampton Town are always assured of one significant entry in the history of the Football League. In 1965 they became the first club to rise from the Fourth to the First Division, a feat they achieved in five remarkable seasons. The tragedy was that their return to the lowest reaches of the League should be even swifter. They lasted only one season in Division One and, almost unbelievably, by 1969 were back in Division Four.

The club first tasted success as Southern League champions in 1909 and the man who guided them to that triumph was Herbert Chapman, later to win much wider managerial fame with Huddersfield Town and Arsenal. Strangely, that was Northampton's only notable football prize until they took the Division Three title in 1962–63.

Dave Bowen, the former Wales and Arsenal wing-half, who managed the club through most of the vicissitudes to the 1970s. Cliff Holton, another previously with Arsenal, Ron Flowers and Jack English are just a few of the experienced players who have starred for the 'Cobblers', whose ground is also the home of Northamptonshire County Cricket Club.

Division 3 Champions: 1962–63.
Record attendance: 24,523 v. Fulham (League), April 1966.
Modern Capacity: 25,000.
Entered Football League: 1920—Div. 3.
Biggest win: 10–0 v. Walsall (Div. 3 South), November 1927.
Heaviest defeat: 0–8 v. Walsall (Div. 3 South), October 1946.
Best in F.A. Cup: 5th Round 1933–34, 1949–50, 1969–70.
Best in Football League Cup: 5th Round 1964–65, 1966–67.
Pitch measurements: 110 × 76 yd.
Highest League Scorer in Single Season: Cliff Holton—36 in 1961–62 (Div. 3).
Transfers—
  Highest fee paid: £27,000—Joe Broadfoot (from Ipswich), November 1965.
  Highest fee received: £45,000—John Roberts (to Arsenal), April 1969.

Norwich City

Carrow Road,
Norwich, NOR 22T.
Norwich 21514/5

Shirts: Yellow, Green Collar and Cuffs
Shorts: Green, Yellow Seam
Stockings: Yellow

The early seventies have been the most significant in Norwich City's history. In 1972 they reached Division One for the first time; in 1973 manager Ron Saunders took them to a first Wembley appearance (they lost the League Cup Final to Tottenham, 1–0); and season 1973–74, during which Saunders moved to Manchester City, ended with the 'Canaries' dropping back into Division Two.

Norwich won the League Cup in only its second season (1961–62), and it is as cup fighters that the East Anglian club are best known. Founded in 1905, they waited only four years before establishing their reputation by knocking out Liverpool at Anfield. Other notable cup 'scalps' included Sunderland in 1910–11, Tottenham in 1914–15, Leeds in 1934–35, Liverpool again in 1950–51, and Arsenal at Highbury in 1953–54.

Their greatest F.A. Cup run came in 1959 when, as a Third Division side, they knocked out Manchester United, Cardiff, Tottenham and Sheffield United before losing 1–0 to Luton after a 1–1 draw in the semi-final.

Norwich, who gained the nickname 'Canaries' when they adopted their green and yellow colours, and moved to a ground called 'The Nest' in 1908, were founder-members of Division Three (South) in 1920. They won promotion to Division Two in 1934, but were relegated in 1939 and stayed down until 1960.

Division 2 Champions: 1971–72.
Division 3 (South) Champions: 1933–34.
League Cup Winners: 1961–62.
Record attendance: 43,984 v. Leicester City (F.A. Cup), March 1963.
Modern Capacity: 42,000.
Entered Football League: 1920—Div. 3.
Biggest win: 10–2 v. Coventry (Div. 3 South), March 1930.
Heaviest defeat: 2–10 v. Swindon Town (S. League), September 1908.
Best in F.A. Cup: Semi-final 1958–59.
Pitch measurements: 114 × 74 yd.
Highest League Scorer in Single Season: Ralph Hunt—31 in 1955–56 (Div. 3 South).
Transfers—
  Highest fee paid: £145,000—Phil Boyer (from Bournemouth), February 1974.
  Highest fee received: £170,000—Graham Paddon (to West Ham), December 1973.

Nottingham Forest

City Ground,
Nottingham, NG2 5FJ.
0602–868236/7/8

Shirts: Red, White Trim
Shorts: White, Red Seam
Stockings: Red with
  White-banded Top

In the strictest sense of the word, Nottingham Forest are the only *true* club in the Football League, run as they are by an elected committee. The other 91 are all limited companies, each with a board of directors. Another oddity is that Forest play outside the city of Nottingham and Notts County play inside the boundary, on the opposite bank of the River Trent.

Forest were founded in 1865, and are the third oldest League club after Notts County and Stoke City. In various ways, Forest helped shape the game's early history. For instance, their England International Sam Widdowson was the first player to wear shinguards, in 1874. It was in a Forest game four years later that a referee used a whistle for the first time—previously signals were given by handkerchief—and in 1891 the crossbar and nets made their first appearance in soccer, at the Forest ground.

The club's first F.A. Cup success came in 1898, and although they won the trophy again in 1959, the Championship has always eluded them.

Yet they have seldom lacked players of International standing, their more recent caps including Terry Hennessey, Joe Baker, Alan Hinton, Jim Baxter and Ian Moore. Bob McKinlay, former centre-half and captain, set the remarkable club record of 614 League appearances between 1951 and 1969.

Division 2 Champions: 1906–07, 1921–22.
Division 3 (South) Champions: 1950–51.
F.A. Cup Winners: 1897–98, 1958–59.
Record attendance: 49,945 v. Manchester Utd (League), October 1967.
Modern Capacity: 49,500.
Entered Football League: 1892—Div. 1.
Biggest win: 14–0 v. Clapton (F.A. Cup), 1890–91.
Heaviest defeat: 1–9 v. Blackburn Rovers (Div. 2), April 1937.
Best in Football League Cup: 4th Round 1960–61, 1969–70.
Pitch measurements: 115 × 78 yd.
Highest League Scorer in Single Season: Wally Ardron—36 in 1950–51 (Div. 3 South).
Transfers—
  Highest fee paid: £100,000—Jim Baxter (from Sunderland), December 1967.
  Highest fee received: £200,000—Ian Moore (to Man. Utd.), March 1972.

Notts County

Meadow Lane Ground,
Nottingham, NG2 3HJ.
Nottingham 864152

Shirts: Black and White Stripes
Shorts: Black
Stockings: White

Notts County is the oldest club in the Football League, formed in 1862 and founder member of the League in 1888. Twice in the next six years they reached the final of the F.A. Cup. They lost 3–1 to Blackburn Rovers at Kennington Oval in 1891, but in 1894 they won the trophy by beating Bolton Wanderers 4–1 at Everton. They spent three separate periods in Division One between 1897 and 1926, but their highest final position was third in 1901.

Few events in County's chequered history have caused greater comment than the sensational signing of centre forward Tommy Lawton from Chelsea in November 1947 for £20,000, a figure which few clubs, let alone a Third Division side, could afford in those days. Yet the deal paid off for club and player. County soon won promotion and Lawton gained further caps for England.

Jackie Sewell went from Meadow Lane to Sheffield Wednesday in March 1951, for the then record fee of £34,500, after scoring nearly 100 League goals.

Another remarkable County character was the 6 ft 5 in Albert Iremonger, rated by some as the finest goalkeeper ever to play for England. He made 564 League appearances for the club from 1904–26.

Division 2 Champions: 1896–97, 1913–14, 1922–23.
Division 3 (South) Champions: 1930–31, 1949–50.
Division 4 Champions: 1970–71.
F.A. Cup Winners: 1893–94.
Record attendance: 47,301 v. York (F.A. Cup), March 1955.
Modern Capacity: 45,000.
Entered Football League: 1888—Div. 1.
Biggest win: 11–1 v. Newport County (Div. 3 South), January 1949.
Heaviest defeat: 1–9 v. Aston Villa (Div. 1), September 1888; 1–9 v. Blackburn Rovers (Div. 1), November 1889; 1–9 v. Portsmouth (Div. 2), April 1927.
Best in Football League Cup: 5th Round 1963–64, 1972–73.
Pitch measurements: $117\frac{1}{2} \times 76$ yd.
Highest League Scorer in Single Season: Tom Keetley—39 in 1930–31 (Div. 3 South).
Transfers—
 Highest fee paid: £40,000—Ray O'Brien (from Man. Utd.), March 1974.
 Highest fee received: £34,500—Jackie Sewell (to Sheffield Wed.), March 1951.

Oldham Athletic

Boundary Park,
Oldham OL1 2PA.
061–624–4972

Shirts: Royal Blue
Shorts: Blue
Stockings: White

Although most of Oldham's modern existence has been spent in the Third and Fourth Divisions, they were in the Championship section half a century ago. Indeed, they narrowly failed to carry off the League title in 1914–15, finishing a point behind Everton.

Eric Gemmell performed a notable goalscoring feat for Oldham in season 1951–52. Playing in a Third Division North match against Chester, he scored seven times in an 11–2 win.

In addition to developing goalscorers, Oldham have found a number of International goalkeepers, notably Jack Hacking, Ted Taylor, Albert Gray and Frank Moss, who was one of seven Arsenal players capped against Italy in 1934.

Season 1970–71 was notable in two ways for Oldham. They earned promotion to Division Three and their players also won the one-season Ford Sporting League, bringing the club total prize money of £80,000 for the improvement of spectator facilities.

With a late-season flourish, Oldham snatched the Third Division championship of 1973–74, returning to the Second Division after an interval of 20 years.

Division 3 (North) Champions: 1952–53.
Division 3 Champions: 1973–74.
Record attendance: 47,671 v. Sheffield Wed. (F.A. Cup), January 1930.
Modern Capacity: 36,500.
Entered Football League: 1907—Div. 2.
Biggest win: 11–0 v. Southport (Div. 4), December 1962.
Heaviest defeat: 4–13 v. Tranmere (Div. 3 North), December 1935.
Best in F.A. Cup: Semi-final 1912–13.
Best in Football League Cup: 2nd Round 1960–61, 1962–63, 1964–65, 1965–66, 1970–71, 1971–72.
Pitch measurements: 110 x 74 yd.
Highest League Scorer in Single Season: Tom Davis—33 in 1936–37 (Div. 3 North).
Transfers—
  Highest fee paid: £20,000—Dennis Stevens (from Everton), December 1965; £20,000—Ian Towers (from Burnley), December 1965; £20,000—George McVitie (from W.B.A.), August 1972.
  Highest fee received: £80,000—David Shaw (to West Bromwich), March 1973.

Orient

Leyton Stadium,
Brisbane Road, Leyton,
London, E10.
01–539–1368/6800

Shirts: Red,
Shorts: Red
Stockings: Red

When Orient sold brilliant young half-back Tommy Taylor to West Ham for £80,000 in October 1970, it was a move of considerable financial significance to a club which three years earlier almost foundered. Orient called a Sunday morning public meeting after disclosing accumulated debts of £100,000. The response was immediate and generous. By 1970 the deficit had been halved, and the sale of Taylor completed an economic recovery.

The club owe their name to the Orient Shipping Company. They were formed in 1881 as Clapton Orient; they became Leyton Orient in 1946 and dropped the prefix 'Leyton' in 1967. Orient made their home at Brisbane Road in 1937, having previously shared Clapton greyhound stadium, the Essex cricket ground at Leyton and the old Lea Bridge speedway stadium.

Alec Stock, who had three spells in charge, took them to second place in Division Three South in 1955 and up into Division Two as Champions 12 months later. Six years later they gained promotion with Liverpool to Div. One, but survived only one season. Under George Petchey—their eleventh post-war manager—Orient just failed to play their way back to top company in 1974, drawing the final game at home to Aston Villa when they needed victory for promotion.

Division 3 (South) Champions: 1955–56.
Division 3 Champions: 1969–70.
Record attendance: 34,345 v. West Ham United (F.A. Cup), January 1964.
Modern Capacity: 35,000.
Entered Football League: 1905—Div. 2 (as Clapton Orient).
Biggest win: 9–2 v. Aldershot (Div. 3 South), February 1934; 9–2 v. Chester (League Cup), October 1962.
Heaviest defeat: 0–8 v. Aston Villa (F.A. Cup), January 1929.
Best in F.A. Cup: 6th Round 1925–26, 1953–54, 1971–72.
Best in Football League Cup: 5th Round 1962–63.
Pitch measurements: 110 × 80 yd.
Highest League Scorer in Single Season: Tom Johnston—35 in 1957–58 (Div. 2).
Transfers—
  Highest fee paid: £60,000—Gerry Queen (from Crystal Palace), September 1972; £60,000—Ricky Heppolette (from Preston), December 1972.
  Highest fee received: £112,000—Dennis Rofe (to Leicester), August 1972.

Oxford United

Manor Ground,
Beech Road,
Headington, Oxford.
0865–61503

Shirts: Gold
Shorts: Gold
Stockings: Gold

One of the oldest established clubs to stay outside the Football League, Oxford United, were formed in 1896 as Headington United but did not turn professional until 1949. They took their present name in 1961 and, after Accrington Stanley withdrew from Division Four in March 1962, Oxford got the chance of Football League status, quickly proving themselves worthy of it. In 1964 they became the first Fourth Division side to reach the sixth round of the F.A. Cup, and in only six seasons of League membership they climbed two divisions into the Second.

In their first year in Division Two (1968–69) Oxford survived by only one place. In the next three seasons they finished just below half-way, and in 1972–73 they attained their highest final Second Division placing—eighth. Improvement was not maintained, however, and with relegation increased to three clubs, Oxford spent an uncomfortable season 1973–74 near the foot of the table, surviving by a late revival.

When United gained promotion from the Fourth Division in 1964–65 with 61 points, they scored 87 goals. Their results that season included a record 7–0 success against Barrow.

Division 3 Champions: 1967–68.
Record attendance: 22,730 v. Preston N.E. (F.A. Cup), February 1964.
Modern Capacity: 19,000.
Entered Football League: 1962—Div. 4.
Biggest win: 7–0 v. Barrow (Div. 4), December 1964.
Heaviest defeat: 0–5 v. Cardiff (Div. 2), February 1969; 0–5 v. Cardiff (Div. 2), September 1973.
Best in F.A. Cup: 6th Round 1963–64.
Best in Football League Cup: 5th Round 1969–70.
Pitch measurements: 112 × 78 yd.
Highest League Scorer in Single Season: Colin Booth—23 in 1964–65 (Div. 4).
Transfers—
  Highest fee paid: £50,000—Hugh Curran (from Wolves), September 1972.
  Highest fee received: £40,000—John Evanson (to Blackpool), February 1974.

Peterborough United

London Road Ground,
Peterborough PE2 8AL.
Peterborough 3623

Shirts: Royal Blue, White Trim
Shorts: Blue
Stockings: Red

When Peterborough United, an ambitious Southern League club with a splendidly appointed ground, won admission to the Football League in 1960–61, the cynics wondered whether they were really equipped to bridge the gap between the two grades of football. The 'Posh', as they are familiarly known, gave the best possible answer: they won the Fourth Division Championship at the first attempt, and in record-breaking style.

Terry Bly was the chief destroyer of defences in Peterborough's first season in League football. His tally of 52 goals in 46 games remains the highest for the division—no other player has topped 50 League goals for any club in post-war football—and the 134 goals obtained by Peterborough is a record for any division of the Football League. Will it ever be beaten?

The following season they threatened to go straight into the Second Division. Finally, however, they took fifth place, though they scored more goals, 107, than either of the promoted teams.

In 1965, Peterborough reached the sixth round of the F.A. Cup, beating Salisbury, Q.P.R., Chesterfield, Arsenal and Swansea before losing to Chelsea.

In 1968 the club was demoted to the Fourth Division because of alleged irregularities in their books, but at the end of his second season in 1974, manager Noel Cantwell had inspired another Peterborough promotion success as Div. 4 winners.

Division 4 Champions: 1960–61, 1973–74.
Record attendance: 30,096 v. Swansea (F.A. Cup), February 1965.
Modern Capacity: 30,000.
Entered Football League: 1960—Div. 4.
Biggest win: 8–1 v. Oldham Athletic (Div. 4), November 1969.
Heaviest defeat: 1–8 v. Northampton (F.A. Cup), December 1946.
Best in F.A. Cup: 6th Round 1964–65.
Best in Football League Cup: Semi-final 1965–66.
Pitch measurements: 113 × 76 yd.
Highest League Scorer in Single Season: Terry Bly—52 in 1960–61 (Div. 4).
Transfers—
  Highest fee paid: £21,000—Derek Dougan (from Aston Villa), June 1963.
  Highest fee received: £30,000—John Wile (to W.B.A.), December 1970.

Plymouth Argyle

Home Park,
Plymouth, Devon.
Plymouth 52561/2/3

Shirts: Green and Black Stripes
Shorts: Black
Stockings: Black

Plymouth Argyle achieved some extraordinary feats in their early years in the old Southern Section of the Third Division. For six consecutive years between 1921 and 1927 they finished runners-up, twice missing promotion by a point and once on goal average; in 1920—21 they drew 21 of their 42 matches and the following season their defence conceded only 24 League goals.

The reward for consistency was finally earned in 1930 when the Devon club took the title with unmistakable authority. They finished seven points clear of the second club, Brentford, and lost only four matches.

Probably no League club has travelled more miles *in England* during their history than Argyle. Yet for all the strain which long journeys inevitably impose on players, the club have gone close to winning First Division status on several occasions. They finished fourth in Division Two in 1932 and 1953, and fifth in seasons 1937 and 1962.

In season 1973—74 Plymouth, despite being in the lower half of Division Three, went closer to Wembley than ever before. They lifted West Country hearts with thrilling League Cup victories away to First Division opponents Burnley, Q.P.R. and Birmingham, and in the semi-final more than 30,000 saw Argyle draw 1—1 with Manchester City at Home Park. But, with Wembley a stride away, Plymouth lost the second leg 2—0.

Division 3 (South) Champions: 1929—30, 1951—52.
Division 3 Champions: 1958—59.
Record attendance: 43,596 v. Aston Villa (League), October 1936.
Modern Capacity: 40,000.
Entered Football League: 1920—Div. 3.
Biggest win: 8—1 v. Millwall (Div. 2), January 1932.
Heaviest defeat: 0—9 v. Stoke City (Div. 2), December 1960.
Best in F.A. Cup: 5th Round 1952—53.
Best in Football League Cup: Semi-final 1964—65, 1973—74.
Pitch measurements: 112 × 75 yd.
Highest League Scorer in Single Season: Jack Cock—32 in 1925—26 (Div. 3 South).
Transfers—
  Highest fee paid: £45,000—Barrie Jones (from Swansea), September 1964.
  Highest fee received: £40,000—Norman Piper (to Portsmouth), May 1970.

Portsmouth

Fratton Park,
Frogmore Road,
Portsmouth, PO4 8RA.
Portsmouth 31204/5

Shirts: White with Two Blue Stripes
Shorts: Royal Blue
Stockings: White, Blue Turnover

Portsmouth spent 25 consecutive seasons in Division One after gaining promotion in 1927 on the strength of a goal average that was 1/250th of a goal better than Manchester City's. Elevation to football's top flight was to be the launching pad for a catalogue of League and Cup successes. Portsmouth were defeated in the 1929 and 1934 F.A. Cup Finals, but beat hot favourites Wolves 4–1 in the 1939 Final.

The famous 'Pompey Chimes' rang out across Fratton Park as the League title was won in 1949, and Portsmouth successfully defended it the following season, becoming only the eighth club in the history of the game to complete such a double.

Thus Portsmouth were the first former Third Division club to win the Championship, but their star waned dramatically and they dropped to Division Three in 1959. They have been in the Second Division since 1962, and in 1973 spent heavily on new stars Peter Marinello, Ron Davies and Paul Went in a bid to regain former eminence.

Jimmy Dickinson, England half-back in 48 post-war Internationals, holds the British record with 764 League appearances —all for Portsmouth, of whom he is now club secretary.

League Champions: 1948–49, 1949–50.
Division 3 (South) Champions: 1923–24.
Division 3 Champions: 1961–62.
F.A. Cup Winners: 1938–39.
Record attendance: 51,385 v. Derby County (F.A. Cup), February 1949.
Modern Capacity: 46,000.
Entered Football League: 1920—Div. 3.
Biggest win: 9–1 v. Notts County (Div. 2), April 1927.
Heaviest defeat: 0–10 v. Leicester City (Div. 1), October 1928.
Best in Football League Cup: 5th Round 1960–61.
Pitch measurements: 116 × 72 yd.
Highest League Scorer in Single Season: Billy Haines—40 in 1926–27 (Div. 2).
Transfers—
  Highest fee paid: £154,000—Paul Went (from Fulham), December 1973.
  Highest fee received: £50,000—George Smith (to Middlesbrough), January 1969.

Port Vale

Vale Park, Burslem,
Stoke-on-Trent, ST6 1AW.
Stoke-on-Trent 87626

Shirts: White, Black Edging
Shorts: White
Stockings: White, Black Hooped Turnover

Port Vale nearly wrote a fresh page in the history of the F.A. Cup in 1954. No Third Division club has reached the final of the competition, but that year Vale looked as though they might be the first to do so. Caught up on a wave of enthusiasm which spread far beyond the Potteries, they beat Q.P.R. away (1–0), Cardiff away (2–0), Blackpool at home (2–0) and Leyton Orient away (1–0) on their way to the semi-finals. Before a crowd of 68,221 at Villa Park, they faced their Black Country neighbours and famed Cup fighters, West Bromwich Albion and, incredibly, led them until the second half through a goal by Albert Leake. In the end, however, the First Division side triumphed 2–1, but as consolation Port Vale won the Third North title that season by a margin of eleven points.

A number of players have given Vale outstanding service, but none more so than local-born Roy Sproson who made 762 League appearances between 1950 and 1972. He was a member of the sides which won the Third Division (North) in 1953–54, the Fourth Division title in 1958–59 and was still an ever-present defender in the team which again won promotion to the Third Division by finishing fourth in 1970.

Division 3 (North) Champions: 1929–30, 1953–54.
Division 4 Champions: 1958–59.
Record attendance: 50,000 v. Aston Villa (F.A. Cup), February 1960.
Modern Capacity: 50,000.
Entered Football League: 1892—Div. 2.
Biggest win: 9–1 v. Chesterfield (Div. 2), September 1932.
Heaviest defeat: 0–10 v. Sheffield Utd (Div. 2), December 1892; 0–10 v. Notts County (Div. 2), February 1895.
Best in F.A. Cup: Semi-final 1953–54.
Best in Football League Cup: 2nd Round 1960–61, 1962–63, 1963–64, 1967–68, 1972–73.
Pitch measurements: 116 × 76 yd.
Highest League Scorer in Single Season: Wilf Kirkham—38 in 1926–27 (Div. 2).
Transfers—
  Highest fee paid: £15,000—Albert Cheesebrough (from Leicester), July 1963; £15,000—Billy Bingham (from Everton), August 1963.
  Highest fee received: £30,000—Terry Alcock (to Blackpool), August 1967.

Preston North End

Deepdale,
Preston, PR1 6RU.
Preston 53818/9

Shirts: White
Shorts: Dark Blue
Stockings: White

Preston North End won the first League Championship of all in 1888–89 without losing a match, and the F.A. Cup the same season without conceding a goal—a 'double' without parallel.

Founder members of the League, Preston justified their title 'Invincibles' until they were relegated in 1901. They returned in 1904, continuing to move ten times up and down between the divisions until, for the first time in their history, in 1970, they found themselves in Division Three. A year later they were Champions of that section.

After being beaten by Sunderland in the 1937 F.A. Cup Final, Preston carried off the trophy in 1938 when George Mutch gave them a 1–0 victory over Huddersfield from the penalty spot with the last kick of Wembley's first extra-time Final.

Tom Finney, who made 433 League appearances (187 goals) and won 76 England caps, was the outstanding figure in Preston football from 1946–60, and in 1973 another of England's greatest post-war forwards, Bobby Charlton, joined the club as manager after an illustrious career with Manchester United. His first season at Deepdale, however, ended with Preston relegated to Div. 3, whereupon Charlton announced that at 36 he would come back on the field as player-manager for 1974–75.

League Champions: 1888–89, 1889–90.
Division 2 Champions: 1903–04, 1912–13, 1950–51.
Division 3 Champions: 1970–71.
F.A. Cup Winners: 1888–89, 1937–38.
The Double (League and F.A. Cup Winners): 1888–89.
Record attendance: 42,684 v. Arsenal (League), April 1938.
Modern Capacity: 40,000.
Entered Football League: 1888—Div. 1.
Biggest win: 26–0 v. Hyde (F.A. Cup), October 1887.
Heaviest defeat: 0–7 v. Blackpool (Div. 1), May 1948.
Best in Football League Cup: 4th Round 1962–63, 1965–66, 1971–72.
Pitch measurements: 112 × 78 yd.
Highest League Scorer in Single Season: Ted Harper—37 in 1932–33 (Div. 2).
Transfers—
  Highest fee paid: £70,000—Mike Elwiss (from Doncaster), February 1974.
  Highest fee received: £150,000—Alex Bruce (to Newcastle), January 1974.

Queen's Park Rangers

South Africa Road,
Shepherd's Bush,
London W12 7PA.
01–743–2618/2670

Shirts: Blue and White Hoops
Shorts: White
Stockings: White

The season of 1966–67 will always be recalled as a vintage one by supporters of Queen's Park Rangers. The club not only took the Third Division title by a margin of twelve points, but became the first outside the first two divisions to win the Football League Cup. In a thrilling decider at Wembley—the first time that venue was used for the League Cup—Rangers beat First Division opponents West Bromwich Albion 3–2 after being two down.

The magic continued under Alec Stock's managership and the following year Rangers completed the greatest period in their history by going up into Division One—thus emulating Charlton's feat (1935 and 1936) of moving from Third to First Division in consecutive years. But Rangers immediately found the highest class too much, and were relegated (1969) for another four years.

But in 1973, managed by Gordon Jago, they swept back to the First Division as the top scorers in the Football League (81 goals) and this time confirmed their readiness to rise by playing some of the best football seen anywhere in season 1973–74, when they were London's most attractive and highest-placed team, standing eighth in the final table.

Division 3 (South) Champions: 1947–48.
Division 3 Champions: 1966–67.
League Cup Winners: 1966–67.
Record attendance: 33,572 v. Chelsea (F.A. Cup), Feb. 1970.
Modern Capacity: 35,000.
Entered Football League: 1920—Div. 3.
Biggest win: 9–2 v. Tranmere Rov. (Div. 3), December 1960.
Heaviest defeat: 1–8 v. Mansfield Town (Div. 3), March 1965; 1–8 v. Manchester Utd (Div. 1), March 1969.
Best in F.A. Cup: 6th Round 1947–48, 1969–70, 1973–74 (also reached last eight—old 4th Round—in 1909–10, 1913–14, 1922–23).
Pitch measurements: 112 × 72 yd.
Highest League Scorer in Single Season: George Goddard—37 in 1929–30 (Div. 3 South).

Transfers—
  Highest fee paid: £165,000—Dave Thomas (from Burnley), October 1972.
  Highest fee received: £200,000—Rodney Marsh (to Manchester City), March 1972.

Reading

Elm Park, Norfolk Road,
Reading, RG3 2EF.
Reading 57878/9

Shirts: Blue and White Hoops
Shorts: White
Stockings: White, Two Blue Rings

The Berkshire club were 100 years old in 1971, but far from celebrating their centenary in style, they were relegated to Division Four for the first time. In the last eight seasons before the war they never finished lower than sixth in Division Three (South) and twice were runners-up. When the Football League resumed in 1946 they twice more occupied second place, in 1949 and 1952. They were particularly unlucky not to gain promotion in season 1951–52 because they obtained their highest points total, 61, and 112 goals.

Between the wars Reading won the Third Division (South) Championship in 1925–26 and lasted in the Second Division for five seasons. During that period the 'Biscuitmen' fielded what many people believe was their finest half-back line of William Inglis, Alf Messer and David Evans.

Many other splendid players have served the club, among them Jack Palethorpe, who later scored in Sheffield Wednesday's Cup-winning side at Wembley in 1935; W. H. McConnell, an Ireland cap; Tony McPhee, a clever, goalscoring leader; George Marks, later Arsenal's goalkeeper; Pat McConnell, another Irish international; Maurice Edelston, an England Amateur international; and Ronnie Blackman, whose 156 League goals between 1947–54 stand as a record for the club.

Division 3 (South) Champions: 1925–26.
Record attendance: 33,042 v. Brentford (F.A. Cup), February 1927.
Modern Capacity: 28,000.
Entered Football League: 1920—Div. 3.
Biggest win: 10–2 v. Crystal Palace (Div. 3 South), September 1946.
Heaviest defeat: 0–18 v. Preston N.E. (F.A. Cup), 1893–94.
Best in F.A. Cup: Semi-final 1926–27.
Best in Football League Cup: 4th Round 1964–65, 1965–66.
Pitch measurements: 112 × 75 yd.
Highest League Scorer in Single Season: Ronnie Blackman —39 in 1951–52 (Div. 3 South).
Transfers—
  Highest fee paid: £20,000—Steve Death (from West Ham), August 1970.
  Highest fee received: £60,000—Tom Jenkins (to Southampton), December 1969.

Rochdale

Spotland,
Sandy Lane,
Rochdale.
Rochdale 44648/9

Shirts: White with Blue and Yellow Diagonal
Shorts: White
Stockings: Blue with Yellow and White Tops

With limited financial and playing resources, Rochdale's efforts have been directed at keeping football alive at Spotland in the face of competition from elsewhere in Lancashire. In 1931–32 they failed to win a Division Three (North) match after 7 November. They played 26 matches, lost 25 and drew one, and a total of 33 defeats that season is the worst on record in League football.

Another lowlight, on Tuesday, 5 February 1974, was what is believed to be the smallest crowd for any post-war League fixture. The club refused to issue an official attendance against Cambridge that afternoon, but the estimate was 450. The season ended with Rochdale relegated to Division Four.

It says much for the resolution and perseverance of those associated with the club that Rochdale have remained in continuous membership of the Football League since being elected to the Northern Section in 1921.

They gained promotion from the Fourth Division in 1969 by taking third place, and made a mark in the Football League Cup as runners-up to Norwich City in 1962; no other Division 4 team has reached the Final.

Record attendance: 24,231 v. Notts County (F.A. Cup), December 1949.
Modern Capacity: 28,000.
Entered Football League: 1921—Div. 3 (North).
Biggest win: 8–1 v. Chesterfield (Div. 3 North), December 1926.
Heaviest defeat: 0–8 v. Wrexham (Div. 3 North), December 1929.
Highest final League position: Runners-up Div. 3 (North) 1923–24, 1926–27.
Best in F.A. Cup: 4th Round 1970–71.
Best in Football League Cup: Runners-up 1961–62.
Pitch measurements: 110 × 72 yd.
Highest League Scorer in Single Season: Albert Whitehurst —44 in 1926–27 (Div. 3 North).

Transfers—
  Highest fee paid: £15,000—Malcolm Darling (from Norwich), October 1971.
  Highest fee received: £40,000—David Cross (to Norwich), October 1971.

Rotherham United

Millmoor Ground,
Rotherham S60 1HR.
Rotherham 2434

Shirts: Red, White Collar and Sleeves
Shorts: White
Stockings: Red

Fortune has certainly played some unkind tricks on Rotherham United during more than 50 years' membership of the Football League. None more so than in 1955, when, by winning eight of the last nine games and finally slamming Liverpool 6–1, they finished level on points at the top of Division Two with Birmingham City and Luton Town. Yet, despite scoring more goals than their rivals, they missed a First Division place on goal average.

In the three seasons directly after the Second World War they were runners-up in Division Three North (only the Champions gained promotion). Their points totals were 64, 59 and 62, all enough to have won the divisional title in many another season. After such close attempts to take the title, Rotherham slipped to sixth the following season (1949–50), but a year later their perseverance paid off. They became Champions by seven points, but 17 seasons in the Second Division ended with relegation in 1968, and five years later they fell into the Fourth.

Rotherham, in company with other small clubs, rely heavily on finding their own players. Among the best known are Danny Williams, a stalwart defender who made 459 League appearances between 1946–60 and Wally Ardron, whose 38 League goals in 1946–47 are still a Rotherham record.

Division 3 (North) Champions: 1950–51.
Record attendance: 25,000 v. Sheffield United (League), December 1952.
Modern Capacity: 24,000.
Entered Football League: 1893—Div. 2.
Biggest win: 8–0 v. Oldham Athletic (Div. 3 North), May 1947.
Heaviest defeat: 1–11 v. Bradford City (Div. 3 North), August 1928.
Best in F.A. Cup: 5th Round 1952–53, 1967–68.
Best in Football League Cup: Runners-up 1960–61.
Pitch measurements: 116 × 76 yd.
Highest League Scorer in Single Season: Wally Ardron—38 in 1946–47 (Division 3 North).
Transfers—
　Highest fee paid: £27,000—John Quinn (from Sheffield Wed.), November 1967.
　Highest fee received: £100,000—David Watson (to Sunderland), December 1970.

Scunthorpe United

Old Show Ground,
Scunthorpe, Lincs. DN15 7RH.
Scunthorpe 2954

Shirts: Red
Shorts: Red
Stockings: Red

Officials of Scunthorpe and Lindsey United were among many surprised by the manner in which the club was elected in 1950 at the time the Football League was extending both Northern and Southern Sections of the Third Division by two clubs. When the 'North' vote was taken Scunthorpe were not even placed second. Workington and Wigan tied and so there was a fresh vote. At the new count Scunthorpe and Wigan tied, so there was another poll. This time Scunthorpe and Wigan tied, and it needed a third vote before the Lincolnshire club finally won election. A few years later the name Lindsey was dropped from their title.

Scunthorpe arrived with the reputation of having been Midland League Champions. They were not long in justifying their place in higher company. After finishing third in 1954, and again in 1955, they won the Northern Section Championship in 1958.

Scunthorpe came close to providing First Division football at their picturesquely-named Old Show Ground in 1961–62, when finishing fourth, but they have since declined, going down to the Third Division in 1964, to the Fourth in 1968, up again in 1972 and back to the Fourth a year later.

Their longest-serving player was Jack Brownsword, who made 657 League and Cup appearances between 1950–65, and was the game's first full-back to score 50 League goals. Among modern stars, Liverpool's goalkeeper Ray Clemence and striker Kevin Keegan were produced by Scunthorpe.

Division 3 (North) Champions: 1957–58.
Record attendance: 23,935 v. Portsmouth (F.A. Cup), January 1954.
Modern Capacity: 25,000.
Entered Football League: 1950—Div. 3 (North).
Biggest win: 9–0 v. Boston U. (F.A. Cup), Nov. 1953.
Heaviest defeat: 0–8 v. Carlisle United (Div. 3 North), December, 1952.
Best in F.A. Cup: 5th Round 1957–58, 1969–70.
Best in Football League Cup: 3rd Round 1962–63, 1968–69.
Pitch measurements: 112 × 78 yd.
Highest League Scorer in Single Season: Barrie Thomas—31 in 1961–62 (Div. 2).
Transfers—
  Highest fee paid: £20,000—Barrie Thomas (from Newcastle), November 1964.
  Highest fee received: £42,500—John Kaye (to W.B.A.), May 1963.

Sheffield United

Bramall Lane Ground,
Sheffield, S2 4SU.
0742–25585

Shirts: Red and White Stripes
Shorts: Black
Stockings: White, Two Red Bands at Top

For all their long Football League history, Sheffield United achieved their greatest feats in the F.A. Cup, by winning the trophy four times by 1925.

In 1925–26 they headed the First Division scorers with 102 goals, beating Cardiff 11–2 and Manchester City 8–3. But after brief moments of glory in the 1920s, 'The Blades' lost their cutting edge and were relegated from the First Division in 1934. Five years later they just beat their neighbours, Wednesday, for second place in the Second Division, but had to wait seven years before actually returning to the First Division, owing to the outbreak of the Second World War.

On three occasions since the war football at Bramall Lane has lost the First Division label. Each time United fought their way back, and since returning in 1971 they have finished consistently in the middle of the table.

The summer of 1973 marked the end of an era as Yorkshire C.C.C. played at Bramall Lane for the last time, and United, redeveloping their home exclusively for football, erected a magnificent stand on the side where, for 118 years, the cricket square had been situated.

League Champions: 1897–98.
Division 2 Champions: 1952–53.
F.A. Cup Winners: 1898–99, 1901–02, 1914–15, 1924–25.
Record attendance: 68,287 v. Leeds (F.A. Cup), Feb. 1936.
Modern Capacity: 55,000.
Entered Football League: 1892—Div. 2.
Biggest win: 11–2 v. Cardiff City (Div. 1), January 1926.
Heaviest defeat: 0–13 v. Bolton W. (F.A. Cup), February 1890.
Best in Football League Cup: 5th Round 1961–62, 1966–67, 1971–72.
Pitch measurements: 115 × 73 yd.
Highest League Scorer in Single Season: Jimmy Dunne—41 in 1930–31 (Div. 1).
Transfers—
  Highest fee paid: £65,000—John Tudor (from Coventry), November 1968.
  Highest fee received: £100,000—Mick Jones (to Leeds), Sept. 1967; £100,000—Alan Birchenall (to Chelsea) Nov. 1967.

Sheffield Wednesday

Hillsborough,
Sheffield, S6 1SW.
0742–343122

Shirts: Blue and White Stripes
Shorts: Blue
Stockings: White

Sheffield Wednesday reached a success peak between 1929 and 1935, winning the F.A. Cup and two League Championships, and finishing third in the First Division on four other occasions. Those two League title triumphs, inspired by the veteran inside-forward Jimmy Seed, were in 1929 and 1930. It was a repetition of a similar Championship double by them in 1903 and 1904.

Wednesday's lavish ground, with seating for 23,500, was used for World Cup matches in 1966 and is a regular F.A. Cup semi-final venue.

Their most celebrated player in recent years was Derek Dooley, who scored 46 goals in season 1951–52 in 30 Division Two matches. A broken leg, which had to be amputated, ended his playing career the following season, and in January 1971 Dooley was appointed team manager of the club for which he had starred so briefly, so spectacularly.

But in December 1973, with Wednesday threatened for the first time by relegation to the Third Division, Dooley was replaced. Until they return to the First Division, Hillsborough will be something of a white elephant—a stately home of soccer in search of a team capable of filling it with football style and football fans as in days gone by.

League Champions: 1902–03, 1903–04, 1928–29, 1929–30.
Division 2 Champions: 1899–1900, 1925–26, 1951–52, 1955–56, 1958–59.
F.A. Cup Winners: 1895–96, 1906–07, 1934–35.
Record attendance: 72,841 v. Manchester City (F.A. Cup), February 1934.
Modern Capacity: 55,000.
Entered Football League: 1892—Div. 1.
Biggest win: 12–0 v. Halliwell (F.A. Cup), January 1891.
Heaviest defeat: 0–10 v. Aston Villa (Div. 1), October 1912.
Best in Football League Cup: 4th Round 1967–68.
Pitch measurements: 115 × 75 yd.
Highest League Scorer in Single Season: Derek Dooley—46 in 1951–52 (Div. 2).
Transfers—
  Highest fee paid: £100,000—Tommy Craig (from Aberdeen), May 1969.
  Highest fee received: £100,000—Wilf Smith (to Coventry), August 1970.

Shrewsbury Town

Gay Meadow,
Shrewsbury.
Shrewsbury 56068

Shirts: Royal Blue, Amber Collar and Cuffs
Shorts: Royal Blue, Amber Seam
Stockings: Amber, Blue Tops

For 64 years Shrewsbury had been in existence, but it was not until 1950 that they were elected to membership of the Football League. They spent the first season in Division Three (North) but then switched to the Southern section, where they remained until the League was extended in season 1958–59. Shrewsbury moved into Division Four and immediately won promotion by finishing fourth. Twice since then the club has missed going up into the Second Division by one place, being third in 1960 and 1968, but by the end of season 1973–74 Town were back in Division Four.

Arthur Rowley's League scoring record of 434 goals included 152 for Shrewsbury and he also holds the club's single-season record with 38 in Division Four during 1958–59.

When the Football League Cup was launched in season 1960–61, Shrewsbury reached the semi-final before losing to Rotherham United 4–3 on aggregate.

Shrewsbury have enjoyed years of comparative success, too, in the F.A. Cup, progressing to the fifth rounds in 1965 and 1966. In January 1968, record receipts of £4962 were paid when Arsenal were held to a 1–1 draw in a third round tie.

Record attendance: 18,917 v. Walsall (League), April 1961.
Modern Capacity: 20,000.
Entered Football League: 1950—Div. 3 (North).
Biggest win: 7–0 v. Swindon Town (Div. 3 South), May, 1955.
Heaviest defeat: 1–8 v. Norwich City (Div. 3 South), September 1952; 1–8 v. Coventry City (Div. 3), October 1963.
Highest final League position: 3rd in Div. 3 1959–60, 1967–68.
Best in F.A. Cup: 5th Round 1964–65, 1965–66.
Best in Football League Cup: Semi-final 1960–61.
Pitch measurements: 116 × 74 yd.
Highest League Scorer in Single Season: Arthur Rowley—38 in 1958–59 (Div. 4).
Transfers—
  Highest fee paid: £30,000—Graham Turner (from Chester), January 1973.
  Highest fee received: £95,000—Jim Holton (to Man. United), January 1973.

Southampton

The Dell,
Milton Road,
Southampton, SO9 4XX
Southampton 23408/28108

Shirts: Red and White Stripes
Shorts: Black
Stockings: Red with White Hoop

Southampton finally achieved First Division status in 1966 after missing promotion in extraordinary circumstances soon after the Second World War. In April 1949 they led the Second Division by eight points. The title seemed theirs for the taking. But an injury to centre-forward Charlie Wayman changed their luck and, incredibly, they finally finished third behind Fulham and West Bromwich.

Ted Bates, who played for the club as an inside-forward just before and after the Second World War, returned as manager in 1956 and was largely responsible for Southampton's modern rise to the heights. He made some shrewd buys and discovered local talent in Terry Paine, Martin Chivers and Mike Channon. Paine holds the appearances record for the club—more than 800 since his début in 1956 and at 35 still playing. He joined Jimmy Dickinson (764), Roy Sproson (762) and Stanley Matthews (701) as the only players to exceed 700 League appearances.

But 1973–74 ended sadly for Paine and for Southampton, with relegation—despite the £275,000 signing of Peter Osgood from Chelsea—after eight seasons in the First Division.

Division 3 (South) Champions: 1921–22.
Division 3 Champions: 1959–60.
Record attendance: 31,044 v. Manchester Utd. (League), October 1969.
Modern Capacity: 31,000.
Entered Football League: 1920—Div. 3.
Biggest win: 11–0 v. Northampton (Southern League), December 1901.
Heaviest defeat: 0–8 v. Tottenham (Div. 2), March 1936; 0–8 v. Everton (Div. 1), November 1971.
Best in F.A. Cup: Runners-up 1899–1900, 1901–02
Best in Football League Cup: 5th Round 1960–61, 1968–69.
Pitch measurements: 110 × 72 yd.
Highest League Scorer in Single Season: Derek Reeves— 39 in 1959–60 (Div. 3).
Transfers—
  Highest fee paid: £275,000—Peter Osgood (from Chelsea), March 1974.
  Highest fee received: £125,000—Martin Chivers (to Tottenham), January 1968.

Southend United

Roots Hall Ground,
Victoria Avenue,
Southend-on-Sea, SS2 6NQ.
Southend 40707

Shirts: Royal Blue
Shorts: Royal Blue,
White Trim
Stockings: White

A succession of ambitious and dedicated Southend United officials have done their best to bring a higher standard of football to London's nearest seaside resort. In 1955 the club moved from Southend Stadium to a new ground at Roots Hall, Prittlewell, and three years later it looked as though Southend United were heading for the Second Division. But though they gained 54 points, they were still six points behind Brighton, the promoted club. Sammy McCrory, who won Northern Ireland honours, scored 31 of their 90 League goals that season, but by 1966 Southend had dropped to the Fourth Division, from which they climbed again six years later.

Twice in their formative years the club finished runners-up in the Second Division of the Southern League, but there have been too few years of glory to satisfy devotees of 'The Shrimpers'. The F.A. Cup competition of 1951–52 produced three months of excitement when, drawn at home five times out of five, Southend fought their way into the last 16 before losing 2–1 to Sheffield United.

Record attendance: 28,059 v. Birmingham City (F.A. Cup), January 1957.
Modern Capacity: 35,000.
Entered Football League: 1920—Div. 3.
Biggest win: 10–1 v. Golders Green (F.A. Cup), November 1934; 10–1 v. Brentwood (F.A. Cup), December 1968.
Heaviest defeat: 1–11 v. Northampton Town (Southern League), December 1909.
Highest final League position: 3rd in Div. 3 (South) 1931–32, 1949–50.
Best in F.A. Cup: 5th Round 1925–26, 1951–52.
Best in Football League Cup: 3rd Round 1963–64, 1964–65, 1969–70.
Pitch measurements: 110 × 74 yd.
Highest League Scorer in Single Season: Jim Shankly—31 in 1928–29 (Div. 3 South); Sammy McCrory—31 in 1957–58 (Div. 3 South).
Transfers—
  Highest fee paid: £16,000—Chris Guthrie (from Newcastle), November 1972.
  Highest fee received: £120,000—Peter Taylor (to Crystal Palace), October 1973.

Southport

Haig Avenue,
Southport.
Southport 5353

Shirts: Gold, Blue Trim
Shorts: Royal Blue, Gold Stripe
Stockings: Gold

Formed in 1881 as Southport Central, the club took their present name in 1919, two years before joining the Northern section of the old Third Division.

Twice they finished in fourth place before the Second World War—in 1924–25 and again in 1938–39. In 1958, Southport transferred to the Fourth Division and after a number of indifferent seasons they gave a much-needed fillip to football interest in the area by gaining promotion in 1967, winning 23 and drawing 13 of their 46 matches, but they were relegated three seasons later.

Season 1972–73 ended with Southport winning their first title as Fourth Division Champions, but they immediately found themselves struggling and went down again in 1974.

Older supporters will recall Southport's splendid run in the 1931 F.A. Cup tournament. Millwall, Blackpool and Bradford were all beaten at Southport. Then the quaintly nicknamed 'Sandgrounders' were drawn to meet Everton at Goodison Park in the sixth round . . . and crashed to a 9–1 defeat. It was a calamitous end to what remains to this day Southport's longest run in the competition.

Division 4 Champions: 1972–73.
Record attendance: 20,010 v. Newcastle (F.A. Cup), January 1932.
Modern Capacity: 21,000.
Entered Football League: 1921—Div. 3 (North).
Biggest win: 8–1 v. Nelson (Div. 3 North), January 1931.
Heaviest defeat: 0–11 v. Oldham Athletic (Div. 4), December 1962.
Best in F.A. Cup: 6th Round 1930–31.
Best in Football League Cup: 2nd Round 1962–63, 1963–64, 1968–69, 1969–70, 1971–72, 1972–73.
Pitch measurements: 113 × 77 yd.
Highest League Scorer in Single Season: Archie Waterston—31 in 1930–31 (Div. 3 North).
Transfers—
  Highest fee paid: £6000—Malcolm Russell (from Halifax), September 1968.
  Highest fee received: £20,000—Tony Field (to Blackburn), October 1971.

Stockport County

Edgeley Park,
Stockport,
Cheshire, SK3 9DD.
061–480–8888/9

Shirts: White, Blue Trim
Shorts: White, Blue Stripe
Stockings: White, Blue Tops

Only 13 people paid to watch a Football League match at Old Trafford in May, 1921. This stranger-than-fiction event came about because Stockport's own ground was under suspension and the club used the nearby Manchester United venue for their Division Two match against Leicester City.

Nearly 13 years later, on 6 January 1934, Stockport scored 13 times without reply against Halifax Town in a Division Three (North) match. This and Newcastle's 13–0 victory over Newport County on 5 October 1946 are the biggest wins in Football League history.

Alex Herd, who played in Manchester City's 1933 and 1934 Cup Final teams, gave Stockport splendid service. He and his son, David, provided a rare instance of father and son playing together in the same League side. They were inside-right and inside-left respectively against Hartlepools at Edgeley Park on 5 May 1951, the last day of the season. It was a proud day for 39-year-old Alex, especially as 17-year-old David scored one of the goals in a 2–0 win.

Sadly, Stockport struggled harder than ever in season 1973–74, when they finished last of the 92 League clubs with gates dropping below 1500.

Division 3 (North) Champions: 1921–22, 1936–37.
Division 4 Champions: 1966–67.
Record attendance: 27,833 v. Liverpool (F.A. Cup), February 1950.
Modern Capacity: 24,000.
Entered Football League: 1900—Div. 2.
Biggest win: 13–0 v. Halifax Town (Div. 3 North), January 1934.
Heaviest defeat: 1–8 v. Chesterfield (Division 2), April 1902.
Best in F.A. Cup: 5th Round 1934–35, 1949–50.
Best in Football League Cup: 4th Round 1972–73.
Pitch measurements: 111 × 73 yd.
Highest League Scorer in Single Season: Alf Lythgoe—46 in 1933–34 (Div. 3 North).
Transfers—
  Highest fee paid: £14,000—Alex Young (from Glentoran), November 1968.
  Highest fee received: £25,000—Paul Hart (to Blackpool), June 1973.

Stoke City

Victoria Ground,
Stoke-on-Trent, ST4 4EG.
0782—44660

Shirts: Red and White Stripes
Shorts: White
Stockings: White, Red Hoops

Until 1972, what success Stoke achieved in a long tradition of football had been linked with the name of Stanley Matthews. In 1933, the young Matthews was a promising winger in the Stoke side that brought back First Division football to the Potteries after an absence of ten years.

After relegation in 1953, Stoke spent another ten-year spell in the Second Division. In 1960 Tony Waddington took over as manager and he recruited several veterans including Matthews, who returned from Blackpool, aged 46, at a bargain £3000 fee. Matthews and company—their average age was the highest in the four divisions—took the club back into the First Division in 1963, and Stoke have remained there.

One of the League's original twelve in 1888, they are the second oldest League club—formed in 1863, the year after Notts County. Into the seventies they had still to reach the F.A. Cup Final or win a trophy, but Wembley 1972 brought them their long-awaited first prize, for in the League Cup Final they beat Chelsea 2–1.

England's Gordon Banks, who played an outstanding part in that achievement, was Stoke goalkeeper for six seasons from 1967 until eye injuries received in a car crash ended his career. In January 1974 manager Waddington showed his appreciation of young talent by paying £240,000 for Chelsea midfield player Alan Hudson, and his arrival inspired City to finish fifth, their highest Championship placing since 1947.

Football League Cup Winners: 1971–72.
Division 2 Champions: 1932–33, 1962–63.
Division 3 (North) Champions: 1926–27.
Record attendance: 51,380 v. Arsenal (League), March 1937.
Modern Capacity: 50,000.
Entered Football League: 1888—Div. 1.
Biggest win: 10–3 v. W.B.A. (Div. 1), February 1937.
Heaviest defeat: 0–10 v. Preston (Div. 1), September 1889.
Best in F.A. Cup: Semi-final 1898–99, 1970–71, 1971–72.
Pitch measurements: $116\frac{1}{2} \times 75$ yd.
Highest League Scorer in Single Season: Freddie Steele—33 in 1936–37 (Div. 1).
Transfers—
  Highest fee paid: £240,000—Alan Hudson (from Chelsea), January 1974.
  Highest fee received: £140,000—Mike Barnard (to Everton), May 1972.

Sunderland

Roker Park Ground,
Sunderland, SR6 9SW.
Sunderland 72077/58638

Shirts: Red and White Stripes
Shorts: Black
Stockings: Red, White Tops

When Bob Stokoe was appointed manager of Sunderland late in November 1972, this club of great tradition was drifting third from bottom of the Second Division. In the months that followed, glory—and the crowds—returned to Roker Park, and after thrilling F.A. Cup victories over Manchester City and, in the semi-final, Arsenal, Sunderland found themselves participating in Wembley's 50th birthday celebrations.

Having reached the final, they had turned back the clock 42 years, for by their 1–0 triumph over Leeds the Cup went outside the First Division for the first time since West Bromwich's victory in 1931.

Ian Porterfield shot the goal that brought victory to the original 250–1 outsiders, and the 11 Sunderland heroes at Wembley were: Montgomery; Malone, Guthrie, Horswill, Watson, Pitt, Kerr, Hughes, Halom, Porterfield, Tueart.

For Sunderland, six times League Champions, this was the first prize they had won since their previous F.A. Cup success in 1937. Until 1958 they could claim, proudly and exclusively, that they had never played outside the First Division. Then they fell on hard times, from which they did not emerge until Bob Stokoe left Blackpool and went back to his native North-east to make a fairy-tale come true.

League Champions: 1891–92, 1892–93, 1894–95, 1901–02, 1912–13, 1935–36.
F.A. Cup Winners: 1936–37, 1972–73.
Record attendance: 75,118 v. Derby County (F.A. Cup), March 1933.
Modern Capacity: 57,500.
Entered Football League: 1890—Div. 1.
Biggest win: 11–1 v. Fairfield (F.A. Cup), 1894–95.
Heaviest defeat: 0–8 v. West Ham (Div. 1), October 1968.
Best in Football League Cup: Semi-final 1962–63.
Pitch measurements: 112 × 72 yd.
Highest League Scorer in Single Season: Dave Halliday—43 in 1928–29 (Div. 1).
Transfers—
  Highest fee paid: £125,000—Tony Towers (from Manchester City), March 1974.
  Highest fee received: £275,000—Dennis Tueart (to Manchester City), March 1974.

Swansea City

Vetch Field,
Swansea, SA1 3SU.
Swansea 42855

Shirts: White, Black Trim
Shorts: White
Stockings: White, Black-hooped Turnover

When Swansea won the Third Division (South) Championship in 1949 by seven points, they fielded seven Internationals in their side. They were Paul, Richards and Lucas (Wales), Feeney, McCrory, Keane and O'Driscoll (Ireland). This title enabled Irish manager Billy McCandless to complete a remarkable 'hat trick' of successes with Welsh clubs. He had previously guided Newport (1938–39) and Cardiff City (1946–47) into the Second Division.

Swansea has always been a reservoir of great soccer talent. Roy John, Trevor Ford, Ivor and Len Allchurch, Cliff Jones and Barrie Jones are just a few of many fine players whom the club have developed.

In season 1963–64, Swansea only just avoided relegation from Division Two, yet almost reached the F.A. Cup Final. They won their way through to the last four with victories over such formidable First Division opponents as Sheffield United, Stoke City and Liverpool (League Champions that season) before going down 2–1 to Preston in the semi-final.

The 'Swans' changed their title from Town to City in 1970 on winning promotion from Division Four, but were relegated again three years later.

Division 3 (South) Champions: 1924–25, 1948–49.
Record attendance: 32,700 v. Arsenal (F.A. Cup), February 1968.
Modern Capacity: 35,000.
Entered Football League: 1920—Div. 3.
Biggest win: 8–1 v. Bristol Rovers (Div. 3 South), April 1922, 8–1 v. Bradford City (Div. 2), February 1926.
Heaviest defeat: 1–8 v. Fulham (Div. 2), January 1938.
Best in F.A. Cup: Semi-final 1925–26, 1963–64.
Best in Football League Cup: 4th Round 1964–65.
Pitch measurements: 110 × 70 yd.
Highest League Scorer in Single Season: Cyril Pearce—35 in 1931–32 (Div. 2).
Transfers—
  Highest fee paid: £26,000—Ronnie Rees (from Nottingham Forest), January 1972.
  Highest fee received: £45,000—Barrie Jones (to Plymouth), September 1964.

Swindon Town

County Ground,
Swindon.
Swindon 22118

Shirts: Red, White Edging
Shorts: Black with White Stripes
Stockings: Black and Red, White Hoop

Enthusiasm reached unprecedented heights in the West Country on 6 March 1969, when Swindon Town became League Cup holders by beating Arsenal 3–1 in extra time at Wembley—and at the end of the season also gained promotion to Division Two, where they remained until 1974.

After 43 years as a Third Division club, Swindon gained promotion as runners-up in 1963. They started off well in Second Division football, being undefeated for their first nine games, but eventually finished the season well down the table, and the following year they were back in the Third Division.

One of the club's earliest stars was Harold Fleming, an inside-forward capped nine times for England. His skills played a major part in Swindon's two F.A. Cup semi-final appearances in 1910 and 1912. Others of renown have included Harry Morris, who scored 47 League goals in 1926–27 and a total of 216 in eight seasons; Maurice Owen, another with goalscoring flair and 554 League appearances for the club (1946–63); Norman Uprichard, Ireland's goalkeeper in the 1950's; England International Mike Summerbee and Under-23 caps Ernie Hunt and Don Rogers; and Dave Mackay (ex-Tottenham and Scotland), player, then manager from November 1971, before moving on to Nottingham Forest and Derby.

League Cup Winners: 1968–69.
Record attendance: 32,000 v. Arsenal (F.A. Cup), January 1972.
Modern Capacity: 32,000.
Entered Football League: 1920—Div. 3.
Biggest win: 10–1 v. Farnham Utd. Breweries (F.A. Cup), November 1925.
Heaviest defeat: 1–10 v. Manchester City (F.A. Cup), January 1930.
Highest final League position: Runners-up Div. 3 1962–63, 1968–69.
Best in F.A. Cup: Semi-final 1909–10, 1911–12.
Pitch measurements: 117 × 78 yd.
Highest League Scorer in Single Season: Harry Morris—47 in 1926–27 (Div. 3 South).
Transfers—
  Highest fee paid: £80,000—Peter Eastoe (from Wolves), March 1974.
  Highest fee received: £140,000—Don Rogers (to Crystal Palace), October 1972.

Torquay United

Plainmoor Ground,
Torquay, Devon, TQ1 3PS.
Torquay 38666/7

Shirts: Gold, Blue Collar and Cuffs
Shorts: Gold
Stockings: Gold, Blue Turnover

Two local amateur clubs, Torquay Town and Babbacombe, joined forces to form the present club which became professional in 1922. In season 1927—28 the Football League clubs recognized Torquay's promise by electing them to the Southern Section of the old Division Three. Their first season ended disastrously—in bottom place—and in the years before and immediately after the Second World War they rarely rose above half-way in the table.

This applied until 1956, when they finished fifth. The following year they were runners-up, missing promotion to the Second Division only on goal average, but by the time the League was extended in 1958 they found themselves in Division Four.

Since then Torquay have alternated between Third and Fourth Divisions without achieving a title. With little money available, and situated in an area of the country where League football has seldom attracted national attention, Torquay United struggle along on depressingly small attendances, which dropped below 3000 last season (1973—74), the lowest level in the club's history.

Record attendance: 21,736 v. Huddersfield Town (F.A. Cup), January 1955.
Modern Capacity: 22,000.
Entered Football League: 1927—Div. 3 (South).
Biggest win: 9—0 v. Swindon Town (Div. 3 South), March 1952.
Heaviest defeat: 2—10 v. Fulham (Div. 3 South), September 1931; 2—10 v. Luton Town (Div. 3 South), September 1933.
Highest final League position: Runners-up Div. 3 (South) 1956—57.
Best in F.A. Cup: 4th Round 1948—49, 1954—55, 1970—71.
Best in Football League Cup: 3rd Round 1967—68, 1971—72.
Pitch measurements: 112 × 74 yd.
Highest League Scorer in Single Season: Sammy Collins— 40 in 1955—56 (Div. 3 South).
Transfers—
  Highest fee paid: £15,000—David Tearse (from Leicester), November 1971.
  Highest fee received: £21,000—Tommy Mitchinson (to Bournemouth), December 1971.

Tottenham Hotspur

748 High Road,
Tottenham,
London, NI7 0AP.
01-808-1020

Shirts: White
Shorts: Navy Blue
Stockings: White

Since the war there have been two truly great Spurs eras—Arthur Rowe's 'push and run' team, which won the Second and First Division titles in successive years (1950 and 1951) and Bill Nicholson's Tottenham.

What happened on 11 October 1958, when Nicholson, former Spurs player and coach, became manager, was a pointer to the successful future. Tottenham beat Everton 10–4 (then their record win) that day. With Danny Blanchflower, Dave Mackay, Cliff Jones and John White the corner-stones, they did the 'double' in 1960–61.

Over the next decade the club spent more than a million pounds on new players, who included Jimmy Greaves, Alan Mullery, Terry Venables, Mike England, Martin Chivers, Martin Peters and Ralph Coates. By the time Spurs took the 1973 League Cup they had contested seven finals in four different competitions under Bill Nicholson's command and won the lot.

League Champions: 1950–51, 1960–61.
Division 2 Champions: 1919–20, 1949–50.
F.A. Cup Winners: 1900–01, 1920–21, 1960–61, 1961–62, 1966–67.
Winners of European Cup-Winners' Cup: 1962–63.
League Cup Winners: 1970–71, 1972–73.
U.E.F.A. Cup Winners: 1971–72.
The Double (League and F.A. Cup Winners): 1960–61.
Record attendance: 75,038 v. Sunderland (F.A. Cup), March 1938. **Modern Capacity:** 57,000.
Entered Football League: 1908—Div. 2.
Biggest win: 13–2 v. Crewe (F.A. Cup), February 1960.
Heaviest defeat: 2–7 v. Liverpool (Div. 1), October 1914; 2–7 v. Newcastle Utd. (Div. 1), September 1951; 2–7 v. Blackburn Rovers (Div. 1), September 1963; 2–7 v. Burnley (Div. 1), April 1964.
Pitch measurements: 111 × 73 yd.
Highest League Scorer in Single Season: Jimmy Greaves—37 in 1962–63 (Div. 1).
Transfers—
  Highest fee paid: £200,000 equivalent—Martin Peters (from West Ham), March 1970—(£146,000 plus Jimmy Greaves).
  Highest fee received: £70,000—Terry Venables (to Q.P.R.), June 1969.

Tranmere Rovers

Prenton Park,
Prenton Road West,
Birkenhead.
051-608-3677/4194

Shirts: White, Blue Trim
Shorts: Royal Blue
Stockings: White, Blue Band

Living in the shadows of those two giant Merseyside clubs, Everton and Liverpool, has meant a continual battle for players and supporters for Tranmere Rovers. Yet the Rovers, formed in 1883 and League members since 1921, have certainly had their moments. They won the Northern Section of the Third Division in fine style in 1937–38, only to suffer an astonishing reversal of form the following season. They lost 31 of their 42 matches and were promptly relegated.

Devotees of the Birkenhead club fondly recall the nine goals by 'Bunny' Bell in a 13–4 Third Division (North) victory over Oldham Athletic on Boxing Day, 1935, the only time 17 goals have been scored in a Football League match.

While 'Bunny' Bell is remembered for his goalscoring feats, centre-half *Harold* Bell also earned a distinguished place in the records for Tranmere. He was ever present for nine seasons between 1946 and 1955, playing 401 consecutive matches—the League record—and altogether made 595 League appearances for the club, the last of them in 1964.

Tranmere were responsible for one of the biggest shocks in League Cup history when, on 2 October 1973, under player-manager Ron Yeats (ex-Liverpool and Scotland centre-half), they beat Arsenal 1–0 in the second round—at Highbury!

Division 3 (North) Champions: 1937–38.
Record attendance: 24,424 v. Stoke City (F.A. Cup), February 1972.
Modern Capacity: 29,000.
Entered Football League: 1921—Div. 3 (North).
Biggest win: 13–4 v. Oldham Athletic (Div. 3 North), December 1935.
Heaviest defeat: 1–9 v. Tottenham Hotspur (F.A. Cup), January 1953.
Best in F.A. Cup: 5th Round 1967–68.
Best in Football League Cup: 4th Round 1960–61.
Pitch measurements: 112 × 72 yd.
Highest League Scorer in Single Season: R. ('Bunny') Bell —35 in 1933–34 (Div. 3 North).
Transfers—
  Highest fee paid: £15,000—George Hudson (from Northampton), January 1967.
  Highest fee received: £35,000—Jim Cumbes (to W.B.A.), August 1969.

Walsall

Fellows Park,
Walsall, WS2 9DB.
Walsall 22791

Shirts: White, Red Trim
Shorts: Red
Stockings: White

Whenever the name of Walsall is mentioned someone is almost certain to remark: 'Do you recall the day they knocked Arsenal out of the F.A. Cup?' Few football events between the two World Wars caused a greater stir than Walsall's famous 2–0 win over Arsenal in the third round on 14 January 1933. The 'Gunners' team, then the most powerful in the land, was packed with internationals; Walsall were a Third Division North side of no special skills. Yet they won that afternoon on their merits. Gilbert Alsop, a centre-forward who gave the club wonderful service, getting one of the goals.

The story and the legends of this game will continue to be told until Walsall achieve something more extraordinary. As it is, the rest of their history recounts few achievements, though they won the Division Four title in 1960 convincingly enough with 65 points, five more than their nearest challengers. A year later Walsall again won promotion to the Second Division, but survived there only two seasons.

Perhaps the best known of their 'home produced' players has been Allan Clarke, of Leeds United and England. Walsall transferred him to Fulham for £35,000 in March 1966, and by the time Clarke joined Leeds via Leicester City, his transfer deals had involved £350,000.

Division 4 Champions: 1959–60.
Record attendance: 25,453 v. Newcastle Utd. (League), August 1961.
Modern Capacity: 25,000.
Entered Football League: 1892—Div. 2.
Biggest win: 10–0 v. Darwen (Div. 2), March 1899.
Heaviest defeat: 0–12 v. Small Heath (Div. 2), December 1892; 0–12 v. Darwen (Div. 2), December 1896.
Best in F.A. Cup: 5th Round 1938–39.
Best in Football League Cup: 4th Round 1966–67.
Pitch measurements: 113 × 73 yd.
Highest League Scorer in Single Season: Gilbert Alsop—40 in 1933–34 and 40 in 1934–35 (both in Div. 3 North).
Transfers—
  Highest fee paid: £17,000—Trevor Smith (from Birmingham), October 1964.
  Highest fee received: £35,000—Allan Clarke (to Fulham), March 1966.

Watford

Vicarage Road Ground,
Watford, WD1 8ER.
Watford 21759

Shirts: Gold
Shorts: Black, Gold Stripe
Stockings: Gold

After spending 49 years in lower grade League football, Watford came out of comparative obscurity in 1969 to win promotion to the Second Division and earn a name as F.A. Cup fighters. They became Third Division champions on goal average over Swindon and held Manchester United to a fourth round draw at Old Trafford in the F.A. Cup.

The following season, Watford enjoyed an even better Cup run, beating Bolton, Stoke and Liverpool before losing 5–1 to Chelsea in the semi-final. But Second Division life was hard and the club were relegated back to the Third in 1972.

Watford moved to their present ground at Vicarage Road in 1919. The following year they became founder members of the Third Division. Apart from two seasons (1958–60) in the newly-formed Fourth Division, Watford spent the whole of their League career up to 1969 in the Third Division.

Before the Second World War, Tommy Barnett made 445 appearances for the club in 12 seasons (1928–39) and scored 164 goals. Cliff Holton broke Watford's scoring record for a single season with 42 goals in 1959–60.

The club's outstanding discovery since the war was Northern Ireland goalkeeper Pat Jennings, sold to Tottenham in June 1964 for £25,000.

Division 3 Champions: 1968–69.
Record attendance: 34,099 v. Manchester Utd. (F.A. Cup), February 1969.
Modern Capacity: 36,500.
Entered Football League: 1920—Div. 3.
Biggest win: 10–1 v. Lowestoft Town (F.A. Cup), November 1926.
Heaviest defeat: 0–10 v. Wolves (F.A. Cup), January 1912.
Best in F.A. Cup: Semi-final 1969–70.
Best in Football League Cup: 3rd Round 1961–62, 1971–72.
Pitch measurements: 112 × 74 yd.
Highest League Scorer in Single Season: Cliff Holton—42 in 1959–60 (Div. 4).
Transfers—
  Highest fee paid: £30,000—Ross Jenkins (from Crystal Palace), November 1972.
  Highest fee received: £60,000—Colin Franks (to Sheffield United), June 1973.

West Bromwich Albion

The Hawthorns,
West Bromwich B71 4LF.
021–553–0095

Shirts: Navy Blue and White Stripes
Shorts: White
Stockings: White

As F.A. Cup winners five times, West Bromwich Albion have a proud record, but League honours have usually eluded them. They have appeared in ten F.A. Cup Finals and 17 semi-finals.

In 1965–66, West Bromwich made a belated entry into the League Cup and won it; they were also Finalists in 1967 and 1970. In the summer of 1971 they appointed as manager their former full-back Don Howe, under whose coaching Arsenal did the 'double' the previous season, but season 1972–73 marked the end of a 24-year stay in Division 1. They were among the promotion runners in 1974, but failed to last the course.

One of the highlights in Albion's history was their 1931 F.A. Cup Final triumph (as a Second Division team) over Birmingham, which earned them the distinction of being the only club to win the Cup and promotion in the same season.

West Bromwich were among the original 12 members of the Football League in 1888, but have won the Championship only once—in 1920—despite long spells in the First Division. England full-back Jesse Pennington was one of their earliest star players. In their Championship season of 1919–20 they often fielded seven Internationals.

League Champions: 1919–20.
Division 2 Champions: 1901–02, 1910–11.
F.A. Cup Winners: 1887–88, 1891–92, 1930–31, 1953–54, 1967–68.
League Cup Winners: 1965–66.
Record attendance: 64,815 v. Arsenal (F.A. Cup), March 1937.
Modern Capacity: 50,000.
Entered Football League: 1888—Div. 1.
Biggest win: 12–0 v. Darwen (Div. 1), April 1892.
Heaviest defeat: 3–10 v. Stoke City (Div. 1), February 1937.
Pitch measurements: 115 × 75 yd.
Highest League Scorer in Single Season: W. ('Ginger') Richardson—39 in 1935–36 (Div. 1).
Transfers—
  Highest fee paid: £135,000—Willie Johnston (from Rangers), December 1972.
  Highest fee received: £75,000—Colin Suggett (to Norwich), February 1973.

West Ham United

Boleyn Ground,
Green Street,
Upton Park,
London, E13.
01-472-0704

Shirts: Claret, Blue
  Sleeves and Trim
Shorts: White
Stockings: Blue

When England won the World Cup in 1966, West Ham provided the captain, Bobby Moore, and two other members of that great team—Geoff Hurst and Martin Peters. The East London club has also produced an 'academy' of players who have become well-known managers, among them Frank O'Farrell, Malcolm Allison, Dave Sexton, Noel Cantwell, Jimmy Bloomfield and John Bond.

In 1923, four years after being elected to the Football League, they gained promotion to the First Division and also reached the first Wembley Cup Final, which they lost 2–0 to Bolton. They were relegated in 1932, and it was 1958 before they returned.

West Ham have had only four managers in their history, and during Ron Greenwood's reign they have been among the most attractive sides in Britain, especially during the sixties, when they won the F.A. Cup (1964) and the European Cup-Winners' Cup (1965). After finishing sixth in the 1972–73 Championship, they surprisingly slipped into the relegation zone last season, but hauled themselves clear with an impressive second half revival.

F.A. Cup Winners: 1963–64.
Winners of European Cup-Winners' Cup: 1964–65.
Division 2 Champions: 1957–58.
Record attendance: 42,322 v. Tottenham Hotspur (League), October 1970.
Modern Capacity: 42,500.
Entered Football League: 1919—Div. 2.
Biggest win: 8–0 v. Rotherham United (Div. 2), March 1958; 8–0 v. Sunderland (Div. 1), October 1968.
Heaviest defeat: 0–10 v. Tottenham Hotspur (Southern League), 1904–05.
Best in Football League Cup: Runners-up 1965–66.
Pitch measurements: 110 × 72 yd.
Highest League Scorer in Single Season: Vic Watson—41 in 1929–30 (Div. 1).
Transfers—
  Highest fee paid: £170,000—Ted MacDougall (from Man. United), February 1973; £170,000 Graham Paddon (from Norwich), December 1973.
  Highest fee received: £200,000 equivalent—Martin Peters (to Tottenham—£146,000 plus Jimmy Greaves in part exchange), March 1970.

Wolverhampton Wanderers

Molineux Grounds,
Waterloo Road,
Wolverhampton, WV1 4QR.
0902–24053

Shirts: Gold, Black Collar and Cuffs
Shorts: Black
Stockings: Gold

Football fame came back to the Wolves in the fifties. Not only did they challenge for the title of Britain's top club, but they also shone in prestige matches against the best of that era in Europe.

Behind their amazing record of success was the genius of manager Stan Cullis, the captaincy of Billy Wright and an all-star team excelling at the long-ball game.

Wolves began the most glamorous period in their history with a 3–1 Wembley win over Leicester City in the 1949 F.A. Cup Final. They went on to become League Champions in 1954, 1958 and 1959, and won the Cup again in 1960.

Then for Wolves, one of the League's founder clubs in 1888, came 14 years of unsuccessful striving for further glory before they returned to Wembley, under manager Bill McGarry, for the 1974 League Cup Final, in which they defeated Manchester City 2–1.

Billy Wright, first England player to complete a century of Internationals (105 appearances) played more League and Cup games—535 between 1946 and 1959—than anyone in Wolves' history.

League Champions: 1953–54, 1957–58, 1958–59.
Division 2 Champions: 1931–32.
Division 3 (North) Champions: 1923–24.
F.A. Cup Winners: 1892–93, 1907–08, 1948–49, 1959–60.
League Cup Winners: 1973–74.
Record attendance: 61,315 v. Liverpool (F.A. Cup), February 1939.
Modern Capacity: 53,500.
Entered Football League: 1888—Div. 1.
Biggest win: 14–0 v. Crosswell's Brewery (F.A. Cup), 1886–87.
Heaviest defeat: 1–10 v. Newton Heath (Div. 1), October 1892.
Pitch measurements: 115 × 72 yd.
Highest League Scorer in Single Season: Dennis Westcott—37 in 1946–47 (Div. 1).
Transfers:
  Highest fee paid: £100,000—Steve Kindon (from Burnley), June 1972.
  Highest fee received: £100,000—Alun Evans (to Liverpool), September 1968.

Workington

Borough Park,
Workington, CA14 2DT.
Workington 2871

Shirts: Red
Shorts: White
Stockings: Black with
　　Red and White Hoops

A continual struggle for existence has failed to daunt the hard core of enthusiasts devoted to the cause of Workington F.C. They have poured money, time and creative ideas into sustaining League football in this outpost of the game on the coast of Cumberland. Such zeal deserves to succeed, but in season 1973–74 gates dropped below 1000 and at the finish the club had to apply for re-election.

Originally founded in 1884, Workington reformed in 1921 and won election to the Third Division (North) in 1951.

Excitement ran high in the area during season 1963–64 when they came third, only a point behind their local rivals, Carlisle. Two seasons later they were among the leading clubs in Division Three, finishing fifth, but this rich promise was not fulfilled the following year when they occupied bottom place.

Several well known personalities have gained valuable managerial experience with Workington, among them Bill Shankly, Joe Harvey and Ken Furphy.

Record attendance: 21,500 v. Manchester Utd. (F.A. Cup), January 1958.
Modern Capacity: 21,000.
Entered Football League: 1951—Div. 3 (North).
Biggest win: 9–1 v. Barrow (League Cup), September 1964.
Heaviest defeat: 0–8 v. Wrexham (Div. 3 North), October 1953.
Highest final League position: 3rd in Div. 4 1963–64.
Best in F.A. Cup: 4th Round 1933–34.
Best in Football League Cup: 5th Round 1963–64, 1964–65.
Pitch measurements: 112 × 76 yd.
Highest League Scorer in Single Season: Jim Dailey—26 in 1956–57 (Div. 3 North).
Transfers—
　Highest fee paid: £6000—Ted Purdon (from Sunderland), March 1957.
　Highest fee received: £35,000—Ian McDonald (to Liverpool), January 1974.

Wrexham

Racecourse Ground,
8 Mold Road, Wrexham.
Wrexham 2414

Shirts: Red, White Trim
Shorts: White, Red Seam
Stockings: Red

Wrexham hold the distinction of being the oldest Association football club in Wales. They were founded in 1873 and have provided a steady flow of players to the International team. Wrexham have also won the Welsh Cup 19 times, yet they are unable to point to a single Championship during their Football League membership which began in 1921.

The two highlights of their League existence are widely separated. In 1932–33 they finished second to Hull in the old Northern Section of Division Three, and 37 years later, in 1970, they were runners-up in Division Four. They did finish third in 1961–62, but returned to Division Four two seasons later.

The Racecourse Ground is still an occasional International venue. A record crowd of 34,445 attended the F.A. Cup fourth round tie on 26 January 1957, when Manchester United beat Wrexham 5–0.

Wrexham provided F.A. Cup sensations in season 1973–74. They beat Second Division leaders Middlesbrough 1–0 to reach the fifth round for the first time in their history, and then did even better by winning 1–0 away to First Division Southampton. Then they were drawn away to another First Division club, Burnley, and went out by the only goal.

Record attendance: 34,445 v. Manchester Utd. (F.A. Cup), January 1957.
Modern Capacity: 36,000.
Entered Football League: 1921 — Div. 3 (North).
Biggest win: 10–1 v. Hartlepools Utd. (Div. 4), March 1962.
Heaviest defeat: 0–9 v. Brentford (Div. 3), October 1963.
Highest final League position: Runners-up Div. 3 (North), 1932–33; runners-up Div. 4 1969–70.
Best in F.A. Cup: 6th Round 1973–74.
Best in Football League Cup: 5th Round 1960–61.
Pitch measurements: 117 × 75 yd.
Highest League Scorer in Single Season: Tommy Bamford —44 in 1933–34 (Div. 3 North).
Transfers—
  Highest fee paid: £15,000 — Mel Sutton (from Cardiff), June 1972.
Highest fee received: £28,000 — David Powell (to Sheffield Utd.), September 1968.

York City

Bootham Crescent,
York, YO3 7AQ.
York 24447

Shirts: Maroon
Shorts: White
Stockings: Maroon

York City are one of only four Third Division clubs who have reached the semi-final round of the F.A. Cup. Millwall (1937), Port Vale (1954) and Norwich City (1959) are the others. City startled the football world in 1955 with an extraordinary Cup run which actually carried them further than any other Third Division side in history; they took Newcastle United to a replay before losing the semi-final 2–0.

York had reached the last eight in 1938 when their team, said to have cost only £50, defeated teams from all four divisions. Some of the club's best performances have been achieved more recently. Three times since the League was extended in 1958 they have won promotion to the Third Division—in 1959, 1965 and 1971.

Between October–December 1973 York equalled a 47-year-old record (Millwall, Div. 3 South 1926) by playing 11 consecutive Third Division matches without conceding a goal. Such defence played a major part in City finishing third and so reaching the Second Division for the first time in their history.

At the start of 1973–74 the prospect of York playing Manchester United for points was no more than a dream . . . but by 1974–75 it was reality.

Record attendance: 28,123 v. Huddersfield Town (F.A. Cup), March 1938.
Modern Capacity: 23,500.
Entered Football League: 1929—Div. 3 (North).
Biggest win: 9–1 v. Southport (Div. 3 North), February 1957.
Heaviest defeat: 0–12 v. Chester (Div. 3 North), Feb. 1936.
Highest final League position: 3rd in Div. 4 1958–59, 1964–65; 3rd in Div. 3 1973–74.
Best in F.A. Cup: Semi-final 1954–55.
Best in Football League Cup: 5th Round 1961–62.
Pitch measurements: 115 × 75 yd.
Highest League Scorer in Single Season: Bill Fenton—31 in 1951–52 (Div. 3 North); Alf Bottom—31 in 1954–55 (Div. 3 North).
Transfers—
  Highest fee paid: £15,000—Barry Lyons (from Nottingham Forest), October 1973.
  Highest fee received: £20,000—Phil Boyer (to Bournemouth), December 1970.

The Scottish League

Aberdeen, the principal club in the north-east of Scotland, were founded in 1903 and from the early years they built a reputation for playing attractive football although rarely achieving top honours.

In 1905 they left the North-east Alliance to enter the Scottish League, and although they stayed in the First Division, it took them half a century to become League Champions. After being runners-up in 1911 and 1937, they at last took the title in 1955. They were runners-up the following year and again in 1971 and 1972.

By 1967 Aberdeen had reached the Scottish Cup Final six times but won the trophy only once—when defeating Hibernian 2–1 in 1947. Their second F.A. Cup triumph came in 1970, when they beat Celtic 3–1 in the Final. They took the League Cup in its inaugural season (1945–46) and won it again ten years later.

Airdrieonians climbed their highest peaks in the early 1920s when they challenged the supremacy of Rangers and Celtic. They were First Division runners-up in four successive seasons (1923–26) and won the Scottish Cup for the only time in 1924, beating Hibernian 2–0 in the Final.

In the League during that era, Airdrie were unbeaten on their own Broomfield Park pitch for more than three years. They fielded six Scottish Internationals, the greatest of them Hughie Gallacher.

Airdrie dropped into the Second Division in 1936 and did not get back into the top class until 1947, since when they have fought an almost constant battle to stay up—or go up.

Albion Rovers' most memorable year was 1920 when, for the only time, they reached the Scottish Cup final, after beating mighty Rangers in the semi-final. In that Rovers team beaten 3–2 by Kilmarnock was Jock White, still their only international, who was capped with them before moving on to Hearts and Leeds. Elected to the First Division in 1919, 'Wee Albion' have had at best a see-saw existence, being relegated three times—the last occasion in 1949. One of their most outstanding players was Jock Stein, subsequently the triumphant manager of Celtic and a star defender at Cliftonhill during the 1940s.

For **Alloa Athletic** the proudest achievement came in season 1921—22, when they won the very first Second Division championship by a margin of 13 points. But a year later they were relegated and have remained in the Second Division ever since. They were, however, harshly affected by the outbreak of the Second World War. They were due for promotion at the end of season 1938—39, but the League was disbanded because of the war, and when it was reformed, Alloa were not elected to the First Division.

The small Scottish coastal town of **Arbroath** is famous for kippers—and the club's 36—0 victory over Bon Accord in a first round cup-tie in September 1885. This stands as the biggest score in a first-class match in Britain. Bon Accord's regular goalkeeper Jimmie Grant was unfit and replaced by wing-half Andrew Lornie. John Petrie scored 13 against him and Arboath totalled 55 goals in the cup that season before losing to Hibernian in the fourth round. The previous year Arbroath were robbed of another place in the history books. They beat Rangers in a fourth round cup-tie, but after protesting that the Gayfield pitch was smaller than regulation size, Rangers won the replayed game 8—1 on their own ground. Arbroath had to wait another 90 years to achieve that first win over Rangers—a stunning 3—2 League victory on 2 February 1974. At Ibrox Park, too!

Ayr United have enjoyed steady support since they entered the Scottish First Division in 1913. They have mostly struggled on the fringe of the First Division. Between 1925 and 1969 they won promotion six times—but since that last elevation they have consolidated, and a place in the top half of the table in seasons 1972—73 and 1973—74 suggested that Somerset Park is heading for its most successful era.

For as long as football is played in Scotland, **Berwick Rangers** 1, Glasgow Rangers 0 will stand high on the list of 'unbelievable' results. The date was 28 January 1967 in the first round of the Cup, and Shielfield Park, home of the little English border-town team of part-timers who play in the Scottish League, was crammed with a record 13,365 crowd for the visit of mighty Rangers.

Sammy Reid, a former Liverpool player, scored the historic 32nd-minute goal, and for the rest of the game Berwick's 35-year-old goalkeeper-manager Jock Wallace (ex-Airdrie and W.B.A.) and his defence heroically resisted all Rangers' pressure to produce Scotland's greatest 'Jock the giantkiller' story.

Never before had Rangers been knocked out of the Cup by Second Division opposition . . . and it is said that many of the 7000 fans who followed them from Glasgow to Tweedmouth that day still refuse to believe it ever happened.

Another club never to have reached the First Division, **Brechin City** has the smallest population (6000) supporting a senior club in Britain. During the 1920s—when Brechin moved to their present ground, Glebe Park—the town was inhabited by more than 10,000 and attendances averaged 3000, but after the war the population fell dramatically, and so did support for Brechin.

Celtic, arch rivals of Rangers as the top club in Scottish football, were formed in 1888 by Irish Catholics living in Glasgow, the first object being to raise money for the poor of the city's East End.

Under former captain Jock Stein (appointed manager in 1965) they have reached astonishing heights, with 1966–67 their greatest season. In an historic clean sweep, they became the first British club to win the European Cup, defeating Inter-Milan 2–1 in the Final; they won the League Championship (scoring 111 goals and losing only one game out of 34); they took the Scottish Cup; and the Scottish League Cup also went to Parkhead.

Celtic's famous green and white strip has long been an emblem of attacking football, and season 1971–72 brought them the Double for the fourth time in six years. A ninth *successive* League Championship (their 29th in all) in 1973–74 equalled a world record by Hungarian club MTK Budapest (1917–25) and the Bulgarians CDNA Sofia (1954–62), a feat celebrated by completion of the Double for the ninth time in their history.

Celtic have won the Scottish Cup a total of 23 times and the League Cup on seven occasions, but they have been defeated in four consecutive League Cup Finals.

Of Celtic's galaxy of star players down the years, Jimmy McGrory was unquestionably the greatest goalscorer. In 378 games between 1922–39 he obtained 397 goals for them—the highest all-time total in the Scottish League—and after a playing career in which his goal aggregate reached 550, he also managed the club.

Clyde were formed in 1877 and took their name from the river and dockyards of Glasgow. Their home, Shawfield Park, is in the East End and they have constantly struggled to keep up with their big city rivals.

Although they have slipped out of the First Division on six occasions, they have always made a rapid return to the top bracket, five times doing so at the first attempt.

Clyde have never been Champions of Scotland, nor have they won the League Cup, but they have triumphed three times in the F.A. Cup.

After defeats in the 1910 and 1912 Finals they at last won the trophy in 1939, when they beat Motherwell 4–0. They were also Cup winners in 1955, defeating Celtic 1–0 in a replay, and in 1958 another single goal gave them victory over Hibernian.

The most-recently founded club in the Scottish League are present-day **Clydebank**, formed in 1967. They had played one season in the Second Division under the name of East Stirlingshire Clydebank, but in 1965 there was a legal dispute and Clydebank became established in their own right.

In the 1920s the original Clydebank FC were a First Division club, but they resigned from the Scottish League in 1931. A team built from their remnants continued under the name of Clydebank Intermediate, but they failed to gain senior status.

After years of Second Division obscurity, **Cowdenbeath** won unexpected promotion in season 1969–70, and within months they were in a League Cup semi-final against Rangers—excitement unheard of at Central Park since the Second Division Championship of 1938–39. But they lasted only one more season in the top class.

Cowdenbeath won the Second Division in 1939 by 12 points, but when League football was resumed seven years later there was no place for them in the First Division.

Season 1972–73 saw **Dumbarton** playing their first match in the First Division for fifty years, while Clyde returned to the Second. It was an ironic twist, for two seasons earlier Dumbarton made a take-over bid for Clyde, but it was rejected as an attempt to buy their way out of the Second Division.

Founded in 1872, Dumbarton were one of the original

members of the Scottish League in 1890. They shared the first Championship title with Rangers, and won it outright the following year. They entered the first Scottish Cup in 1873–74 and have done so ever since—a record equalled only by Queen's Park and Kilmarnock. They won the Cup in 1883.

Dundee, a First Division club for most of their history, did not win the League Championship until 1962—after four times being runners-up. That is still their only League title to date, but they were F.A. Cup winners in 1910, and their three League Cup successes were gained in seasons 1951–52, 1952–53 and 1973–74 (when they shocked Celtic 1–0 in the Final).

In 1963 Dundee were close to becoming the first British club to win the European Cup, losing in the semi-finals to AC Milan, who went on to win the competition. They have a good record in European football, having beaten such celebrated clubs as Sporting Lisbon, Anderlecht, Standard Liège and Zürich.

Dundee United, founded in 1910, have constantly struggled to emulate the deeds of their next-door neighbours, Dundee —and are still trying to win their first major prize. Originally known as Dundee Hibernian, they changed their name in 1923 on gaining election to the Second Division of the Scottish League. Two years later they won promotion but they led an up-and-down existence (relegated 1927–30–32) until stability was brought to the side at the start of the 1960s.

First Division football returned to Tannadice Park in 1960, since when United have consistently maintained a place halfway, or just above, in the Scottish Championship.

In 1974 they reached the F.A. Cup Final for the first time, and although they lost 3–0 to Celtic their presence at Hampden Park encouraged hopes at Tannadice that honours would not be delayed much longer.

Dunfermline Athletic did not 'arrive' as a top club in Scotland until the sixties, although they were formed as long ago as 1907. Their real rise began in 1960, when Jock Stein was appointed manager. The following year they reached the Scottish Cup Final for the first time, and after a goalless draw beat Celtic 2–0 in a replay. Their second F.A. Cup victory came in 1968 when they defeated Hearts 3–1 in the Final.

Although Stein left, Dunfermline remained strong and

Plate 1 They Did the 'Double' (1) Since the Football League was formed in 1888, four clubs have performed the League Championship & F.A. Cup double by winning both competitions in the same season. First were **Preston North End** in the League's inaugural year (1888–89). They won the Championship undefeated and the Cup without conceding a goal. *Standing:* R. Holmes, N. Ross, D. Russell, R. Howarth, J. Graham, Dr R. H. Mills-Roberts. *Seated:* J. Gordon, J. Ross, J. Goodall, F. Dewhurst, G. Drummond.

Plate 2 They Did the 'Double' (2) Aston Villa were the second double-event club in 1896–97. *Back row:* R. Chat, H. Spencer, A. Evans, T. Wilkes, J. Campbell. *Middle row:* C. Athersmith, J. Devey, F. Wheldon, S. Smith. *Front:* J. Crabtree, J. Cowan.

Plate 3 They Did the 'Double' (3) Tottenham Hotspur, 1960–61
Standing: Bill Brown, Peter Baker, Ron Henry, Danny Blanchflower, Maurice Norman, Dave Mackay.
Seated: Cliff Jones, John White, Bobby Smith, Les Allen, Terry Dyson.

Plate 4 They Did the 'Double' (4) Arsenal 1970–71 *Standing:* Fred Street (physiotherapist), Pat Rice, Peter Marinello, Sammy Nelson, Bob Wilson, Geoff Barnett, Charlie George, Eddie Kelly, George Armstrong, Steve Burtenshaw (coach). *Seated:* John Roberts, Bob McNab, Peter Storey, Frank McLintock, Bertie Mee (manager), Peter Simpson, George Graham, Ray Kennedy, John Radford. **Trophies** (*l. to r.*) League Championship, Footballer of the Year (Frank McLintock) Manager of the Year (Bertie Mee), F.A. Cup. (Street and Burtenshaw were appointed physiotherapist and coach respectively after the double was completed. Don Howe was coach to the 1970–71 team, then left Arsenal to manage West Bromwich.)

Moments (1) The first Wembley Final

This was the scene on 28 April 1923 at the time Bolton Wanderers and West Ham United should have kicked off, with a crowd estimated at nearly 200,000 invading the stadium. Eventually the pitch was cleared, the match started 40 minutes late, and Bolton won 2–0. How many attended the first Wembley could only be guessed. The official crowd figure given as 126,047 (still the biggest for a match in England), but the railway companies said that 241,000 passengers booked to the ground from London stations. Cup Finals at Wembley have been all-ticket ever since.

Plate 6 Historic Moments (2) Wembley's most dramatic penalty With the 1938 F.A. Cup Final into the last seconds of extra time, there was still no score between Preston North End and Huddersfield Town. Then Preston forward George Mutch was brought down in the penalty-area. He took the spot-kick himself and beat goalkeeper Hesford with a shot that

Plate 7 Historic Moments (3)
29 June 1950 was the day the football world turned upside down. In the World Cup at Belo Horizonte, Brazil, England were beaten 1–0 by the United States of America. The goal was scored by centre-forward Gaetjens, and at the end he was carried shoulder-high from the pitch by jubilant fans. More than 20 years after football's most unbelievable result, the game has still not become established in the USA.

Plate 8 Historic Moments (4) Sunderland win the Cup for the Second Division
When the 1972–73 F.A. Cup competition began, Leeds United were 10–1 favourites and Second Division Sunderland were among the 250–1 outsiders. But, come Cup Final Day on May 5, 1973, Sunderland delivered an even bigger shock than they produced in getting to Wembley under revivalist manager Bob Stokoe—they beat Leeds 1–0. Here is the goal, shot by Ian Porterfield (obscured by Leeds player Trevor Cherry, wearing No. 3 right) that ended an F.A. Cup monopoly which First Division clubs

**Plate 9
Champions of Champions** By winning the first five European Cup competitions (1956–60) Real Madrid earned the title of the 'world's greatest-ever club side', and this was their all-star team of 1960. *Back row:* Dominguez, Miera, Marquitos, Pachin, Vidal, Santisteban. *Front row, players from left.* Canario, Del Sol, Di Stefano, Puskas, Gento.

Plate 10 England's World Cup (1) Wembley, 30 July 1966. With almost the last kick of extra time, Geoff Hurst shoots the final goal against West Germany at Wembley, and England have triumphed 4–2 to win the World Cup for the first time.

**Plate 11
England's
World Cup (2)**
West Germany,
the match
officials and
England line up
before the 1966
World Cup Final
at Wembley.
(England, dark
shirts). *From
right*:
Jack Charlton,
Martin Peters,
Geoff Hurst
(partly hidden),
Bobby Charlton,
Nobby Stiles,
Ray Wilson,
Roger Hunt,
Gordon Banks,
Alan Ball,
George Cohen,
Bobby Moore.

**Plate 12
England's
World Cup (3)**
England
manager
Alf Ramsey,
subsequently
knighted, joins
the 1966
World Cup-
winning
celebrations
with his captain
Bobby Moore,
Nobby Stiles
and reserve
Jimmy Armfield.

**Plate 13
Britain's First European Cup**
In May 1967, Celtic became the first British club to win the European Cup, beating Inter-Milan 2–1 in Lisbon. This was the scene when they returned to Glasgow, to the acclaim of thousands of supporters waiting to greet them at their Parkhead home.

Plate 14 A Dream Comes True for Matt Busby Manchester United win the European Cup for the first time. In the Final at Wembley in May 1968 they beat Benfica 4–1 in extra time, and as he raises the trophy, the smile on the face of United's manager—who became Sir Matt a few months later—reflects the joy that Britain shared at his club's success.

Plate 15 The Big Three

F.A. Cup

Football League Championship Trophy

Football League Cup

Plate 16 Leeds win F.A. Cup Centenary Final
The 1972 F.A. Cup marked the Centenary of the competition, and a new name went on the trophy—that of Leeds United. To a background of flags representing all the previous winners, manager Don Revie leads United into the Wembley arena alongside Bertie Mee and his Arsenal team. Ninety minutes later Leeds, having scored the only goal, added their name to the list of winners, and two nights later they just missed completing the Double.

were only two points from putting their name on the First Division title in 1964–65, when third to champions Kilmarnock and Hearts. They finished third again in 1968–69.

In 1969, Dunfermline reached the semi-finals of the European Cup-Winners' Cup, eventually losing 1–2 on aggregate to Slovan Bratislava.

East Fife are unique in having won the Scottish Cup while members of the Second Division. That highest peak came in 1938, when they beat Kilmarnock 4–2 in a Final replay after a 1–1 draw.

As a Second Division side, East Fife had sprung a surprise in 1927 by reaching the Final, but were beaten 3–1 by Celtic. In their only other F.A. Cup Final they lost 3–0 to Rangers in 1950.

Third has been their highest final position in the Championship (in 1952 and 1953), and the League Cup has been East Fife's most successful tournament with three triumphs—in 1948, 1950 and 1954.

East Stirlingshire have clearly shown the potential to be successful, for in their only post-war First Division season, 1963–64, they attracted crowds of 10,000 to Firs Park. In 1964, after relegation, they merged with Clydebank, but after only one season they reverted to their original identity.

Many fine players have begun their careers at Firs Park, and in 1962 Eddie McCreadie, later capped 23 times by Scotland at full-back, Tommy Knox and Jim Mulholland were all transferred to Chelsea.

Falkirk's closest bid for the Scottish League Championship was made at the start of the century, when they finished runners-up to Celtic in 1908 and 1910. Since the last war they have four times been relegated to the Second Division.

In the Scottish F.A. Cup they have had two successes, beating Raith 2–0 in the 1913 Final and then, after a gap of 44 years, taking the trophy again in 1957 with a replay victory by 2–1 against Kilmarnock.

Falkirk have produced many star players—for English as well as bigger Scottish clubs—and none better than Scottish International inside-forward John White, who moved to Tottenham for £20,000 in October 1959.

Although **Forfar Athletic** were formed as long ago as 1884, they are not to be found anywhere on the list of League or

Cup honours. Indeed, their highest final position remains sixth in the Second Division in season 1967–68, and even then their average gate was less than 1500. Yet the fact that they are approaching their centenary is a tribute to their perseverance and good housekeeping despite all the odds, and as a developing ground for young footballers in the area Forfar are among the clubs ready to welcome a re-organization of the Scottish League.

Unique in title among first-class clubs in Britain, **Hamilton Academicals** owe their derivation to the local academy at the time of their formation in 1870. No major honours have gone to Douglas Park, but Hamilton were Scottish Cup Finalists in 1911 and 1935.

The club's best period was in the 1930s when, besides reaching the Cup Final—in which Rangers beat them 2–1—they finished in the top eight in the First Division five times in seven seasons.

Over the years Hamilton have often had to transfer star players to help finances, and probably their most famous 'discovery' was forward Alec Herd, who went on to a great career with Hearts, Manchester City and Scotland.

Heart of Midlothian were among the founder-members of the Scottish League in 1890 and have never been out of the First Division—a wonderful record, even if it is more than a decade since they won the last of their four Championships in 1960.

Hearts' Scottish Cup triumphs number five (1891, 1896, 1901, 1906 and 1956) and the League Cup has been won by the famous Maroons of Tynecastle Park, Edinburgh, on four occasions—1955, 1959, 1960 and 1963. The 1960 success gave them a double, because they were League Champions as well that season.

Among more than 50 Scottish Internationals to represent the club, there has been no greater artist than Tommy Walker, ace inside-forward of the 1930s and beyond. After a spell with Chelsea just after the war, he returned to Tynecastle and managed Hearts through one of the most spectacular phases in their history.

Other players of truly star quality to serve Hearts with distinction have included Tom Purdie (the club's first captain), Bobby Walker, Charlie Thomson, 'Barney' Battles, Alec Massie, Dave McCulloch, Willie Bauld and Dave Mackay.

Hibernian form with Hearts the football strength in the city of Edinburgh, and although their combined records do not begin to measure up to those of the Glasgow 'big two', they have nevertheless made an invaluable contribution to the Scottish soccer scene. Hibs' two Scottish F.A. Cup victories were achieved long ago, in 1887 and 1902. The first of four occasions when they have taken the League title was in 1903.

Apart from two seasons at the start of the thirties, they have spent the whole of this century as members of the First Division, with the Championship won in 1948, 1951 and 1952. Season 1972–73 marked Hibs' first League Cup success.

The first British team to take part in the European Cup when it was launched in 1955, Hibernian, like most Scottish clubs, have at times been forced for financial reasons to sell star players. Forward 'exports' have been their speciality— Colin Stein was sold to Rangers for £100,000 in October 1968. Peter Marinello went to Arsenal at the same fee in January 1970, and two months later the transfer of Peter Cormack to Nottingham Forest fetched £85,000.

But in February 1974 Hibs used the transfer market in the opposite way to make history—they signed Scotland striker Joe Harper from Everton for £120,000, the highest Scottish fee ever paid to an English club.

No one could say that **Kilmarnock** were winning out of turn when they took the Scottish League title in 1965; they had been runners-up in four of the previous five seasons.

That remains the only League honour to go so far to Rugby Park, and the League Cup has still to be won, but Kilmarnock have had two successes in the Scottish Cup, in 1920 and 1929.

Over the years they have become almost the champion runners-up of Scottish football; besides those four 'seconds' in the League in the early 1960s, they have been beaten F.A. Cup Finalists five times and three times losers of the League Cup Final. And at the start of season 1973–74 they faced the task of winning back a First Division place lost after 19 years—and achieved that objective first time.

Montrose belong among the Scottish clubs never to have competed in the First Division, and between 1947 and 1955 they dropped into Division C. The club's most noteworthy achievements were in reaching the Cup quarter-finals on two occasions—losing to Rangers in 1930 and to Celtic in 1948.

The only major honour to come to Greenock **Morton** was the Scottish Cup in 1922 by a shock 1—0 win over Rangers in the Final. But they are very much part of the fabric of Scottish football with their home at Cappielow Park close to the shipyards and sugar refineries of Clydeside.

In 1964, Morton became the first Scottish club to recruit Scandinavian players by taking on goalkeeper Eric Sorenson, a Dane. The idea came from director-manager Hal Stewart, who took over in 1962 when they were a dying club—the last but one in the Second Division with only two signed players on the staff.

Under his guidance, they reached the League Cup Final in 1963—64, and at the end of the season were Second Division Champions by the record margin of 14 points. At one stage that winter Morton won 23 games in a row (a new Scottish League record). Three years later in 1967, they were Second Division winners again, with 69 points another record.

Until season 1931—32, Celtic and Rangers had monopolized Scottish League football for 27 years, but then **Motherwell** came upon the scene as new champions—a reward for the attractive football they had played for many years without winning any major honours.

The previous season, Motherwell reached the Scottish Cup Final for the first time and would have won it but for a tragic last-minute own goal allowing Celtic the chance of a replay which they won 4—2.

Motherwell had to wait another 21 years for their F.A. Cup Final victory which came in 1952 (4—0 against Dundee), but the year before they put their name on the League Cup for the first time.

In the 1973 close season Motherwell placed their managership in the hands of their former star player, Ian St John, who returned to Fir Park after an illustrious career with Liverpool. His immediate task was to revive interest, but although St John brought Motherwell to life on the field, the Lanarkshire public were still sceptical about giving solid support after more than 20 years without success.

On 23 October 1971 **Partick Thistle** caused the biggest sensation in Scottish football for years by thrashing odds-on favourites Celtic 4—1 in the League Cup Final. With an average age of 22—and just six months after winning back their First Division place following one season in the Second

—Thistle astonished a crowd of 62,740 at Hampden Park by scoring four goals in a 30-minute spell. It was their first major success in 50 years.

Skipper Alex Rae started the goal rush, left-winger Bobby Lawrie scored the second, right-winger Denis McQuade made it three, and centre-forward Jimmy Bone shot the fourth ... and mighty Celtic, playing in their eighth successive League Cup Final, were humbled.

Thistle's only other triumph since being formed in the north-west of Glasgow in 1876 was a Cup Final victory in 1921, when they beat Rangers 1–0.

In the League Championship Partick's highest final placing has been third, three times—in 1948, 1954 and 1963.

Queen of the South's most successful period was between 1933 and 1950, when they competed in the First Division. During that period they reached the Cup quarter-finals three times, and in the relegation season of 1949–50 they reached the semi-final. They were formed in 1919 when three local sides, Dumfries, the King's Own Scottish Borderers and Arrol Johnston, amalgamated. Their outstanding discovery was Hughie Gallacher—later to become one of the greatest Scottish forwards—who played two seasons for the 'Queens' before joining Airdrie on his way to a spectacular career with Newcastle, Chelsea, Derby and Scotland.

Queen's Park, for long the only amateur club competing in Britain's big professional leagues, are unique in many other ways. From their year of formation in 1867 they went unbeaten for seven years (in the first five of which goalkeeper Jock Grant did not have a goal scored against him).

They won the Scottish Cup **ten** times between 1874–93, before the Scottish F.A. legalized professionalism, and in addition Queen's Park were English F.A. Cup finalists in 1884 and 1885.

Except for winning the 1955–56 Second Division championship and the honour of continuing to supply the big majority of Scotland's amateur international players, Queen's Park have had no post-war claims to fame. They were last relegated in 1958 and, though seldom watched nowadays by more than a few hundred spectators, this club of great tradition have gone on playing their home games in Britain's biggest arena, Hampden Park.

Raith Rovers can claim the most goals ever scored in a

league season by a British club: 142 in 34 matches when they won the Scottish Second Division championship in 1937–38. It is a record that, short of a tactical revolution within the game, may never be beaten.

Third in 1922, behind Celtic and Rangers, is the closest Raith have ever been to the First Division title; in knockout football they were beaten finalists in the Scottish Cup in 1913 and runners-up in the League Cup in season 1948–49.

Easily the outstanding player produced by the Kirkcaldy club was Alex James, who became a classic inside-forward with Preston, Arsenal and Scotland in the 1920s and 1930s.

Although their great rivals Celtic have dominated Scotland's honours list in modern times, **Rangers** are still ahead in the overall Championship-winners' table with 34 titles. The Scottish F.A. Cup has gone to Ibrox 20 times, and the 'Gers' have won seven League Cups, giving them a grand total of 61 prizes in the three tournaments.

Rangers' richest phase came just after the first war with the appointment of Willie Struth as manager in 1920. In 33 years under his command—until at 79 he went on the board—Rangers won the League 18 times, the Cup ten times and the League Cup twice. Some record!

Under Struth's successor, Scot Symon, Rangers continued triumphantly until in 1967, Celtic became predominant. Davie White followed him, lasted two years and was succeeded in the managerial chair by Willie Waddell, whose first success was of double value in that it came against Celtic in the 1970–71 League Cup Final.

In European campaigns, Rangers are one of Britain's most experienced clubs, failing to qualify only three times in the past 18 seasons. In 1961 and 1967 they were runners-up in the Cup-Winners' Cup, but season 1971–72 proved third time lucky in this particular final, with Rangers beating Moscow Dynamo 3–2 to take the trophy. Their triumph was tarnished, however, by the misconduct of Glaswegian supporters who invaded the Barcelona pitch during the final, with the sequel that U.E.F.A. banned Rangers from Europe for the following season.

St Johnstone, one of the sturdy provincials of Scottish football, were formed in 1884 but, apart from three times winning the Second Division championship, they made no mark for 85 years.

Then in season 1969–70, they reached the Final of the

League Cup and football fever gripped the picturesque and usually quiet Tayside town of Perth. At Hampden Park, however, the mighty Celtic beat them, though only by the lone goal of a fiercely fought game.

Before being relegated in 1971, **St Mirren** had spent only two seasons outside the First Division (1936–37, 1967–68) —a remarkable record considering the club have only once finished as high as third in the championship, and that as long ago as 1893. They were Scottish Cup winners in 1926 and 1959.

In modern times English clubs have come to regard St Mirren as something of a source for transfer bargains—such as Jimmy Robertson to Tottenham (£25,000), Archie Gemmill to Preston (£13,000), Gordon McQueen to Leeds (£35,000) and Jim Blair to Norwich (£18,000).

Since their formation in 1884 **Stenhousemuir** have failed to win a major honour and have never moved above the Second Division. But they could claim a part in Scotland's qualification for the 1974 World Cup Finals in Munich, for national team manager Willie Ormond began his playing career at Ochilview Park.

Stirling Albion owed their formation in 1945 to the miscalculations of a German bomb-aimer some five years earlier. In 1940 an enemy aircraft discharged its cargo over the town of Stirling, and the Forth Bank ground—home of King's Park FC—was destroyed. Local feeling demanded the formation of a new club and under the leadership of coal merchant Tom Fergusson, Stirling Albion was born after the war. Their ground became Annfield Park, with the dressing-rooms located in a huge mansion.

In their first season Stirling won the inaugural post-war Scottish Division C Championship. The pattern of an up-and-down existence has continued ever since.

Stranraer, situated on the south-west coast, have the smallest ground capacity (6000) on Scotland's league club circuit. Formed in 1870, they have passed their centenary without achieving a major prize, but their ambition and undying hopes were reflected by the appointment of Eric Caldow, former Scotland captain and Rangers full-back, as manager in 1973.

Prominent European Clubs

(Details as at 1 January, 1974)

Ajax Amsterdam: Formed in 1900 and came to prominence only after professionalism introduced in 1953. Have a tiny ground of their own (22,000) but play their big matches at the Olympic Stadium (capacity 65,000). Dutch Champions 16 times (a record) including a hat-trick between 1966 and 1968, and also F.A. Cup winners 1969–70 (when they completed the double), 1970–71 and 1971–72. Have won the Cup seven times altogether. Finalists in the European Cup in 1969, their open attacking play foundered against the *cattenacio* defence of AC Milan. After crashing 1–4, they were more cautious when they reached the Final again in 1971 and won the trophy 2–0 against Panathinaikos at Wembley, the start of a run of three consecutive European successes. Managed through most of their triumphs by former player Rinus Michels (now with CF Barcelona). Stars: Piet Keizer (left wing) and, in midfield, Arie Haan, Johan Neeskens and Gerrie Muhren.

RSC Anderlecht: Formed in 1908, the Royal Sporting Club Anderlecht play at their own Parc Astrid in Brussels (capacity 28,000) with the 60,000 Stade de Heysel reserved for big games. Champions of Belgium 14 times (a record) and Cup winners in 1965, 1972 and 1973. Recorded a spectacular success in the sixties when they won the championship five times in a row (another record) between 1964 and 1968. Crashed 0–10 to Manchester United in their first venture into the European Cup (1956–57), but improved later to become one of the few teams to have the distinction of eliminating Real Madrid in Di Stefano's time. Fairs Cup Finalists 1970. Best known players: Jeff Mermans (56 caps) in the fifties; Joseph Jurion (64 caps) in the sixties; today, Paul Van Himst.

Atletico Madrid: Founded in 1923 and adopted by the Spanish forces in the thirties, when known as Aviaciones Atletico. Champions of Spain seven times and F.A. Cup winners five times. Most recent success—champions in 1972–73 and the Cup in 1972. Built the futuristic Estadio Manzanares in the sixties, intended to rival Real's Chamartin, but still incomplete, with a capacity of 70,000. Won the European Cup-Winners' Cup in 1962 and were Finalists again in 1963. Perhaps their most meritorious achievement came in

1959 when, with international stars Vava (centre-forward in Brazil's 1958 World Cup-winning team) and Portuguese schemer Jorge Mendonca in the side, they took Real Madrid, then at their peak, to a third game in the European Cup semi-final and lost 3–4 overall. Current stars: centre-forward Garate and the Argentinians Ayala and Heredia.

CF Barcelona: Formed in 1899 and today the wealthiest club in Spain with their Nou Camp Stadium (completed in 1968) accommodating 90,000. Spanish champions eight times and F.A. Cup winners 17 times. Most recent successes in the Spanish Cup were in 1968 and 1971. Also Latin Cup winners in 1949 and 1951. European Cup Finalists in 1961; Cup-Winners' Cup Finalists in 1969 and the only club to win the Fairs Cup three times—in 1958, 1960 and 1966. Their most successful phase was 1959–61 when, under the guidance of Helenio Herrera, they won the championship two years in succession. Best known stars of the sixties: Luis Suarez, Sandor Kocsis (Hungary), Ladislav Kubala (Hungary). Today: Johan Cruyff (Holland) and Hugo Sotil (Peru).

FC Bayern München: The outstanding West German team of recent years but omitted from the Bundesliga when it was formed in 1963, preference being given to neighbours München 1860, who were subsequently relegated. Bayern were promoted in 1965 and quickly established themselves by winning the F.A. Cup in 1966. A year later they added the European Cup-Winners' Cup to their trophies and also retained the F.A. Cup. Champions of West Germany four times, the most recent successes being in 1972 and 1973, and Cup winners on five occasions (a record), four of those times since 1966. Yugoslav coach Zlatko Cajkovski led the club to promotion and their early triumphs but resigned in 1969. Current stars: Gerd Muller and Franz Beckenbauer.

Benfica: Champions of Portugal 20 times and F.A. Cup winners 18 times—both records. Also Latin Cup winners 1950. Formed in 1904 and play at the 75,000-capacity Estadio da Luz. Their most successful period was in the sixties when champions eight times in ten seasons. Most recent successes: champions 1972–73 and Cup-winners 1971–72. Rose to international eminence soon after professionalism was introduced and under guidance of Hungarian-born manager Bela Guttman twice won the European Cup—1961 and 1962. Also reached the Final in 1963, 1965 and

1968. Beaten in the World Club Championship by Penarol (1961) and Santos (1962). Mario Coluna (captain) and Jose Aguas best-known stars of their triumphs, with Eusebio their ace striker in his hey-day.

Borussia Mönchengladbach: Like their West German rivals Bayern, they failed to gain a Bundesliga place on its inception in 1963 but won promotion in 1965. Steadily developed since then and at their best are today one of the Continent's strongest teams. Champions of West Germany twice—1969–70 and 1970–71 and F.A. Cup winners twice. Thrashed Internazionale-Milan 7–1 in a European Cup-tie in 1971 only to have U.E.F.A. demand a replay in Berlin because of crowd trouble. Star players: full-back Berti Vogts (1971 Footballer of the Year in West Germany), forward Josef Heynckes. Manager Hennes Weisweiler brought them to the forefront and keeps them there.

C.S.K.A. Sofia: Formed in 1948 as the team of the Bulgarian Army and immediately successful. Champions sixteen times (a record) and Cup winners nine times. Pulled off an incredible run of success when winning the championship nine times in a row between 1954 and 1962. Most recent success—Bulgarian champions and Cup winners 1972–73. Took part 12 times in European Cup, reaching the semi-finals in 1967 and taking Inter-Milan to a third game. Inside-left Ivan Kolev was the big star of the sixties with a record 76 caps. Centre-forward Petar Jekov and inside-left Dimiter Yakimov, each capped more than 50 times starred later. C.S.K.A. made a name for themselves in 1973 when they ended Ajax's three-year run of unbroken European success.

Dukla Prague: The Sports Club of the Czechoslovak Army, formerly known as U.D.A. and later A.T.K. Prague. Champions eight times (a post-war record) under manager Jaroslav Vejvoda, and Cup winners four times (the competition started only in 1961). Most recent successes, champions in 1965–66 and Cup winners 1968–69, but they slumped when Vejvoda left to take over Legia (Poland). Seven times in European Cup but never progressed beyond the quarter-finals; twice (1961 and 1962) won the International Cup staged in New York. Best-known players of the sixties: wing-halves Josef Masopust and Svatopluk Pluskal, and left-back Ladislav Novak. Now managed by Josef Masopust, who is rejuvenating the side.

Dynamo Kiev: Achieved a unique double in being the first provincial club to break the Moscow clubs' stranglehold on the major Russian honours—winning the F.A. Cup for the first time in 1954 and taking the league title in 1961. They have gone on to win five league championships and the F.A. Cup three times. Most recent honours: champions three times in a row (1966 to 1968) and again in 1971. The stars who contributed most to these successes were goalkeeper Jevgueni Rudakov, star spearhead Anatoli Bychevetz and an exceptionally skilful midfield trio—Josif Szabo (Hungarian-born), Viktor Serebrianikov and Vladimir Muntjan. Runners-up in both Cup and League in 1973 with Victor Kolotov, their big new star, playing in midfield with Muntjan. Also discovered striker Oleg Blokhin, top league scorer in 1973.

Dynamo Moscow: Formed in 1887 and today the team of the Electrical Trades Union in Moscow. League champions ten times (a Russian record) and F.A. Cup winners four times. Most recent successes—four times champions in the fifties, champions again in 1963 and Cup winners in 1967 and 1970. Gained world-wide fame when in November 1945, they toured briefly and very successfully in Britain, but 12 years of isolation followed for Russian football. Made their bow in international competition in 1971–72 Cup-Winners' Cup. Most famous player Alexei 'Tiger' Khomich, goalkeeper in the fifties, and they provided another world-class goalkeeper, Lev Yashin, and right-winger Igor Chislenko for the 1966 World Cup. Best current players: forwards Kozlov and Jevruchkin.

Dynamo Zagreb: Known before the last war as Gradjanska SK and reorganized in 1945. Champions of Yugoslavia eight times and F.A. Cup winners on five occasions. Most recent success: F.A. Cup winners 1973. Won the Fairs Cup in 1967 and did it the hard way, eliminating Dunfermline, Dynamo Bucharest, Juventus, Eintracht Frankfurt and Leeds United in the Final 2–0 and 0–0. Stars of the sixties: Skoric, Perusic, Brncic and Zambata, who all moved to West European clubs. Rudolf Belin, Yugoslavia's Footballer of the Year in 1964, was transferred to Olimpija. After Branko Zebec left to manage Bayern München, Dynamo had a lean spell, but in 1973 recovered their position among the top clubs in Yugoslavia.

Ferencvaros: Formed in 1899 as an athletics and gymnastic club. Champions of Hungary 21 times (a record) and winners of the F.A. Cup twice, the most recent triumph being in 1972. Also Mitropa Cup winners in 1928 and 1937. Most recent successes: champions in 1968 and league runners-up in 1973. The first East European club to win a modern international tournament when they won the Fairs Cup in 1965—beating AS Roma, Bilbao, Manchester United and Juventus (in the Final). Finalists again in 1968. Best known stars of the sixties: Florian Albert (centre-forward); Mate Fenyvesi (left wing) and Sandor Matrai (stopper), who all gained more than 70 caps. Current stars: Szoke, Branikovics and Mucha.

Feyenoord: Founded 1908 and established as top club in Holland during the thirties, they built a superb 64,000-capacity stadium in Rotterdam in 1938. Champions nine times and F.A. Cup winners four times (the Cup was abandoned in the fifties because of lack of public interest). Most recent successes: a double in 1968–69 and champions 1970–71. Surprised everyone by winning the European Cup in 1970, beating Celtic 2–1 in the Final in Milan after extra time. Star of that team, Swedish centre-forward Ove Kindvall. Pre-war, Puck Van Heel was their big name, winning a record 64 caps. Stars of the sixties: Coen Moulijn and Rinus Israel. Currently Wim Van Hanegem and Wim Jansen are the big names.

Fiorentina: Formed relatively late in 1926 and champions of Italy three times. Also Cup winners three times. Most recent successes: F.A. Cup winners 1965–66 and champions in 1968–69. Won the European Cup-Winners' Cup in 1961 and were Finalists in 1962. Their most distinguished performances came when they ran away with the 1955–56 Italian championship—they were unbeaten until the last day of the season—and the following year (1956–57) when they reached the European Cup Final, only to meet Real Madrid playing on their home ground and lost 0–2. Best known stars: Julinho (Brazil) and Michelangelo Montuori (Argentina), who played in the fifties. Current star: Giancarlo De Sisti, who played for Italy in 1970 World Cup Final v. Brazil.

Gornik Zabrze: Gornik, meaning 'Miners', have established themselves as the leading club in Poland since the war and built something of an international reputation, too. Champions nine times and Cup winners six times, they have been consistently successful in recent years, winning the league five times in a row (1963–67) and five consecutive F.A. Cups

(1968–72). In the European Cup reached the quarter-final in 1968, falling to Manchester United (1–2 on aggregate) directly after their three-month winter lay-off. Responded better to this challenge in 1970 and reached the 1970 Cup-Winners' Cup Final, losing 1–2 to Manchester City. In the sixties their stars were Ernst Pohl (inside-forward) and Stanislas Oslizlo (stopper), who both earned 60 caps. Current star: Wlodzimierz Lubanski.

Grasshoppers FC: Based in Zürich and one of the old-established Swiss clubs, they have been champions 16 times (a record) and F.A. Cup winners 13 times (another record). In 1937 won an F.A. Cup Final 10–0 against Lausanne and went on to take the Cup six times in seven seasons between 1937 and 1943 under Austrian-born manager Karl Rappan, who devised the Swiss 'bolt' defensive system. In 1955–56 they achieved a Cup and League double, with Yugoslav star Vukosaljevic scoring 33 league goals. In 1970–71 beat FC Basle 4–3 in a play-off after extra time to win the league once more. Most capped players: Josef Minelli (79) and Fredy Bickel (71). Current star: Rainer Ohlhauser (West German international).

Internazionale FC: Formed in 1909 as a breakaway from AC Milan and known before the war as Ambrosiana-Inter. Champions of Italy 11 times (including three successes in the sixties) but they have never won the F.A. Cup. Most recent success: champions 1970–71. Reached international prominence under manager Helenio Herrera, winning the European Cup in 1964 and 1965. Also finalists in 1967 and 1972. Their peak achievement came in 1964, when they won the Italian championship, the European Cup and the World Club Championship—and they retained the World title in 1965 by beating Independiente (Argentina) a second time; Hélenio Herrera returned as manager in 1973 after a spell in Rome. Current stars: Sandro Mazzola, Roberto Boninsegna and Giacinto Facchetti, who all appeared for Italy in the 1970 World Cup Final, plus *libero* Tareisio Burgnich, who took on a new lease of life with the national team in 1973, and a young stopper Mauro Bellugi, capped regularly in 1973.

Juventus: Founded in 1897 and share the Stadio Communale in Turin (75,000) with AC Torino. Known affectionately throughout Italy as the 'Old Lady', they have been champions of Italy 15 times and F.A. Cup winners five times (both records). Most recent successes: champions in 1972 and 1973, when they also reached the Cup Final and European Cup Final. F.A. Cup winners 1964–65. Fairs Cup Finalists in 1965 and 1971, the last being a frustrating experience when they lost the trophy to Leeds on the away goals rule. Rarely outside the top four in the Italian league, they have imported some of the world's outstanding players over the years; their best period was perhaps in the early sixties, when John Charles (Wales) and Enrico Sivori (Argentina) spearheaded their attack. Current stars: Pietro Anastasi, goalkeeper Dino Zoff and Italy's right wing pair Fabio Capello and Franco Causio.

AC Milan: Formed in 1899 as Milan Cricket and Football Club, they play at the 90,000-capacity San Siro stadium. Italian champions nine times and F.A. Cup-winners three times—they went on to win the European Cup-Winners' Cup the following season (1967–68). Most recent successes: European Cup Winners 1963 and in 1973 won a double: European Cup-Winners' Cup and Italian F.A. Cup. Won the World Club title in 1969 against Estudiantes (Argentina) in Buenos Aires. Also won the now defunct Latin Cup in 1951 and 1956. Best-ever team was probably in 1955. Studded with stars, their line-up included Nils Liedholm and Gunnar Nordahl (Sweden), Eduardo Ricagni (Argentina), Arne Soerensen (Denmark) and Juan Schiaffino (Uruguay). Current stars: Gianni Rivera, right-back Giuseppe Sabadini and left-winger Luciano Chiarugi.

Partizan Belgrade: The team of the Yugoslav Army who took over Belgrade S.K. (five times pre-war champions) in 1946. Play at the Partizan Stadium, capacity 60,000. Champions 11 times and F.A. Cup winners on five occasions. Won the league five times in five seasons in the sixties. Their best side of recent years was probably that of 1965–66 which eliminated Manchester United in the European Cup semi-final with a superb rearguard action. They were then beaten in the Final 1–2 by Real Madrid after leading. Stars of the sixties: goalkeeper Milutin Soskic and full-back Fahrudin Jusufi (both now in Germany) and centre-half Velibor Vasovic, who recently retired after helping Ajax Amsterdam win the European Cup in 1971. Current stars: defender Blagoje Paunovic and striker Nenad Bjekovic.

SC Rapid: Vienna's traditional masters of the Austrian game, formed in 1898 and champions 25 times (a record). Also F.A. Cup winners seven times. Champions four times in the sixties. Cup winners in 1969 and did the Cup and League double in 1967–68. Also had the unique distinction of winning the German Championship and Cup during the war when Austria was annexed. Eliminated Real Madrid from the European Cup in 1969. Gerhardt Hanappi, a play-anywhere type, has been their greatest post-war star with 92 caps. Most recent success: F.A. Cup Winners in 1971, but beaten Cup finalists in 1972 and 1973, and overshadowed recently in the league by Wacker Innsbruck.

Real Madrid: Founded in 1898 and rose to world eminence under chairmanship of Santiago Bernabeu, who built the 120,000-capacity Chamartin Stadium and signed Alfredo Di Stefano in the fifties. Champions of Spain 15 times (a record) and F.A. Cup winners ten times. Champions five times in succession (1961–65), a record, and again in 1967, 1968 and 1969. Also Cup winners 1969–70, they went on to reach the European Cup-Winners' Cup Final in 1971. Latin Cup Winners 1955 and 1957, but best known for their fabulous team of the fifties which won the first five European Cup tournaments (1956 to 1960) with Di Stefano, Ferenc Puskas and Jose Santamaria the stars. Won the European Cup again in 1966 and Finalists in 1962 and 1964. First World Club Champions in 1960. Most recent success: champions in 1972. Current stars: Gunter Netzer (W. Germany), Oscar Mas (Argentina) and Spanish internationals Garcia Remon, Jose Luis, Benito Pirri and Amancio.

Red Star Belgrade: Known pre-war as Jugoslawija FK, they were reformed in 1945 as the sports club of Belgrade University. Champions of Yugoslavia 12 times (a record) and F.A. Cup winners nine times (all in the post-war period). Most recent successes in seasons 1967–68, 1968–69 and 1969–70, when they achieved a league title hat-trick, adding the F.A. Cup to their honours in 1968 and 1970 to pull off two 'doubles': Champions again in 1973 and beaten Cup finalists. Best known players: Vladimir Beara (goalkeeper) and Rajko Mitic (inside-forward) in the fifties; Dragoslav Sekularec (inside-forward) in the sixties. Current stars: Petar Krivokuca (right-back) and Dragan Dzajic (left-wing), the most-capped Yugoslav of all time.

Spartak Moscow: Founded in 1922 and over the years one of the most consistent Russian clubs. Champions nine times and F.A. Cup-winners on ten occasions. Most recent honours: Cup winners 1965, champions in 1969 and Cup winners again in 1971. Took the championship four times in the fifties (and the Cup three times) with star centre-forward Nikita Simonian the key man. His career record of 156 league goals for Spartak seems unassailable in the defence-dominated game played in Russia today.

Spartak Trnava: Firmly established as a Division II club, Trnava, a small town team in Slovakia, leapt into prominence in the 1960s. Under the guidance of former player Anton Malatinsky they won promotion and went on to dominate Czech football. Since 1966 they have never finished lower than the top three. Their first honour was the Czech F.A. Cup in 1967 and the Mitropa Cup. They took the F.A. Cup again in 1971 to complete a Cup and League double. From 1967–68 they took the championship five times in six seasons. In 1970, when they failed in the league, Malatinsky was in Austria, working for Admira but returned to lead them to a double in 1971. Star players: Josef Adamec, Ladislav Kuna, Karol Dobias and Vladimir Hagara, all now nearing the veteran stage.

Sporting Lisbon: Eternal rivals of Benfica, they play at the 45,000 Estadio Jose Alvalade. Champions of Portugal 13 times and F.A. Cup winners also on 13 occasions. Most recent successes: champions in 1969–70 and, after Benfica had overshadowed them in the 1970–71 title race, they had the satisfaction of crushing their neighbours 4–1 in the 1971 Cup Final. Also won the Cup in 1973. In the international arena their best performance was to win the European Cup-Winners' Cup in 1964, beating Atalanta (Italy), Manchester United, Lyon (France) and, in the Final, MTK (Hungary). After losing 1–4 at Old Trafford that year, they produced an astonishing 5–0 victory over Manchester United in Lisbon. Provided seven men for Portugal's 1966 World Cup squad. Current stars: goalkeeper Damas and the Argentinian striker Hector Yazalde, who succeeded Eusebio as Portugal's top scorer and got six goals in one game in 1973.

Standard Liège: Playing at the Stade de Sclessin (capacity 40,000), they have been pace-makers in the Belgian game since professionalism came into the open. Champions six times and F.A. Cup winners three times. In recent years have won the Cup in 1967, and the championship in successive seasons 1969, 1970 and 1971. The only Belgian club to reach the European Cup semi-finals, they did so in 1962, beating Real Madrid 2–0 in their home leg but losing 0–4 in Madrid. Best-known players of the sixties were Paul Bonga Bonga (Congo), Johnny Crossan (N. Ireland) and Istvan Sztani (Hungary). The current team includes six Belgian internationals headed by goalkeeper Christian Piot, stopper Nico Dewalque and midfield dynamo Wilfried Van Moer. In attack, Leon Semmeling and the Yugoslavs Sylvestre Takacs and Josip Bukal shine.

Ujpest Dozsa: Founded in 1899 and now the team of the Hungarian Ministry of the Interior. The Dozsa stadium, which holds 40,000, is probably the best-equipped club ground in Budapest. Champions 14 times and F.A. Cup winners twice (the knockout competition began only in the last decade). Most recent successes: 1969—Cup and League double; 1970—Cup and League double, 1970–71 (changeover season)—champions. League winners five times in succession, 1969 to 1973. Also winners of the Mitropa Cup in 1929 and 1939. Ujpest reached the Fairs Cup Final in 1969, losing 2–6 on aggregate to Newcastle United. Star players: Ferenc Bene (centre-forward) and Antal Dunai (inside-left).

Valencia: Founded in 1902, their Estadio Mestalla holds 70,000 and their reserves (Mestalla CF) play in Spanish Division II. Champions of Spain four times and F.A. Cup winners on four occasions. Most recent successes—champions in 1970–71 and F.A. Cup Finalists—beaten by Barcelona after extra time. Cup finalists again in 1972. Twice winners of the Fairs Cup (1962 and 1963) and beaten Finalists in 1964. Best-known players of the sixties: Waldo a free-scoring centre-forward from Brazil; Didi, who had a brief spell with them, and another Brazilian inside-forward, Walter, who was tragically killed in a road accident. Present manager: Alfredo Di Stefano, who guided the club to the championship in his first season. Current stars: Keita (Mali), Valdez (Argentina) and Spaniards Sol and Claramunt.

World Stars of 1974–75 *(Career details as at 1 January 1974)*

Anastasi, *Pietro:* Centre-forward of Juventus and Italy. A native of Sicily which, unlike most of the poorer regions of Europe, produces few top-class players. From the local club Catania he was transferred, as a teenager, for a small fee in 1966 to First Division Varese, apparently the only club to recognize his potential. Two years later, with all the wealthy Italian clubs after him, he set a world transfer record when signed by Juventus (Turin) for £440,000. Now, at 26, one of the key men in the talented Juventus side. Quick, skilful, strong in the air and a regular scorer of spectacular goals, he is the complete spearhead, helping Juventus win successive championships in 1972 and 1973. 19 caps for Italy.

Beckenbauer, *Franz:* Centre-half of Bayern München and West Germany. Rose to stardom overnight during the 1966 World Cup as an attacking wing-half but switched to the role of covering centre-back by 1971. With his intelligent anticipation and great range of skills he added another dimension to the game and gave the word *libero* a new meaning. Though the last line of defence, he really is the first man in attack, even going forward himself to score goals regularly. Twice voted the West German Footballer of the Year, he took the European award in 1972. At the age of 28 he set a new record number of caps (73) for West Germany in 1973. Played magnificently in the German team that won the European Championship in 1972.

Anastasi   **Beckenbauer**

Bonev

Bremner

Bonev, *Christo:* A one-club man with Lokomotive Plovdiv and the star of Bulgaria's national team. Began as a forward but switched to midfield to earn his first caps. Stayed there for club and country to become an all-rounder of real ability. Skilful, intelligent and industrious, he plays behind the centre-forward and breaks through to score goals himself. In style and build as well as ability resembles the German star Gunter Netzer. Creates havoc going forward with the ball, feinting and weaving past opponents. At 26 already holds two records—26 goals for Bulgaria (60 caps) and voted Bulgarian Footballer of the Year three times, in 1969, 1972 and 1973.

Bremner, *Billy:* Captain of Leeds United and Scotland. One of the outstanding players in British post-war football, he has been the consistent, dynamic, abrasive leader of Leeds in their triumphs and many near-triumphs, and also inspired Scotland to a place in the 1974 World Cup Finals. Joined Leeds at fifteen from school at Stirling—originally an inside-forward, but quickly converted to right-half, from which position he has captained Leeds to success in the League Championship, Fairs Cup, League Cup and F.A. Cup, exceeding 500 club appearances (43 International caps). England's Footballer of the Year in 1970. He is, at 31, brave as they come, technically superb, easy to find, skilful at distributing middle-distance passes and often drives forward to shoot vital right-foot goals.

Cruyff, *Johan:* Centre-forward of CF Barcelona and Holland. Top Dutch scorer with 33 goals in Holland in his first full season with Ajax when only 18, he played a vital role in the club's three consecutive European Cup Final wins in 1971–72–73. Superbly skilful, fast and with deceptive feints, he is not merely a spearhead but a general who organizes, too, and keeps the attack in top gear. Twice Dutch Footballer of the Year and given the supreme title of European Footballer of the Year in 1971 and 1973, he shares Di Stefano's record of having won this award twice. Transferred to Barcelona in the autumn of 1973 for more than half a million pounds and his guaranteed earnings exceed £75,000 a year in Spain. 26 years old (26 caps).

Deyna, *Kazimierz:* Inside-right of Legia Warsaw and Poland. One of the main-springs behind the growth to full stature of the game in Poland and an enterprising, skilful and elegant ball-player. The inspiration of Legia Warsaw, the Army Club, whom he helped to championship successes in 1969 and 1970 before taking over the mantle of schemer-scorer. In 1972 he scored both goals when Poland beat Hungary 2–1 in the Olympics Final and took a Polish F.A. Cup-winner's medal in 1973. Never at his best in a tough-tackling game, Deyna came through the World Cup qualifying tests of 1973 with flying colours and scored the all-important goal in the 1–1 prestige draw with Holland. 26 years old (49 caps).

Cruyff

Deyna

Dzajic   **Facchetti**

Dzajic, *Dragan:* Outside-left of Red Star (Belgrade) and Yugoslavia. Only world-class natural left-winger in the modern game, a schoolteacher by profession and a supremely elegant player who scores goals himself and creates many more for his colleagues with his speed, dribbling technique and superb passes. Made a big impact in 1968 when, largely as a result of his promptings, Yugoslavia reached the Final of the European Championship and took Italy (the host country) to a replay. Now 28 years old with more than 60 caps, he led his country to third place in Brazil's 1972 mini-cup before breaking a leg in 1973.

Facchetti, *Giacinto:* Left-back of Internationale and Italy, but in his younger days made headlines by breaking forward to score spectacular goals. Has a tremendous physique and no mean skill. Born at Treviglio in Northern Italy and joined Inter-Milan in 1960 as a teenager. Developed by Helenio Herrera into a revolutionary full-back. Standing 6 ft 3 in, he is virtually unbeatable in the air and his long raking stride carried him over the ground in near Olympics time—10.5 seconds for 100 metres. Now 31, he set an all-time Italian record in 1971 when winning his 60th cap and has since stretched that total to more than 70. Captain of Italy's World Cup side, he played a vital role in a defence that did not concede an international goal in 1973.

Jairzinho *(real name Jair Ventura Filho):* Centre-forward of Botafogo and Brazil. Born in Rio de Janeiro 30 years ago, he has been with Botafogo since he was ten. Strong, quick, courageous and with a fierce shot, he made his début for Brazil in 1964, but with the advent of Tostao was successfully switched from centre to a striking role on the right wing for the Mexico World Cup. Brazil's top scorer there with seven goals, netting in all six matches from qualifying group to Final. Went on strike for three months in 1973, demanding a better contract from Botafogo. 80 caps.

Jairzinho

Jennings

Jennings, *Pat:* Goalkeeper of Tottenham Hotspur and Northern Ireland. First played in Ireland for Newry Town after switching from Gaelic football. Third Division Watford were the first to recognize his potential and signed him, only to transfer him to Tottenham for £27,000. Gained his first full cap in 1964 and would have had many more had club fixtures not clashed with Irish internationals. Is particularly strong in dealing with the high cross, often going out to win the ball one-handed on the 18-yard line while most clubs are happy if their 'keeper can dominate the six-yard area. Earned U.E.F.A. Cup and two League Cup Final honours with Spurs and was voted England's Footballer of the Year in 1973. 29 years old (45 caps).

Lubanski, *Wlodzimierz:* The most accomplished player Poland has ever produced, first capped at 16 and scorer of innumerable international hat-tricks. Guided by inside-forward Ernst Pol in his early years with Gornik Zabrze, this local product went on to excel his master. In 1963, when only 16, made his bow in the First Division, gained his first full cap and played in the European Cup. Intelligent anticipation, supreme ball control at top speed and a crashing shot are his big attributes. Starred in Poland's 1972 Olympic Games triumph and in the same year scored four Cup Final goals in Gornik's 5—2 win over arch rivals Legia. Played a substantial part in eliminating England from the 1974 World Cup. Though not fully fit, he snatched the vital second goal in Chorzow. 26 years old with two Polish international records: most caps (67) and most goals (46).

Luis Pereira *(Luis Edmondo Pereira):* A product of Bahia but played all his football in Sao Paulo, finally establishing himself with Palmeiras and helping them to win the 1973 Brazilian championship. Originally a centre-forward, he was converted via wing-half to centre-back and, once settled, began to move forward Beckenbauer-style. Is dominant in the air, skilful and supremely confident, and his talents are most obvious when he breaks upfield to score goals. Made his bow for Brazil on their European tour in 1973 and was an immediate success, solving a problem at the heart of their World Cup defence. 24 years old (8 caps) and seemingly destined for a great future.

Lubanski

Luis Pereira

Muller   **Netzer**

Muller, *Gerd:* Centre-forward of Bayern München and West Germany. Frequently outjumps all challengers for balls in the air, and on the ground his shooting, particularly left foot, is deadly. He is quick off the mark, strong on the ball and volleys superbly, but above all it is an uncanny instinct for the goal-chance and his aggressive determination that make him king of the scorers in West Germany. With 40 goals in 34 league matches, he was Europe's top scorer in 1971—72 and at 28 he had scored 62 goals for West Germany in his first 50 internationals. Leading scorer for the 1970 World Cup tournament in Mexico with ten goals, he has helped Bayern win five German Cup Finals, the Cup-Winners' Cup and three Championships. Top German scorer four times.

Netzer, *Gunter:* Inside-forward of West Germany and Real Madrid. Rose to stardom with his local club Borussia Mönchengladbach and played a vital part in their successes. Won his first full cap in October 1965, helping beat Austria 4—1, but it was not until 1972 that he really exploded into the national arena. Was the key man in West Germany's 3—1 win over England at Wembley, scoring himself from a penalty. With supreme skill, bending and swerving his shots and passes, master-minding the midfield and sending the strikers away, he now commands world-wide recognition. 29 years old (32 caps).

Riva, *Luigi:* Left-winger (nominally) for US Cagliari and Italy, but more often to be found scoring spectacular goals from centre-forward. Predominantly left-footed, he specializes in first-time shooting and diving headers. Three times the top league scorer in Italy, he has also achieved a 'double' in recovering from two broken legs. He was a bargain buy by Cagliari when they signed him for £3,000 in 1963 from Division III club Legnano, and his goalscoring took the 1970 Italian Championship to Cagliari—and to the Mediterranean island of Sardinia—for the first time. It also brought a world record transfer bid of £1 million from Juventus, which Cagliari turned down. Riva is 29 years old and his 35 goals in 40 internationals set a new Italian record.

Rivelino, *Roberto:* Inside-left of Corinthians (Sao Paulo) and Brazil. At first he failed to shine for Brazil as an orthodox inside-forward, but in the 1970 World Cup in Mexico he was cast in a dual role. He lined up on the left wing but played a half-and-half game, dropping back to forage but frequently becoming an orthodox spearhead on the wing. The result was devastating, with stamina, left-foot shooting and superb ball control combining to make him a world-class star. Next to Pele he is reputedly the world's best-paid player at £120 a day. 27 years old (60 caps).

Riva

Rivelino

Rivera, *Gianni:* Inside-left of AC Milan and Italy. An accountant with extensive business interests outside football and one of the most devastating players in world football. He can destroy the best organized defences with his tantalizing dribbles and pin-point passes. Elegantly skilful, he differs from many ball artists in knowing exactly when to release the ball to greatest advantage; uses the long pass superbly and often scores himself. Rivera was the subject of an unusual transfer when only 16; his club Alessandria (Division 1—but now Division III) sold a half-interest to AC Milan for £20,000 and a year later the other 'half' cost £60,000! Now 30 years old with 55 caps.

Sandberg, *Roland:* Probably the most skilful player Sweden has produced in recent years, following the tradition of Gren, Nordahl, Liedholm. He is the most gifted Swede of his generation, scoring goals freely and combining well with the giant Ralf Edstrom. Came to the fore with Atvidaberg FF when they won the Swedish Cup in 1971 and the championship a year later. In both seasons Sandberg was top scorer in Sweden's First Division. Lines up as an inside-outside left, has a deceptive body swerve and although he has only 17 full caps has scored many fine international goals. One of the most valuable was the first in the 2–1 win over Austria in a World Cup qualifying round play-off which took Sweden to the 1974 Finals. By that time he had been transferred to the West German club 1st FC Kaiserslautern. 27 years old.

Rivera

Sandberg

Vogts   **Zoff**

Vogts, *Berti:* Outstanding international defender and one-club man with Borussia Mönchengladbach whom he helped win the West German Bundesliga title in 1969–70 and 1970–71. Rose to stardom with his club colleague of that time, Gunter Netzer, and established himself long before Netzer became known internationally. Has also helped Borussia win the German F.A. Cup. His best position is right-back, where he has won all his 47 caps, but for Borussia he plays on either flank, as stopper, in midfield and even attacking Beckenbauer-style. Played in the 1970 World Cup but missed West Germany's triumphs of 1972 because of a cartilage operation. Was voted West German Footballer of the Year in 1971.

Zoff, *Dino:* Goalkeeper of Juventus and Italy, having earlier played for Naples, Mantova and Udinese. Helped Juventus win the Italian championship in 1971–72 and again the following season, when they also reached the European Cup Final. Played for Italy in 1968 when they won the European Championship, but lost his place temporarily to Albertosi for the 1970 World Cup Final. Later returned, and between the autumn of 1972 and the spring of 1974 played eleven consecutive international matches for Italy without conceding a goal. Deals very capably with the high cross, and has the priceless knack for a goalkeeper of being able to hold almost everything he gets both hands to. 32 years old with more than 30 caps, and by popular consent was judged Europe's best goalkeeper in 1973.

The World Cup

THE ORIGINAL WORLD CUP
Jules Rimet Trophy

THE NEW F.I.F.A. WORLD CUP
First contested in 1974

The greatest football show on earth, the most prized possession in the soccer universe, is the World Cup, staged every four years. For the first 40 years of its existence it was known as the Jules Rimet trophy, after the French lawyer who aired the idea of a world football championship among nations when he became president of F.I.F.A. in 1920.

Ten years later the dream turned to reality with the launching of the World Cup in Montevideo, Uruguay . . . but when the tenth tournament was staged in West Germany in 1974, the prize at stake was of new design and titled not the Jules Rimet Cup but the F.I.F.A. World Cup.

The reason for the change of trophy dates from the time the rules were framed for the very first tournament in 1930. Included was a clause to the effect that if any country won the Jules Rimet Cup three times, it would become theirs permanently—and Brazil's success in Mexico in 1970 was their third world conquest in the last four series. Amid unprecedented scenes of welcome and celebration, they took home to Rio the original World Cup—made of solid gold and weighing nine pounds, though standing only a foot high—to keep for ever.

In Britain the tournament was not regarded as truly representative of world football until 1950 when, having rejoined F.I.F.A. after lengthy disagreement over amateurism and broken-time payments, the Home Countries became eligible to compete for the first time. The prize remained beyond British reach for another 16 years; then, in 1966, England became the third host country to triumph, the first since 1934. They took it from Brazil with football that was functional, disciplined and supremely efficient. In Mexico four years later Brazil, committed to all-out attack to cover their suspect defence and weakness in goal, won it back with the magic and flair of Pele, Gerson, Jairzinho and Rivelino. No country could more worthily have won the World Cup outright.

The 1930 World Cup: Uruguay staged and won the first World Cup. Only 13 countries took part, and all 17 matches were played in Montevideo. Because of travelling difficulties and the lengthy absence involved in a trip by sea to South America and back, Europe's representatives were restricted to France, Yugoslavia, Rumania and Belgium. Uruguay, who had trained their players in isolation for two months, and Argentina each won their semi-final by 6–1 (against U.S.A. and Yugoslavia respectively), and in the first World Cup Final, played on 30 July 1930, the host country rallied from 2–1 down at half-time to triumph 4–2, to the delight of a 90,000 crowd.

The 1934 World Cup: The holders, Uruguay, refused to go to Italy to defend their title, as so few European countries had participated in the first tournament. Of the 16 nations who qualified from an entry of 29, 12 were from Europe. The 'group qualifying' method up to the semi-finals was replaced by an unsatisfactory knock-out system throughout—defeat at the first attempt meant that Brazil, Argentina and U.S.A. travelled halfway across the world for only one match each. Italy kicked off with the 7–1 thrashing of U.S.A., then beat Spain and Austria, both 1–0, to reach the Final against Czechoslovakia in Rome. There the unfancied Czechs took a surprise lead with 20 minutes left, but Italy scored a late equalizer and in extra time they squeezed home 2–1 to emulate Uruguay's feat as the second successive host nation to take the World Cup.

The 1938 World Cup: Now it was Argentina's turn to stay out, in protest over their request to stage the tournament being rejected. Instead, the series was held in Europe for the second successive series, this time in France, and Italy impressively retained the trophy. Victories over Norway, France and Brazil carried them to the Final, in which Hungary were well beaten by 4–2. Once again Italy, under the managership of Vittorio Pozzo, had done it, and with the Second World War soon to break out, they were to hold the Cup longer than anyone before or after— until 1950.

The 1950 World Cup: After an interval of 12 years, the war having erased two tournaments, the world football championship was resumed in Brazil. The British Associations had rejoined F.I.F.A. in 1946, so were eligible for the first time, but only England entered; Scotland could have done so as runners-up in the Home Championship, but all along they had declared they would take part only if they were British Champions. In their first World Cup, England suffered their greatest-ever humiliation, for after beating Chile 2–0 in their opening match in Rio, they took the same eleven to Belo Horizonte on Sunday, 25 June and ludicrously lost one—nil to the United States' part-timers. America won by a 30th-minute goal by their centre-forward Gaetjens, miraculously surviving a rearguard action that lasted all the second half. England contributed an equal part to their own destruction by missing so many chances. The team was: Williams; Ramsey, Aston, Wright, Hughes, Dickinson, Finney, Mannion, Bentley, Mortensen, Mullen. England's elimination was complete when Spain beat them 1–0 in Rio. This was the only time that the competition was based on four qualifying groups, whose winners went into a final pool which comprised Brazil, Spain, Sweden and Uruguay (participating for the first time since the inaugural tournament). After magnificent wins against Sweden (7–1) and Spain (6–1) in the final pool, Brazil needed only to draw with Uruguay in the grand finale to be crowned World Champions for the first time, and in anticipation the all-time world record attendance of 200,000 filled the Maracana Stadium. Brazil began brilliantly and scored first, directly after half-time, but with a superbly marshalled defence Uruguay gradually wore them down, then hit them with two smoothly taken goals to triumph 2–1 and bring their World Cup record to two conquests in two attempts spanning 20 years.

The 1954 World Cup: The fifth World Championship, in Switzerland, established the tournament format that was to be used until 1974, with four groups each providing two qualifiers to contest the quarter-finals and beyond on a knock-out system. Hungary, with Puskas, Hidegkuti and Kocsis superb in attack, were rated 'unbeatable'. In the previous six months they had shattered England's unbeaten home record against foreign countries with an astonishing 6–3 victory at Wembley and completed the double by 7–1 in Budapest. So England were hardly in better shape to face the world than when they had left Brazil demoralized four years earlier, and after topping their group with little conviction, they went out in the quarter-final 4–2 to Uruguay, who had still to be beaten in the World Cup after 24 years! Scotland's entry meant that Britain was doubly represented for the first time, but theirs was no more than a token appearance. In the qualifying group they failed to register a goal or a point, being humbled 7–0 by Uruguay and losing 1–0 to Austria. Meanwhile, Hungary clinched their group by slamming Korea 9–0 and Germany 8–3, and went through to the Final with 4–2 victories over both Brazil and Uruguay; but Germany countered their mastery with guile off the field and then deprived them of the World Cup on it. In their group match against Hungary, the Germans purposely fielded a weak team and did not mind losing 8–3 because they were confident that they could still qualify for the quarter-finals by beating Turkey in a play-off—and did so 7–2. Thus the easier passage to the Final was open to them, and they took it with wins by 2–0 against Yugoslavia and 6–1 against Austria. Yet, for all their strategy, Germany seemed to be heading for defeat in the Final as Puskas (playing for the first time since being injured in the group match against Germany) and Czibor gave Hungary a 2–0 lead. But skipper Fritz Walter rallied his side magnificently, and goals by Morlock and Rahn (2) earned Germany an extraordinary victory by 3–2, which made them the only country in World Cup history to win the trophy after being beaten during the final series.

The 1958 World Cup: In Sweden, Britain was represented for the only time by all four Home Countries, but England (apart from holding Brazil 0–0) and Scotland made no show. Surprisingly, it was the outsiders, Northern Ireland and Wales, who reached the quarter-finals. There, however, a catalogue of injuries proved insurmountable to Ireland, who lost 4–0 to France, and Brazil's one goal was too much for Wales. Hosts Sweden delighted their supporters by reaching the Final, then sent them almost delirious by scoring the first goal, but Brazil answered with one of the greatest exhibitions ever seen in a World Cup Final, devastatingly using 4–2–4 to stamp their mark on the tournament. Garrincha, Didi, Vava and a 17-year-old named Pele showed the world a new conception of attacking play, which brought them the biggest-ever World Cup victory by 5–2—Vava and Pele each scored twice—and a spectacular first success in the competition.

The 1962 World Cup: In contrast to Sweden, Chile staged the least memorable contest for the Jules Rimet Cup since it became a truly world-wide tournament. There was a saturation of negative, defence-ridden football and England, Britain's lone representatives, went out 3–1 to Brazil in the quarter-finals. Pele was lost to Brazil through injury early in the competition, but, although now an ageing side and far less impressive than four years previously, they retained the trophy, beating Czechoslovakia in the Final 3–1 after being a goal down.

The 1966 World Cup: Four months before they staged and won the World Cup, England literally lost it. For 36 years the solid gold cup had been in existence. While in Italy's possession it had survived the war years hidden under the bed of Italian F.A. vice-president Dr Ottorino Barassi. Since 1958 it had been in the safe keeping of Brazil, and London saw it ceremonially for the first time in January 1966, at the making of the draw for the qualifying rounds of the final series. Two months later, at about midday on Sunday, 20 March, it vanished in a daring daylight theft from a padlocked cabinet while on display at a £3-million stamp exhibition at the Central Hall, Westminster. For seven days the football world was held spellbound with conjecture that the game's greatest trophy—like the F.A. Cup stolen in 1895—might never be seen again. Then a black and white mongrel dog named Pickles sniffed at a parcel lying under a laurel bush in the garden of his home in Upper Norwood, London—and the World Cup had been found intact! The motive for the theft had been a ransom demand for £15,000 to Football Association chairman Joe Mears; one of the accomplices, a London dock labourer, was jailed for two years, while Pickles earned some £6000 in rewards for his owner and a medal for himself. And England, having lost and found the Jules Rimet Cup, won it at Wembley on 30 July in the most sensational World Cup Final of all

The start of their march to glory, a 0—0 draw against Uruguay, could hardly have been less exciting for Wembley's 75,000 crowd. Then came two 2—0 wins to stir the blood a little, against Mexico (scorers Bobby Charlton and Roger Hunt) and France (Hunt 2). Argentina in the quarter-final posed the toughest problem yet, and England's World Cup hopes might have ended there had not Antonio Rattin, captain of the Argentinians, got himself sent off towards half-time for rough play and arguing with West German referee Rudolf Kreitlein. During a seven-minute hold-up before Rattin finally departed, the entire Argentine team threatened to walk off. The ten who eventually decided to stay stepped up their spoiling tactics and England struggled through 1—0 with a 77th-minute header by Geoff Hurst, replacing the injured Jimmy Greaves.

Brazil's hopes of a World Cup hat-trick dived when Pele was injured in the opening game against Bulgaria, and they failed to survive the qualifying stage. While England were playing that nasty quarter-final with Argentina at Wembley, up at Goodison Park, Portugal and rank outsiders North Korea produced a match straight out of the realms of fiction. Having shocked Italy 1—0 at Middlesbrough to qualify, Pak Doo Ik and his happy-go-lucky Korean team-mates went one . . . two . . . three up against Portugal. But they lacked the tactical know-how to hold such an advantage, and Eusebio, striking irresistible form, scored the first four goals (two of them penalties) in Portugal's eventual victory by 5—3. At Hillsborough, Sheffield, West Germany comprehensively beat Uruguay 4—0, and in the other quarter-final at Sunderland Russia defeated Hungary 2—1.

The semi-finals provided an enormous contrast. At Goodison, West Germany scored a laborious 2—1 win against Russia (who were quickly reduced to ten fit men by injury to Sabo, and to nine when Chislenko was sent off for retaliation after a foul that injured him, too). At Wembley the following night the score was also 2—1, but this game between England and Portugal put the seal of world stature back on the competition. In terms of technique it was the finest match of the whole series in England. Bobby Charlton cracked both England goals; late on, brother Jack handled and from the spot Eusebio explosively took his only chance of the game—the first time Banks's net had been stretched in the tournament.

For only the second time, the first since 1934, the Final went to an extra half-hour. Haller shot West Germany ahead after 13 minutes, but Hurst equalized six minutes later with a splendid header from Bobby Moore's free-kick and, with 13 minutes left, victory seemed assured as Martin Peters scored at close range after Hurst's shot had been blocked. But in the last seconds Weber slammed Germany level from a disputed free-kick by Emmerich, and at two-all the match went into extra-time. England found the inspiration they needed to win the game all over again in the ceaseless running of Ball. His was the centre which Hurst hammered in off the crossbar for the third goal—Swiss referee Gottfried Dienst awarded it after what seemed a timeless consultation with his Russian linesman Tofik Bakhramov—and through to the closing seconds Moore and his men clung desperately to their lead. Then, in a last-fling attack, West Germany left themselves uncovered at the back and Hurst pounded away down the left flank from halfway and finished with a lashing left-foot shot past Tilkowski from 20 yards. Moments later, England fans in their thousands swept across the Wembley pitch to acclaim the incongruously unemotional Alf Ramsey, who had promised, predicted and fashioned the triumph with his wingless, 4—3—3 tactics; to mob the three-goal hero Hurst, first man to score a hat-trick in the World Cup Final; and to salute the whole team with chants of 'Eng-land! Eng-land!' that billowed across the vast arena as Bobby Moore collected the world's greatest soccer prize.

The 1970 World Cup: By winning all six matches they were required to play in Mexico, Brazil worthily became the first country to take the World Cup three times and, in doing so, they won the trophy outright. Compared with the lowest-ever aggregate of 89 goals in each of the two previous tournaments, the 32-match programme now produced 95, with Brazil responsible for 19 of them. It mattered not that they had a suspect defence; their game was based on creation in midfield and a flair for all-out attack in which Pele, kicked out of the two previous World Cups, once again touched his spectacular best in this his fourth tournament. England, as indeed most of the European countries did, overcame the problems of altitude and heat better than expected. They were based at Guadalajara, and Hurst began as he had finished in 1966—on the scoresheet. England's three group qualifying matches each produced a 1–0 result, with wins against Rumania (Hurst) and Czechoslovakia (Clarke, penalty), and defeat by Jairzinho's goal against Brazil. It was enough to take them through to the quarter-finals as group runners-up to Brazil. Then, with the venue switching to Leon, England were paired with West Germany. For an hour England played as splendidly as they had done against them in the 1966 Final, and when Martin Peters added to Alan Mullery's first-half goal directly after halftime, a lead of 2–0 looked unassailable. But it was far from over. Beckenbauer put Germany back in the game with a diagonal shot that flashed under Bonetti (Banks was in his bed, the victim of a stomach bug) and England were shaken again as Seeler scored with a back-header when the odds were stacked against an equalizer. So, again as in the Wembley Final, the sides went into extra time at 2–2, and in the second period Muller, right in front of the target, smashed in the goal that gave Germany victory by 3–2 and avenged 1966. There were inevitable questionmarks—over the tactical substitution of Bobby Charlton (in his record-breaking 106th International) and Norman Hunter, as well as over two of the German goals—but nothing could alter the fact that the World Champions had been dethroned.

In the other quarter-finals Brazil overcame some difficult moments to beat Peru 4–2 in Guadalajara; Uruguay dismissed Russia 1–0 on a disputed goal in the last minute of extra time in Mexico City; and Italy, having scored only one goal in three matches to head their qualifying group, threw away caution when a goal down, to the hosts Mexico in Toluca, and won 4–1.

Goals were cheap, in extra time, anyway, in the Mexico City semi-final between Italy and West Germany. Boninsegna gave Italy an early lead, and that was still the only goal as the match went into injury time. Then Schnellinger equalized, and West Germany went ahead with the first of five goals scored in the extra half-hour, which finished with Italy winners of an extraordinary match by 4–3. In the other semi-final in Guadalajara Cubilla gave Uruguay a shock lead, but Brazil, albeit belatedly turned on the full range of talents and won 3–1, with goals by Clodoaldo, Jairzinho and Rivelino.

The Azteca Stadium, home of Mexican football, did not see Brazil until the Final itself. Their performance in beating Italy 4–1 was well worth the wait. It started with Pele heading in Rivelino's cross after 18 minutes, and although Italy were level by halftime, Boninsegna punishing one of those defensive mistakes to which Brazil were prone, midfield general Gerson restored the lead with a magnificent shot from outside the penalty-area. Gerson and Pele combined to set up the third goal for Jairzinho, and the final scene was stolen by Brazil's captain, Carlos Alberto. He shot a stunning last goal from Pele's perfect pass, and three minutes later he stepped forward to receive the Jules Rimet Cup that was to be Brazil's for ever. Their hat-trick was an incredible achievement for Mario Zagalo, a member of the winning teams in 1958 and 1962, and now triumphant again only a few months after succeeding Joao Saldanha as Brazil's manager.

WORLD CUP SUMMARIES

1930 World Cup—First Tournament—in Uruguay

Winners: Uruguay. **Runners-up:** Argentina. **Third:** U.S.A. **Entries:** 13.
Other countries taking part: Belgium, Bolivia, Brazil, Chile, France, Mexico, Paraguay, Peru, Rumania, Yugoslavia.
All matches played in Montevideo.
Top scorer in tournament: Stabile (Argentina) 8 goals.

Final:
Uruguay 4 (Dorado, Cea, Iriarte, Castro), *Argentina* 2 (Peucelle, Stabile).
Half-time: Uruguay 1, Argentina 2. *Attendance:* 90,000.
Uruguay: Ballesteros; Nasazzi, Mascheroni, Andrade, Fernandez, Gestido, Dorado, Scarone, Castro, Cea, Iriarte.
Argentina: Botasso; Della Torre, Paternoster, Evaristo (J), Monti, Suarez, Eucelle, Varallo, Stabile, Ferreira, Evaristo (M).

1934 World Cup—Second Tournament—in Italy

Winners: Italy. **Runners-up:** Czechoslovakia. **Third:** Germany. **Entries:** 29 (16 qualifiers).
Other countries taking part in final series: Argentina, Austria, Belgium, Brazil, Egypt, France, Holland, Hungary, Rumania, Spain, Sweden, Switzerland, U.S.A.
Venues: Rome, Naples, Milan, Turin, Florence, Bologna, Genoa, Trieste.
Top scorers in tournament: Schiavio (Italy), Nejedly (Czechoslovakia), Conen (Germany) each 4 goals.

Final (Rome):
Italy 2 (Orsi, Schiavio), *Czechoslovakia* 1 (Puc). After extra time.
Half-time: Italy 0, Czechoslovakia 1. *Score after 90 minutes:* 1–1. *Attendance:* 50,000.
Italy: Combi; Monzeglio, Allemandi, Ferraris, Monti, Bertolini, Guaita, Meazza, Schiavio, Ferrari, Orsi.
Czechoslovakia: Planicka; Zenisek, Ctyroky, Kostalek, Cambal, Krcil, Junek, Svoboda, Sobotka, Nejedly, Puc.

1938 World Cup—Third Tournament—in France

Winners: Italy. **Runners-up:** Hungary. **Third:** Brazil. **Entries:** 25 (15 qualifiers).
Other countries taking part in final series: Belgium, Cuba, Czechoslovakia, Dutch East Indies, France, Germany, Holland, Norway, Poland, Rumania, Sweden, Switzerland.
Venues: Paris, Marseilles, Bordeaux, Lille, Antibes, Strasbourg, Le Havre, Reims, Toulouse.
Top scorer in tournament: Leonidas (Brazil) 8 goals.

Final (Paris)
Italy 4 (Colaussi 2, Piola 2), *Hungary* 2 (Titkos, Sarosi).
Half-time: Italy 3; Hungary 1. *Attendance:* 45,000.
Italy: Olivieri; Foni, Rava, Serantoni, Andreolo, Locatelli, Biavati, Meazza, Piola, Ferrari, Colaussi.
Hungary: Szabo; Polgar, Biro, Szalay, Szucs, Lazar, Sas, Vincze, Sarosi, Szengeller, Titkos.

1950 World Cup—Fourth Tournament—in Brazil

Winners: Uruguay. **Runners-up:** Brazil. **Third:** Sweden. **Entries:** 29 (13 qualifiers).
Other countries taking part in final series: Bolivia, Chile, England, Italy, Mexico, Paraguay, Spain, Switzerland, U.S.A., Yugoslavia.
Venues: Rio de Janeiro, São Paulo, Recife, Curitiba, Belo Horizonte, Porto Alegre.
Top scorer in tournament: Ademir (Brazil) 7 goals.

*Deciding Match (Rio de Janeiro):
Uruguay 2 (Schiaffino, Ghiggia), *Brazil* 1 (Friaca).
Half-time: 0–0. *Attendance:* 200,000.
Uruguay: Maspoli; Gonzales, Tejera, Gambetta, Varela, Andrade, Ghiggia, Perez, Miguez, Schiaffino, Moran.
Brazil: Barbosa; Augusto, Juvenal, Bauer, Danilo, Bigode, Friaca, Zizinho, Ademir, Jair, Chico.
* For the only time, the World Cup was decided on a Final Pool system, in which the winners of the four qualifying groups met in a six-match series. So, unlike previous and subsequent tournaments, there was no official Final as such, but Uruguay v. Brazil was the deciding final match in the Final Pool.

1954 World Cup—Fifth Tournament— in Switzerland

Winners: Germany. **Runners-up:** Hungary. **Third:** Austria. **Entries:** 35 (16 qualifiers).
Other countries taking part in final series: Belgium, Brazil, Czechoslovakia, England, France, Italy, Korea, Mexico, Scotland, Switzerland, Turkey, Uruguay, Yugoslavia.

Venues: Berne, Zürich, Lausanne, Basle, Geneva, Lugano.
Top scorer in tournament: Kocsis (Hungary) 11 goals.

Final (Berne):
Germany 3 (Morlock, Rahn 2), *Hungary* 2 (Puskas, Czibor).
Half-time: 2–2. *Attendance:* 60,000.
Germany: Turek; Posipal, Kohlmeyer, Eckel, Liebrich, Mai, Rahn, Morlock, Walter (O), Walter (F), Schaefer.
Hungary: Grosics; Buzansky, Lantos, Boszik, Lorant, Zakarias, Czibor, Kocsis, Hidegkuti, Puskas, Toth.

1958 World Cup—Sixth Tournament—in Sweden

Winners: Brazil. **Runners-up:** Sweden. **Third:** France.
Entries: 47 (16 qualifiers).
Other countries taking part in final series: Argentina, Austria, Czechoslovakia, England, Hungary, Mexico, Northern Ireland, Paraguay, Russia, Scotland, Wales, West Germany, Yugoslavia.
Venues: Stockholm, Gothenburg, Malmö, Norrköping, Borås, Sandviken, Ekilstuna, Cerebro, Västeras, Hälsingborg, Halmstad.
Top scorer in tournament: Fontaine (France) 13 goals.

Final (Stockholm):
Brazil 5 (Vava 2, Pele 2, Zagalo), *Sweden* 2 (Liedholm, Simonsson).
Half-time: Brazil 2, Sweden 1. *Attendance:* 50,000.
Brazil: Gilmar; Santos (D), Santos (N), Zito, Bellini, Orlando, Garrincha, Didi, Vava, Pele, Zagalo.
Sweden: Svensson; Bergmark, Axbom, Boerjesson, Gustavsson, Parling, Hamrin, Gren, Simonsson, Liedholm, Skoglund.

1962 World Cup—Seventh Tournament—in Chile

Winners: Brazil. **Runners-up:** Czechoslovakia. **Third:** Chile.
Entries: 53 (16 qualifiers).
Other countries taking part in final series: Argentina, Bulgaria, Colombia, England, Hungary, Italy, Mexico, Russia, Spain, Switzerland, Uruguay, West Germany, Yugoslavia.
Venues: Santiago, Vina del Mar, Rancagua, Arica.
Top scorers in tournament: Garrincha (Brazil), Vava (Brazil), Sanchez (Chile), Albert (Hungary), Ivanov (Russia), Jerkovic (Yugoslavia) each 4 goals.

Final (Santiago):
Brazil 3 (Amarildo, Zito, Vava), *Czechoslovakia* 1 (Masopust).
Half-time: 1–1. *Attendance:* 69,000.
Brazil: Gilmar; Santos (D), Mauro, Zozimo, Santos (N), Zito, Didi, Garrincha, Vava, Amarildo, Zagalo.
Czechoslovakia: Schroiff; Tichy, Novak, Pluskal, Popluhar, Masopust, Pospichal, Scherer, Kvasniak, Kadraba, Jelinek.

1966 World Cup—Eighth Tournament—in England

Winners: England. **Runners-up:** West Germany. **Third:** Portugal. **Entries:** 53 (16 qualifiers).
Other countries taking part in final series: Argentina, Brazil, Bulgaria, Chile, France, Hungary, Italy, Mexico, North Korea, Russia, Spain, Switzerland, Uruguay.
Venues: London (Wembley and White City), Sheffield (Hillsborough), Liverpool (Goodison Park), Sunderland, Middlesbrough, Manchester (Old Trafford), Birmingham (Villa Park).
Top scorer in tournament: Eusebio (Portugal) 9 goals.

Final (Wembley):
England 4 (Hurst 3, Peters), *West Germany* 2 (Haller, Weber). After extra time.
Half-time: 1–1. *Score after 90 minutes:* 2–2 *Attendance:* 100,000.
England: Banks; Cohen, Wilson, Stiles, Charlton (J), Moore, Ball, Hurst, Hunt, Charlton (R), Peters.
West Germany: Tilkowski; Hottges, Schnellinger, Beckenbauer, Schulz, Weber, Haller, Held, Seeler, Overath, Emmerich.

1970 World Cup—Ninth Tournament—in Mexico

Winners: Brazil. **Runners-up:** Italy. **Third:** West Germany. **Entries:** 68 (16 qualifiers).
Other countries taking part in final series: Belgium, Bulgaria, Czechoslovakia, El Salvador, England, Israel, Mexico, Morocco, Peru, Rumania, Russia, Sweden, Uruguay.
Venues: Mexico City, Guadalajara, Leon, Puebla, Toluca.
Top scorer in tournament: Muller (West Germany) 10 goals.

Final (Mexico City):
Brazil 4 (Pele, Gerson, Jairzinho, Carlos Alberto), *Italy* 1 (Boninsegna).
Half-time: 1–1. *Attendance:* 107,000.
Brazil: Felix; Carlos Alberto, Brito, Piazza, Everaldo, Clodoaldo, Gerson, Jairzinho, Tostao, Pele, Rivelino.
Italy: Albertosi; Burgnich, Facchetti, Cera, Rosato, Bertini (substitute Juliano), Domenghini, De Sisti, Mazzola, Boninsegna (substitute Rivera), Riva.

1974 World Cup—Tenth Tournament—in West Germany

(not completed at time of going to press).

OTHER WORLD CUP FACTS
(Excluding the 1974 tournament)

The 1970 World Cup in Mexico set a new attendance record for the final series with an aggregate of 1,673,975 spectators attending the 32 matches. The previous record was 1,458,043 present when England staged the tournament in 1966.

Brazil's success in Mexico gave South America the edge against Europe in the balance of World Cup power. It was their fifth triumph (Brazil three wins, Uruguay two) against four by Europe (Italy two wins, West Germany and England one each). With one exception (Brazil's triumph in Sweden in 1958) the World Cup has always been won by a country from the hemisphere in which the Finals are staged.

The individual goalscoring record for a World Cup final series is 13 by Just Fontaine (France) in the 1958 tournament in Sweden. Two other players have reached a double-figure total: Sandor Kocsis with 11 goals for Hungary (Switzerland, 1954 tournament) and Gerd Muller with 10 for West Germany (Mexico, 1970).

Host countries have won three of the nine World Cup tournaments: Uruguay in 1930, Italy in 1934 and England in 1966. This is how the other host nations have fared: 1938—France, unplaced; 1950—Brazil, runners-up; 1954—Switzerland, unplaced; 1958—Sweden, runners-up; 1962—Chile, third; 1970—Mexico, unplaced.

Hungary set two records that still stand when they were runners-up to West Germany in the 1954 World Cup in Switzerland. Their 9–0 win against Korea was the highest score in any Final series, and their total of 27 goals remains the most ever scored by one country in any series of the World Cup proper.

Highest match aggregates in World Cup Final series: 12—Austria 7, Switzerland 5 (Switzerland, 1954); 11—Brazil 6, Poland 5 (France, 1938) and Hungary 8, Germany 3 (Switzerland, 1954).

Mexican goalkeeper Antonio Carbajal holds a World Cup record that may never be equalled. He represented his country in *five* tournaments: in Brazil 1950, Switzerland 1954, Sweden 1958, Chile 1962 and, finally, at Wembley in 1966.

England did not enter the first three World Cup tournaments (1930, 1934 and 1938). This is how they have fared in the competition:

1950 finished second in qualifying group; 1954 beaten in quarter-final; 1958 beaten in play-off for quarter-final place;

1962 beaten in quarter-final; 1966 Winners; 1970 beaten in quarter-final. 1974 failed to qualify for first time.
Scotland's record: 1954 bottom in qualifying group; 1958 bottom in qualifying group, 1974 Britain's only qualifiers.
Northern Ireland's record: 1958 beaten in quarter-final.
Wales's record: 1958 beaten in quarter-finals.
Britain has only twice been represented by more than one country in the World Cup Final series—in 1954, when England and Scotland participated in Switzerland, and in 1958, when England, Scotland, Northern Ireland and Wales all qualified for the tournament held in Sweden.

In seven of the nine World Cup Finals the eventual winners have been behind at one stage of the match. The exceptions: Italy 1938 and Brazil 1970.

World Cup Final Results

1930	(Montevideo)	Uruguay	4	Argentina 2
1934	(Rome)	Italy	2	Czechoslovakia 1
		(after extra time)		
1938	(Paris)	Italy	4	Hungary 2
1950	(Rio de Janeiro)	Uruguay	2	Brazil 1
1954	(Berne)	Germany	3	Hungary 2
1958	(Stockholm)	Brazil	5	Sweden 2
1962	(Santiago)	Brazil	3	Czechoslovakia 1
1966	(Wembley)	England	4	West Germany 2
		(after extra time)		
1970	(Mexico City)	Brazil	4	Italy 1

Venues for the three World Cup tournaments *after* West Germany in 1974 have been arranged as follows: 1978 Argentina, 1982 Spain, 1986 Yugoslavia.

THE 1974 WORLD CUP

World Cups take a deal of preparation, and the beginning of the tenth global tournament that reached its climax with the Final in Munich on 7 July 1974 was made precisely three years earlier—in July 1971, when the draw for the qualifying competition took place in Düsseldorf.

It involved 98 of F.I.F.A.'s 138 then affiliated members—the biggest-ever World Cup entry, comprising 33 from Europe (including West Germany, the host country), 10 from South America (including reigning World Champions Brazil who, like West Germany, qualify automatically), 17 from the Asian group,

24 from Africa and 14 from the group combining Central and North America, and the Caribbean.

The original completion date for the qualifying round was 31 December 1973, but the last of the 16 countries to contest the Final series was not known until 13 February 1974 when Yugoslavia beat Spain 1–0 in Frankfurt in a Group 7 play-off.

The full qualifying round draw, with eventual group winners in bold type, was made in 1971 as follows:

Europe
Group 1 **Sweden**, Hungary, Austria, Malta.
Group 2 **Italy**, Switzerland, Turkey, Luxembourg.
Group 3 Belgium, **Holland**, Norway, Iceland.
Group 4 Rumania, **East Germany**, Albania, Finland.
Group 5 England, **Poland**, Wales.
Group 6 **Bulgaria**, Portugal, Northern Ireland, Cyprus.
Group 7 **Yugoslavia**, Spain, Greece.
Group 8 Czechoslovakia, Denmark, **Scotland**.
Group 9 **Russia**, France, Republic of Ireland.

South America
Group 1 **Uruguay**, Colombia, Ecuador.
Group 2 **Argentina**, Paraguay, Bolivia.
Group 3 Peru, **Chile**, Venezuela.

Asia
Winners of the two groups to play off for place in Finals.
Group 1 Israel, Thailand, Malaysia, Philippines, Hong Kong, Republic of Korea, Japan, South Vietnam.
Group 2 Iran, Iraq, Kuwait, Ceylon, Syria, India, Indonesia, plus winners of **Australia** v. New Zealand.

Africa
Pairs to play on a knock-out system, with one winner of the section to go forward to the Finals.
Group 1 Morocco and Senegal; Guinea and Algeria; United Arab Republic and Tunisia; Ivory Coast and Sierra Leone.
Group 2 Sudan and Kenya; Mauritius and Madagascar; Ethiopia and Tanzania; Zambia and Lesotho.
Group 3 Nigeria and Congo-Brazzaville; Ghana and Dahomey; Togo and **Zaire**; Cameroun and Gabon.

Central America, North America & Caribbean
Regional tournament to decide one winner.
Group 1 Canada, U.S.A., Mexico.
Group 2 Guatemala, El Salvador.
Group 3 Honduras, Costa Rica.
Group 4 Jamaica, Netherlands Antilles.

Group 5 **Haiti**, Puerto Rico.
Group 6 Surinam, Trinidad, Antigua.

The draw for the tenth World Cup Final series was made in Frankfurt on 5 February 1974. The 16 countries taking part were: West Germany (hosts), Brazil (holders), Sweden, Italy, Holland, East Germany, Poland, Bulgaria, Yugoslavia, Scotland, Uruguay, Argentina, Chile (who qualified on Russia's disqualification for refusing to go to Chile for a group play-off match), Australia, Haiti and Zaire.

This was how the countries were grouped:

Group 1 West Germany, Chile, East Germany, Australia. Dates June 14, 18, 22. Venues, Berlin, Hamburg.

Group 2 Brazil, Scotland, Zaire, Yugoslavia. Dates June 13, 14, 18, 22. Venues Frankfurt, Dortmund, Gelsenkirchen.

Group 3 Uruguay, Holland, Bulgaria, Sweden. Dates June 15, 19, 23. Venues Hanover, Dusseldorf, Dortmund.

Group 4 Italy, Argentina, Poland, Haiti. Dates June 15, 19, 23. Venues Munich, Stuttgart.

Each country played the other three nations in its section, and the two top teams in each group advanced to semi-final sections A and B, which were also played on a league system. So, for the first time since 1950, there were to be no quarter-finals.

The runners-up in semi-final Groups A and B were to play off for third and fourth places in Munich on 6 July, and the Final was to be between the winners of those groups in Munich on 7 July.

(*Note:* This publication went to press before the 1974 World Cup tournament opened.)

The European Championship

Originally known as the Henri Delaunay Cup, after its French founder, later as the Nations Cup, and now as the European Championship, it was introduced in 1958. The tournament takes two years to complete, with the Final scheduled to take place exactly halfway between one World Cup and the next. The qualifying competition is divided into eight groups, with quarter-final ties decided on a home-and-away basis. The semi-finals and Final are staged in one of the last four surviving countries. Semi-final and Final results:

1958–60: in France
Semi-finals: Yugoslavia 5, France 4 (Paris); Russia 3, Czechoslovakia 0 (Marseilles).
Final (Paris): *Russia* 2, Yugoslavia 1 (after extra time).

1962–64: in Spain
Semi-finals: Russia 3, Denmark 0 (Barcelona); Spain 2, Hungary 1 (Madrid).
Final (Madrid): *Spain* 2, Russia 1.

1966–68: in Italy
Semi-finals: Yugoslavia 1, England 0 (Florence); Italy 0, Russia 0 (Naples) after extra time—Italy won on toss.
Final (Rome): *Italy* 2, Yugoslavia 0 in replay after 1–1 draw.

1970–72: in Belgium

Semi-finals: Russia 1, Hungary 0 (Brussels); West Germany 2, Belgium 1 (Antwerp).

Final (Brussels): *West Germany* 3, Russia 0.

1974–76—draw:

Group 1   England, Czechoslovakia, Portugal, Cyprus.
Group 2   Wales, Hungary, Austria, Luxembourg.
Group 3   N. Ireland, Yugoslavia, Sweden, Norway.
Group 4   Scotland, Denmark, Rumania, Spain.
Group 5   Italy, Holland, Poland, Finland.
Group 6   Republic of Ireland, Russia, Turkey, Switzerland.
Group 7   Belgium, East Germany, France, Iceland.
Group 8   West Germany, Bulgaria, Greece, Malta.

Groups to be completed by 31 January 1976; Quarter-finals April–May 1976; Semi-finals and Final June 1976

The European Cup

In its 19-year history, the European Cup has presented a standard of international club football that could hardly have been imagined when it was launched in 1955. The idea was conceived by French soccer journalist Gabriel Hanot, a former international player, and developed rapidly after a meeting which he and the proprietors of his newspaper, L'Equipe, called in Paris in the spring of 1955 among all the leading European clubs. Six months later the dream became reality, and so began a contest bringing together the champion clubs of all the European countries and now long-established as football's greatest outside the World Cup.

In 1949 Hanot had been a prominent figure in the introduction of the Latin Cup, featuring the champion clubs of France, Spain, Italy and Portugal. As long ago as 1927 a similar competition, the Mitropa Cup, had been started in Central Europe among the principal clubs of Austria, Czechoslovakia, Hungary, Italy and Yugoslavia. By combining those two tournaments, and inviting the champion teams of North and Western Europe to participate, Hanot found the formula for the European Cup.

The champions of 17 countries entered the opening tournament in season 1955—56, but Chelsea subsequently withdrew under pressure from the Football League, who saw the new venture as a threat to their own competition. A year later Manchester United, disregarding the Establishment, both entered and took part. Fittingly, in 1968, they became the first English club to win the trophy—ten years after a European Cup journey had decimated the Old Trafford club with the Munich air disaster.

Ironically, although France was the birthplace of the European Cup and the first final was staged in Paris, no French club has taken the prize.

With bewildering football, Spanish champions Real Madrid made the competition their own 'spectacular', winning it for the first five years (1956–60). In the last of that astonishing sequence of finals, they beat the German champions, Eintracht Frankfurt, by 7–3 at Hampden Park, Glasgow with one of the most dazzling displays in the game's history. Outshining all others in a magnificent team performance were Real's legendary strikers Ferenc Puskas, who scored four goals, and Alfredo di Stefano, who got the other three.

Real Madrid appeared in eight of the first eleven European Cup finals and won the trophy on six of those occasions. Either as its holders or as champions of Spain, they took part in the first 15 seasons of the competition and the following year (1970–71) reached the final of the European Cup-Winners' Cup.

Until the inception of the European Cup, Real Madrid were little known outside Spain. Suddenly they found themselves the centre of world-wide acclaim—and if Real Madrid made the European Cup, it can also be said that the 'European Coupe des Clubs Champions' made Real. Their vast profits from the competition were invested in a permanent monument to their triumphs with the construction of the 120,000-capacity Bernabeu Stadium in the Chamartin suburb of Madrid.

For the first 11 years the European Cup was the 'Latins' Cup', with Spanish, Portuguese and Italian clubs dominating the tournament. During that period its winners came exclusively from three cities: Madrid, Lisbon and Milan.

Britain, through the medium of Glasgow Celtic, finally broke the Latin grip in 1967. Entering the competition for the first time, they had a comfortable passage through the rounds against Zurich, Nantes, Vojvodina and Dukla. The final, in Lisbon, brought them opposition of the strongest calibre in Inter-Milan, and after falling behind to an early penalty, Celtic saved the tie with Gemmell's second-half equalizer and, five minutes from the end, won it with a goal by Chalmers.

Thus Jock Stein's magnificent Celtic put Britain's hand on the European Cup for the first time. At Wembley a year later England took possession of it from Scotland with a wonderful extra-time victory by Manchester United against Benfica. Three times before —in 1957, 1958 and 1966—Matt Busby's men had been foiled at the semi-final stage. Now, in 1968, they beat their bogey, winning the first leg against Real Madrid by Best's only goal at Old Trafford and storming back from 3–1 down with 18 minutes left to draw the return match in Madrid 3–3, so winning the tie 4–3 on aggregate.

The Final, on 29 May 1968, produced at Wembley an emotional occasion which approached England's 1966 World Cup triumph. Remembering how close Manchester United had been to European success in the past, unable to forget how the European Cup had destroyed the famous 'Busby Babes' in the snows of Munich Airport in 1958, everyone, it seemed, was willing them to victory over Benfica, the Eagles of Lisbon.

Charlton's dipping header early in the second half looked to be sufficient when, with 11 minutes left, that was still the only goal. Then Graca smashed Benfica level, and Stepney miraculously held Eusebio's shot to earn extra time. It was a save that lifted the hearts of United and, with fresh wind in their sails, they moved majestically to victory. Aston demoralized Benfica's right defensive flank, and from the moment Best beat one man, then dribbled the 'keeper, to put United back in front, the European Cup was destined for Old Trafford, the margin stretching to 4–1 as Kidd celebrated his 19th birthday by heading in a crossbar rebound and Charlton himself, shooting the final goal.

A year later AC Milan took the European Cup back to Italy, thus sharing four successes in the competition for that country equally with Inter-Milan. In 1970 Celtic were finalists again, and following Arsenal's victory in the Fairs Cup and Manchester City's success in the Cup-Winners' Cup, there was the prospect of a clean sweep by Britain in all three European tournaments.

In anticipation, 25,000 fanatical Celtic supporters travelled to Milan—the biggest following any British team has ever had abroad—for the final against Dutch 'outsiders' Feyenoord. In the semi-final Celtic had twice beaten Leeds United; in Milan full-back Gemmell shot them ahead after half an hour and the Cup seemed to be heading for Glasgow again. But Feyenoord equalized, dominated the second half, and deservedly triumphed.

In 1971 Wembley staged its third European Champion Clubs' Final, in which Ajax (Amsterdam) kept the prize in Dutch possession by beating Panathinaikos, of Greece, 2–0. Ajax retained the trophy in 1972 and 1973, again without conceding a goal in either Final, and so became the first club to win the European Cup in three successive seasons since Real Madrid in the competition's early years.

Results of European Cup Finals

Year	Venue	Winners	Runners-up	Score
1956	Paris	Real Madrid	Reims	4–3
1957	Madrid	Real Madrid	Fiorentina	2–0
1958	Brussels	Real Madrid	AC Milan	3–2
1959	Stuttgart	Real Madrid	Reims	2–0
1960	Glasgow	Real Madrid	Eintracht	7–3
1961	Berne	Benfica	CF Barcelona	3–2
1962	Amsterdam	Benfica	Real Madrid	5–3
1963	Wembley	AC Milan	Benfica	2–1
1964	Vienna	Inter-Milan	Real Madrid	3–1
1965	Milan	Inter-Milan	Benfica	1–0
1966	Brussels	Real Madrid	Partizan	2–1
1967	Lisbon	Celtic	Inter-Milan	2–1
1968	Wembley	Manchester United	Benfica	4–1
1969	Madrid	AC Milan	Ajax Amsterdam	4–1
1970	Milan	Feyenoord	Celtic	2–1
1971	Wembley	Ajax Amsterdam	Panathinaikos	2–0
1972	Rotterdam	Ajax Amsterdam	Inter-Milan	2–0
1973	Belgrade	Ajax Amsterdam	Juventus	1–0
1974	Brussels	Bayern Munich	Atletico Madrid	4–0

(After 1–1 draw)

The European Cup-Winners' Cup

Staged for the first time in season 1960–61, the Cup-Winners' Cup is the youngest of the three European club tournaments, but in prestige it stands second to the Champions' Cup and British teams have done much to popularize it. In nine seasons between 1963 and 1971 the Cup of Cups was won by Football League clubs no fewer than four times, with Tottenham, West Ham, Manchester City and Chelsea all using victory in the F.A. Cup one year as the passport to European success the following season, and in 1972 Rangers became the first Scottish name on the list of winners—compensation for being beaten finalists in 1961 and 1967.

The enormous success of the Champions' Cup clearly indicated scope for another European competition, and in 1959 the organizers of the Mitropa Cup succeeded in their campaign to launch a knock-out competition for national cup-winners.

It started the following year with only ten entries, the initial problem being that in few Continental countries was the domestic cup greeted with the same enthusiasm and regarded with the same seriousness as the F.A. and Scottish Cups. For instance, Spain played their F.A. Cup at the end of the season, Italy in mid-week (like the Football League Cup), France on neutral grounds and Portugal on a home-and-away basis.

By the third season (1962–63), however, 24 clubs took part in the Cup-Winners' Cup and there is now a regular entry of 32 teams. Not only has the Cup of Cups grown to full maturity; its development pepped up the national cup competitions in many countries, because success brought prospects of a lucrative campaign in Europe.

After the first final, in which Fiorentina triumphed for Italy by beating Rangers home and away, U.E.F.A. took over the competition and one of their first decisions was to do away with two-leg finals. But two matches were still needed to decide the 1962 winners—Atletico Madrid, who held the holders Fiorentina 1–1 in Glasgow and, four months later, triumphed 3–0 in Stuttgart.

In 1963 Tottenham Hotspur put themselves, and the Cup-Winners' Cup, truly on the European map. At the Feyenoord

Stadium in Rotterdam a capacity 65,000 crowd saw them take the trophy from Atletico in tremendous style by 5–1, scorers Greaves (2), Dyson (2) and White.

The following year Sporting Lisbon won the cup for Portugal, but in 1965 it was back in England, with Wembley housing the first 100,000 crowd in the history of the competition and West Ham celebrating the occasion by 2–0 against TSV Munich (scorer Sealey, 2).

Britain also supplied a finalist in each of the next two seasons, but twice West German opposition proved too powerful. Liverpool losing 2–1 to Borussia Dortmund in Glasgow in 1966 and a year later, Rangers going down by the only goal to Bayern Munich in Nuremberg.

Season 1965–66, the year following West Ham's success, may not have retained the trophy for Britain, but a record was established by providing three of the semi-finalists: Liverpool, West Ham and Celtic. But in 1970 the Cup-Winners' Cup did return to England . . . and stayed for two seasons.

Manchester City's 2–1 victory over the Polish mining team Gornik Zabrze in Vienna was earned with goals from Young and Lee, who celebrated his 25th birthday with what proved to be the winner from the penalty spot. Thus City completed a spectacular cup double, for they had already won the Football League Cup that season.

On the night they lifted the Cup-Winners' Cup in the rain-lashed Prater Stadium in Vienna, Chelsea were in Manchester, winning the F.A. Cup in the replayed final against Leeds United —a success that paved the way for them to take over the Cup of Cups from Manchester City in 1971.

Some 4000 supporters journeyed to Athens to cheer Chelsea in the final against the old masters of Europe, Real Madrid. Osgood's lone goal looked all over the winner until, in the most dramatic climax to any European final, Zoco equalized with the last kick of normal time. Webb's goal-line clearance kept Chelsea alive in extra time, and two nights later in the same Karaiskaki Stadium it began all over again.

This time Chelsea, putting the emphasis on attack from the start, took a two-goal lead through Dempsey and Osgood, and although Real Madrid replied 15 minutes from the end, the experience and tradition of eight previous European finals was not enough to save them.

So Chelsea won their first European prize, but the possibility of them becoming the first club to lift the Cup of Cups in successive seasons was quickly shattered in the 1971–72 season. In the first round Chelsea smashed the scoring record for all three European tournaments by beating Luxembourg Cup-holders Jeunesse Hautcharage 21–0 on aggregate (8–0 away, 13–0 at home). The next hurdle seemed to be there for Chelsea's taking when they were paired with the Swedish part-timers Atvidaberg, but after being kept to a goalless draw in Luxembourg, Chelsea became victims of one of the biggest shocks in European football. They could only draw 1–1 at home, missing a penalty in the process, and Atvidaberg went through on the away goals rule.

That 1971–72 tournament ended with Rangers giving Scotland its first sight of the Cup-Winners' Cup. They beat Moscow Dynamo 3–2 in the final in Barcelona, but the Russians protested that their players had been handicapped by the pitch invasions of supporters from Glasgow. It was several weeks before Rangers' victory was confirmed by U.E.F.A., but because of their supporters' misconduct they were barred from European football for two years—a ban subsequently reduced to one season.

Results of European Cup-Winners' Cup Finals

Year	Venue	Winners	Runners-up	Score
1961	—	Fiorentina	Rangers	4–1 aggregate

(Fiorentina won first leg 2–0 in Glasgow, second leg 2–1 in Florence)

Year	Venue	Winners	Runners-up	Score
1962	Stuttgart	Atletico Madrid	Fiorentina	3–0

(In replay after 1–1 draw in Glasgow)

Year	Venue	Winners	Runners-up	Score
1963	Rotterdam	Tottenham Hotspur	Atletico Madrid	5–1
1964	Antwerp	Sporting Lisbon	MTK Budapest	1–0

(In replay after 3–3 draw in Brussels)

Year	Venue	Winners	Runners-up	Score
1965	Wembley	West Ham United	TSV Munich	2–0
1966	Glasgow	Borussia Dortmund	Liverpool	2–1
1967	Nuremberg	Bayern München	Rangers	1–0
1968	Rotterdam	AC Milan	Hamburg	2–0
1969	Basle	Slovan Bratislava	CF Barcelona	3–2
1970	Vienna	Manchester City	Gornik Zabrze	2–1
1971	Athens	Chelsea	Real Madrid	2–1

(In replay after 1–1 draw, also in Athens)

Year	Venue	Winners	Runners-up	Score
1972	Barcelona	Rangers	Dynamo Moscow	3–2
1973	Salonika	AC Milan	Leeds Utd.	1–0
1974	Rotterdam	FC Magdeburg	AC Milan	2–0

The U.E.F.A. Cup

Season 1971–72 marked the innovation of the U.E.F.A. Cup in succession to the European Fairs Cup, which was originally known as the European Inter-City Industrial Fairs Cup. This was the forerunner of the three major European football competitions although in Britain at least it is ranked No. 3 behind the European Cup and Cup-Winners Cup.

For many years before the Fairs Cup was launched in 1955 matches were played between cities on the Continent, but it was not until 1950 that Ernst B. Thommen, of Switzerland, suggested a competition for cities regularly holding industrial and trade fairs.

Thommen, a vice-president of F.I.F.A., had to wait four years for his idea to take shape because there was no suitable organizing body at the time. The competition got off the ground largely through the initiative of F.I.F.A. president Sir Stanley Rous, and until 1971 it ran independently of U.E.F.A. under an organizing committee.

Some cities (e.g. London) at first entered representative teams but others preferred to nominate club sides, and as the competition grew in prestige and popularity, club sides took over.

Although the first Fairs Cup tournament was begun in 1955 it was not completed until 1958. The reason for staggering the schedule was to avoid a clash with long-standing domestic fixtures. But interest could not be sustained over such a long period, and the competition almost ground to a halt.

The organizers, recognizing this weakness, staged the second series over two years, and since season 1960–61 the competition has been an annual event on the football calendar.

Spain provided five of the first six winners, starting with two triumphs for Barcelona. They won the drawn-out 1955–58 series, beating a representative London side 6–0 in Barcelona and by what was to remain the record aggregate of 8–2. In the 1958–60 series Barcelona went through to the finals without losing a single game and won the trophy again by defeating Birmingham City 5–2 on aggregate.

Birmingham were also the losing finalists in the 1960–61 series, when they held AS Roma to a 2–2 draw in Birmingham but lost 2–0 in Rome.

Valencia were the high-scoring winners in 1961–62, defeating

Barcelona 7-3 on aggregate. They won the trophy again the following season and went close to completing a hat-trick in 1963-64, when for the first time it was decided to play a one-match final on a neutral ground. In an all-Spanish decider they lost 2-1 to Real Zaragoza in Barcelona.

But single-leg finals were not a success and after Ferencvaros had beaten Juventus 1-0 in Turin in 1965 — Hungary's first Fairs Cup conquest — the 1965-66 final reverted to two matches. It was held over until the following season and, when it was eventually played, Barcelona became the only team to win the Fairs Cup three times, beating their Spanish rivals Real Zaragoza after losing the home leg.

In 1967 Leeds United became the first British team to reach the final for six years. The toss of a coin took them through the quarter-finals against Bologna after the teams had deadlocked 1-1. In the final, again delayed until the next season, Leeds went down 2-0 on aggregate to Dynamo Zagreb.

A year later, however, Leeds became the first British winners of the trophy. In the first leg they gained a slender 1-0 lead and then held Ferencvaros to a goalless draw in Budapest.

In the last competition under the original title of Inter-Cities Fairs Cup, another British team took the prize — Newcastle United in season 1968-69. It was Newcastle's first venture into Europe, and the Geordies' theme song, 'Blaydon Races', rang out as the crowds thronged St James's Park to see the Tynesiders beat crack Continental clubs Feyenoord, Sporting Lisbon, Real Zaragoza and Vitoria Setubal.

There was an all-British semi-final between Newcastle and Rangers. United fought a rearguard action to hold Rangers 0-0 at Ibrox and then won 2-0 at St James's Park. With their team two down in the second leg, Rangers followers invaded the field intent on getting the game abandoned and play was held up for 18 minutes. There were 31 arrests, 60 spectators were taken to hospital and the match was played out with 1000 police surrounding the pitch.

In the final, Newcastle beat the Hungarians Ujpest Dozsa 3-0 in the home leg, but even that advantage began to look inadequate when Ujpest quickly pulled back two goals in the return game in Budapest. A storming rally by Newcastle, however, produced three goals and an impressive 6-2 victory on aggregate.

In 1970 Arsenal scored a dramatic victory over Belgium's Anderlecht which kept the Fairs Cup in England for the third successive season. They lost the first leg of the final 3-1 in Brussels, but the second match was won 3-0, and a 51,000 Highbury crowd went wild at Arsenal's first success of any sort for 17 years.

A year later Leeds United became the first British club to win the competition twice. In what was the last European Fairs Cup tournament, they were its first winners on the 'away goals' rule, drawing 2–2 against Juventus in Turin and 1–1 at Elland Road.

Season 1971–72 produced the first all-British final in any European contest, Tottenham beating Wolves 3–2 on aggregate and by the same score Liverpool defeated Borussia Moenchengladbach in the 1973 final.

Results of Fairs Cup/U.E.F.A. Cup Finals

1955–58 **Barcelona** beat *London* 8–2 on aggregate (London 2, Barcelona 2; Barcelona 6, London 0)
1958–60 **Barcelona** beat *Birmingham* 5–2 on aggregate (Birmingham 1, Barcelona 1; Barcelona 4, Birmingham 1)
1961 **AS Roma** beat *Birmingham City* 4–2 on aggregate (Birmingham 2, AS Roma 2; AS Roma 2, Birmingham 0)
1962 **Valencia** beat *Barcelona* 7–3 on aggregate (Valencia 6, Barcelona 2; Barcelona 1, Valencia 1)
1963 **Valencia** beat *Dynamo Zagreb* 4–1 on aggregate (Dynamo Zagreb 1, Valencia 2; Valencia 2, Dynamo Zagreb 0)
1964 **Real Zaragoza** 2, *Valencia* 1 (in Barcelona)
1965 **Ferencvaros** 1, *Juventus* 0 (in Turin)
1966 **Barcelona** beat *Real Zaragoza* 4–3 on aggregate (Barcelona 0, Real Zaragoza 1; Real Zaragoza 2, Barcelona 4)
1967 **Dynamo Zagreb** beat *Leeds United* 2–0 on aggregate (Dynamo Zagreb 2, Leeds 0; Leeds 0, Dynamo Zagreb 0)
1968 **Leeds United** beat *Ferencvaros* 1–0 on aggregate (Leeds 1, Ferencvaros 0; Ferencvaros 0, Leeds 0)
1969 **Newcastle United** beat *Ujpest Dozsa* 6–2 on aggregate (Newcastle 3, Ujpest Dozsa 0; Ujpest Dozsa 2, Newcastle 3)
1970 **Arsenal** beat *Anderlecht* 4–3 on aggregate (Anderlecht 3, Arsenal 1; Arsenal 3, Anderlecht 0)
1971 **Leeds United** beat *Juventus* on away goals after 3–3 draw on aggregate (Juventus 0, Leeds 0—abandoned 51 min., rain; Juventus 2, Leeds 2; Leeds 1, Juventus 1).
1972 **Tottenham Hotspur** beat *Wolverhampton Wanderers* 3–2 on aggregate (Wolves 1, Tottenham 2; Tottenham 1, Wolves 1)
1973 **Liverpool** beat *Borussia Moenchengladbach* 3–2 on aggregate (Liverpool 3, Borussia 0; Borussia 2, Liverpool 0).
1974 **Feyenoord** beat *Tottenham Hotspur* 4–2 on aggregate (Tottenham 2, Feyenoord 2; Feyenoord 2, Tottenham 0).

The World Club Championship

This unofficial inter-continental tournament is played each season between the winners of the European Cup and the winners of the South American Cup.

1960 Real Madrid (Spain) beat *Penarol* (Uruguay). (In Montevideo—Penarol 0, Real Madrid 0; in Madrid—Real Madrid 5, Penarol 1).

1961 Penarol (Uruguay) beat *Benfica* (Portugal). (In Lisbon—Benfica 1, Penarol 0; in Montevideo—Penarol 5, Benfica 0; play-off in Montevideo—Penarol 2, Benfica 1).

1962 Santos (Brazil) beat *Benfica* (Portugal). (In Rio de Janeiro—Santos 3, Benfica 2; in Lisbon—Benfica, 2 Santos 5).

1963 Santos (Brazil) beat *AC Milan* (Italy). (In Milan—AC Milan 4, Santos 2; in Rio de Janeiro—Santos 4, AC Milan 2; play-off in Rio—Santos 1, AC Milan 0).

1964 Internazionale Milan (Italy) beat *Independiente* (Argentina). (In Buenos Aires—Independiente 1, Internazionale 0; in Milan—Internazionale 2, Independiente 0; play-off in Madrid—Internazionale 1, Independiente 0, after extra time).

1965 Internazionale Milan (Italy) beat *Independiente* (Argentina). (In Milan—Internazionale 3, Independiente 0; in Buenos Aires—Independiente 0, Internazionale 0)

1966 Penarol (Uruguay) beat *Real Madrid* (Spain). (In Montevideo—Penarol 2, Real Madrid 0; in Madrid—Real Madrid 0, Penarol 2).

1967 Racing Club (Argentina) beat *Celtic* (Scotland). (In Glasgow—Celtic 1, Racing Club 0; in Buenos Aires—Racing Club 2, Celtic 1; play-off, Montevideo—Racing Club 1, Celtic 0).

1968 Estudiantes (Argentina) beat *Manchester United* (England) (In Buenos Aires—Estudiantes 1, Manchester United 0; in Manchester—Manchester United 1, Estudiantes 1).

1969 AC Milan (Italy) beat *Estudiantes* (Argentina) 4—2 on aggregate. (In Milan—AC Milan 3, Estudiantes 0, in Buenos Aires—Estudiantes 2, Milan 1).

1970 Feyenoord (Holland) beat *Estudiantes* (Argentina) 3—2 on aggregate. (In Buenos Aires—Estudiantes 2, Feyenoord 2; in Rotterdam—Feyenoord 1, Estudiantes 0).

1971 Nacional (Uruguay) beat *Panathinaikos* (Greece) 3—2 on aggregate. European Champions Ajax (Holland) declined to take part and were replaced by runners-up Panathinaikos. (In Athens—Panathinaikos 1, Nacional 1; in Montevideo—Nacional 2, Panathinaikos 1).

1972 Ajax Amsterdam (Holland) beat Independiente (Argentina) 4—1 on aggregate. (In Buenos Aires—Independiente 1, Ajax 1; in Amsterdam—Ajax 3, Independiente 0).

1973 Independiente (Argentina) beat Juventus (Italy) 1—0 in Rome—one match only. European Champions Ajax (Holland) declined to play, and runners-up Juventus substituted.

Records Section
ENGLAND'S COMPLETE RECORD IN FULL INTERNATIONALS

Key: WC = World Cup proper; WCQ = World Cup qualifying round; EC = European Championship proper; ECQ = European Championship qualifying round.

Date	Opponents	Venue	Result
Season 1872–73			
Nov. 30	Scotland	Glasgow	D 0–0
Mar. 8	Scotland	Oval	W 4–2
Season 1873–74			
Mar. 7	Scotland	Glasgow	L 1–2
Season 1874–75			
Mar 6	Scotland	Oval	D 2–2
Season 1875–76			
Mar. 4	Scotland	Glasgow	L 0–3
Season 1876–77			
Mar. 3	Scotland	Oval	L 1–3
Season 1877–78			
Mar. 2	Scotland	Glasgow	L 2–7
Season 1878–79			
Jan. 18	Wales	Oval	W 2–1
Apr. 5	Scotland	Oval	W 5–4
Season 1879–80			
Mar. 13	Scotland	Glasgow	L 4–5
Mar. 15	Wales	Wrexham	W 3–2
Season 1880–81			
Feb. 26	Wales	Blackburn	L 0–1
Mar. 12	Scotland	Oval	L 1–6
Season 1881–82			
Feb. 18	Ireland	Belfast	W 13–0
Mar. 11	Scotland	Glasgow	L 1–5
Mar. 13	Wales	Wrexham	L 3–5
Season 1882–83			
Feb. 3	Wales	Oval	W 5–0
Feb. 24	Ireland	Liverpool	W 7–0
Mar. 10	Scotland	Sheffield	L 2–3
Season 1883–84			
Feb. 23	Ireland	Belfast	W 8–1
Mar. 15	Scotland	Glasgow	L 0–1
Mar. 17	Wales	Wrexham	W 4–0

Date	Opponents	Venue	Result
		Season 1884–85	
Feb. 28	Ireland	Manchester	W 4–0
Mar. 14	Wales	Blackburn	D 1–1
Mar. 21	Scotland	Oval	D 1–1
		Season 1885–86	
Mar. 13	Ireland	Belfast	W 6–1
Mar. 29	Wales	Wrexham	W 3–1
Mar. 31	Scotland	Glasgow	D 1–1
		Season 1886–87	
Feb. 5	Ireland	Sheffield	W 7–0
Feb. 26	Wales	Oval	W 4–0
Mar. 19	Scotland	Blackburn	L 2–3
		Season 1887–88	
Feb. 4	Wales	Crewe	W 5–1
Mar. 17	Scotland	Glasgow	W 5–0
Mar. 31	Ireland	Belfast	W 5–1
		Season 1888–89	
Feb. 23	Wales	Stoke	W 4–1
Mar. 2	Ireland	Everton	W 6–1
Apr. 13	Scotland	Oval	L 2–3
		Season 1889–90	
Mar. 15	Wales	Wrexham	W 3–1
Mar. 15	Ireland	Belfast	W 9–1
Apr. 5	Scotland	Glasgow	D 1–1
		Season 1890–91	
Mar. 7	Wales	Sunderland	W 4–1
Mar. 7	Ireland	Wolverhampton	W 6–1
Apr. 6	Scotland	Blackburn	W 2–1
		Season 1891–92	
Mar. 5	Ireland	Belfast	W 2–0
Mar. 5	Wales	Wrexham	W 2–0
Apr. 2	Scotland	Glasgow	W 4–1
		Season 1892–93	
Feb. 25	Ireland	Birmingham	W 6–1
Mar. 13	Wales	Stoke	W 6–0
Apr. 1	Scotland	Richmond	W 5–2
		Season 1893–94	
Mar. 3	Ireland	Belfast	D 2–2
Mar. 12	Wales	Wrexham	W 5–1
Apr. 7	Scotland	Glasgow	D 2–2
		Season 1894–95	
Mar. 9	Ireland	Derby	W 9–0
Mar. 18	Wales	Kensington	D 1–1
Apr. 6	Scotland	Everton	W 3–0

Date	Opponents	Venue	Result
		Season 1895–96	
Mar. 7	Ireland	Belfast	W 2–0
Mar. 16	Wales	Cardiff	W 9–1
Apr. 4	Scotland	Glasgow	L 1–2
		Season 1896–97	
Feb. 20	Ireland	Nottingham	W 6–0
Mar. 29	Wales	Sheffield	W 4–0
Apr. 3	Scotland	Crystal Palace	L 1–2
		Season 1897–98	
Mar. 5	Ireland	Belfast	W 3–2
Mar. 28	Wales	Wrexham	W 3–0
Apr. 2	Scotland	Glasgow	W 3–1
		Season 1898–99	
Feb. 18	Ireland	Sunderland	W 13–2
Mar. 20	Wales	Bristol	W 4–0
Apr. 8	Scotland	Birmingham	W 2–1
		Season 1899–1900	
Mar. 17	Ireland	Dublin	W 2–0
Mar. 26	Wales	Cardiff	D 1–1
Apr. 7	Scotland	Glasgow	L 1–4
		Season 1900–01	
Mar. 9	Ireland	Southampton	W 3–0
Mar. 18	Wales	Newcastle	W 6–0
Mar. 30	Scotland	Crystal Palace	D 2–2
		Season 1901–02	
Mar. 3	Wales	Wrexham	D 0–0
Mar. 22	Ireland	Belfast	W 1–0
May 3	Scotland	Birmingham	D 2–2
		Season 1902–03	
Feb. 14	Ireland	Wolverhampton	W 4–0
Mar. 2	Wales	Portsmouth	W 2–1
Apr. 4	Scotland	Sheffield	L 1–2
		Season 1903–04	
Feb. 29	Wales	Wrexham	D 2–2
Mar. 12	Ireland	Belfast	W 3–1
Apr. 9	Scotland	Glasgow	W 1–0
		Season 1904–05	
Feb. 25	Ireland	Middlesbrough	D 1–1
Mar. 27	Wales	Liverpool	W 3–1
Apr 1	Scotland	Crystal Palace	W 1–0
		Season 1905–06	
Feb. 17	Ireland	Belfast	W 5–0
Mar. 19	Wales	Cardiff	W 1–0
Apr 7	Scotland	Glasgow	L 1–2

Date	Opponents	Venue	Result
		Season 1906–07	
Feb. 16	Ireland	Everton	W 1–0
Mar. 18	Wales	Fulham	D 1–1
Apr. 6	Scotland	Newcastle	D 1–1
		Season 1907–08	
Feb. 15	Ireland	Belfast	W 3–1
Mar. 16	Wales	Wrexham	W 7–1
Apr. 4	Scotland	Glasgow	D 1–1
June 6	Austria	Vienna	W 6–1
June 8	Austria	Vienna	W 11–1
June 10	Hungary	Budapest	W 7–0
June 13	Bohemia	Prague	W 4–0
		Season 1908–09	
Feb. 13	Ireland	Bradford	W 4–0
Mar. 15	Wales	Nottingham	W 2–0
Apr. 3	Scotland	Crystal Palace	W 2–0
May 29	Hungary	Budapest	W 4–2
May 31	Hungary	Budapest	W 8–2
June 1	Austria	Vienna	W 8–1
		Season 1909–10	
Feb. 12	Ireland	Belfast	D 1–1
Mar. 14	Wales	Cardiff	W 1–0
Apr. 2	Scotland	Glasgow	L 0–2
		Season 1910–11	
Feb. 11	Ireland	Derby	W 2–1
Mar. 13	Wales	Millwall	W 3–0
Apr. 1	Scotland	Everton	D 1–1
		Season 1911–12	
Feb. 10	Ireland	Dublin	W 6–1
Mar. 11	Wales	Wrexham	W 2–0
Mar. 23	Scotland	Glasgow	D 1–1
		Season 1912–13	
Feb. 15	Ireland	Belfast	L 1–2
Mar. 17	Wales	Bristol	W 4–3
Apr. 5	Scotland	Chelsea	W 1–0
		Season 1913–14	
Feb. 14	Ireland	Middlesbrough	L 0–3
Mar. 16	Wales	Cardiff	W 2–0
Apr. 4	Scotland	Glasgow	L 1–3
		Season 1919–20	
Oct. 25	Ireland	Belfast	D 1–1
Mar. 15	Wales	Highbury	L 1–2
Apr. 10	Scotland	Sheffield	W 5–4

Date	Opponents	Venue	Result
Season 1920–21			
Oct. 23	Ireland	Sunderland	W 2–0
Mar. 14	Wales	Cardiff	D 0–0
Apr. 9	Scotland	Glasgow	L 0–3
May 21	Belgium	Brussels	W 2–0
Season 1921–22			
Oct. 22	Ireland	Belfast	D 1–1
Mar. 13	Wales	Liverpool	W 1–0
Apr. 8	Scotland	Aston Villa	L 0–1
Season 1922–23			
Oct. 21	Ireland	West Bromwich	W 2–0
Mar. 5	Wales	Cardiff	D 2–2
Mar. 19	Belgium	Highbury	W 6–1
Apr. 14	Scotland	Glasgow	D 2–2
May 10	France	Paris	W 4–1
May 21	Sweden	Stockholm	W 4–2
May 24	Sweden	Stockholm	W 3–1
Season 1923–24			
Oct. 20	Ireland	Belfast	L 1–2
Nov. 1	Belgium	Antwerp	D 2–2
Mar. 3	Wales	Blackburn	L 1–2
Apr. 12	Scotland	Wembley	D 1–1
May 17	France	Paris	W 3–1
Season 1924–25			
Oct. 22	Ireland	Everton	W 3–1
Dec. 8	Belgium	West Bromwich	W 4–0
Feb. 28	Wales	Swansea	W 2–1
Apr. 4	Scotland	Glasgow	L 0–2
May 21	France	Paris	W 3–2
Season 1925–26			
Oct. 24	Ireland	Belfast	D 0–0
Mar. 1	Wales	Crystal Palace	L 1–3
Apr. 17	Scotland	Manchester	L 0–1
May 24	Belgium	Antwerp	W 5–3
Season 1926–27			
Oct. 20	Ireland	Liverpool	D 3–3
Feb. 12	Wales	Wrexham	D 3–3
Apr. 2	Scotland	Glasgow	W 2–1
May 11	Belgium	Brussels	W 9–1
May 21	Luxembourg	Luxembourg	W 5–2
May 26	France	Paris	W 6–0
Season 1927–28			
Nov. 22	Ireland	Belfast	L 0–2
Nov. 28	Wales	Burnley	L 1–2
Mar. 31	Scotland	Wembley	L 1–5

Date	Opponents	Venue	Result
May 17	France	Paris	W 5–1
May 19	Belgium	Antwerp	W 3–1

Season 1928–29

Date	Opponents	Venue	Result
Oct. 22	Ireland	Everton	W 2–1
Nov. 17	Wales	Swansea	W 3–2
Apr. 13	Scotland	Glasgow	L 0–1
May 9	France	Paris	W 4–1
May 11	Belgium	Brussels	W 5–1
May 15	Spain	Madrid	L 3–4

Season 1929–30

Date	Opponents	Venue	Result
Oct 19	Ireland	Belfast	W 3–0
Nov. 20	Wales	Chelsea	W 6–0
Apr. 5	Scotland	Wembley	W 5–2
May 10	Germany	Berlin	D 3–3
May 14	Austria	Vienna	D 0–0

Season 1930–31

Date	Opponents	Venue	Result
Oct 20	Ireland	Sheffield	W 5–1
Nov. 22	Wales	Wrexham	W 4–0
Mar. 31	Scotland	Glasgow	L 0–2
May 14	France	Paris	L 2–5
May 16	Belgium	Brussels	W 4–1

Season 1931–32

Date	Opponents	Venue	Result
Oct. 17	Ireland	Belfast	W 6–2
Nov. 18	Wales	Liverpool	W 3–1
Dec. 9	Spain	Highbury	W 7–1
Apr. 9	Scotland	Wembley	W 3–0

Season 1932–33

Date	Opponents	Venue	Result
Oct. 17	Ireland	Blackpool	W 1–0
Nov. 16	Wales	Wrexham	D 0–0
Dec. 7	Austria	Chelsea	W 4–3
Apr. 1	Scotland	Glasgow	L 1–2
May 13	Italy	Rome	D 1–1
May 20	Switzerland	Berne	W 4–0

Season 1933–34

Date	Opponents	Venue	Result
Oct. 14	Ireland	Belfast	W 3–0
Nov. 15	Wales	Newcastle	L 1–2
Dec. 6	France	Tottenham	W 4–1
Feb. 6	Ireland	Everton	W 2–1
Apr. 14	Scotland	Wembley	W 3–0
May 10	Hungary	Budapest	L 1–2
May 16	Czechoslovakia	Prague	L 1–2

Season 1934–35

Date	Opponents	Venue	Result
Sept. 29	Wales	Cardiff	W 4–0
Nov. 14	Italy	Highbury	W 3–2
Apr. 6	Scotland	Glasgow	L 0–2

Date	Opponents	Venue	Result
Season 1935–36			
Oct. 19	Ireland	Belfast	W 3–1
Dec. 4	Germany	Tottenham	W 3–0
Feb. 5	Wales	Wolverhampton	L 1–2
Apr. 4	Scotland	Wembley	D 1–1
May 6	Austria	Vienna	L 1–2
May 9	Belgium	Brussels	L 2–3
May 18	Holland	Amsterdam	W 1–0
Season 1936–37			
Oct. 17	Wales	Cardiff	L 1–2
Nov. 18	Ireland	Stoke	W 3–1
Dec. 2	Hungary	Highbury	W 6–2
Apr. 17	Scotland	Glasgow	L 1–3
May 14	Norway	Oslo	W 6–0
May 17	Sweden	Stockholm	W 4–0
May 20	Finland	Helsinki	W 8–0
Season 1937–38			
Oct. 23	Ireland	Belfast	W 5–1
Nov. 17	Wales	Middlesbrough	W 2–1
Dec. 1	Czechoslovakia	Tottenham	W 5–4
Apr. 9	Scotland	Wembley	L 0–1
May 14	Germany	Berlin	W 6–3
May 21	Switzerland	Zürich	L 1–2
May 26	France	Paris	W 4–2
Season 1938–39			
Oct. 22	Wales	Cardiff	L 2–4
Oct. 26	F.I.F.A.	Highbury	W 3–0
Nov. 9	Norway	Newcastle	W 4–0
Nov. 16	Ireland	Manchester	W 7–0
Apr. 15	Scotland	Glasgow	W 2–1
May 13	Italy	Milan	D 2–2
May 18	Yugoslavia	Belgrade	L 1–2
May 24	Rumania	Bucharest	W 2–0
Season 1946–47			
Sept. 28	Ireland	Belfast	W 7–2
Sept. 30	Rep. Ireland	Dublin	W 1–0
Nov. 13	Wales	Manchester	W 3–0
Nov. 27	Holland	Huddersfield	W 8–2
Apr. 12	Scotland	Wembley	D 1–1
May 3	France	Highbury	W 3–0
May 18	Switzerland	Zurich	L 0–1
May 25	Portugal	Lisbon	W 10–0
Season 1947–48			
Sept. 21	Belgium	Brussels	W 5–2
Oct. 18	Wales	Cardiff	W 3–0

Date	Opponents	Venue	Result
Nov. 5	Ireland	Everton	D 2–2
Nov. 19	Sweden	Highbury	W 4–2
Apr. 10	Scotland	Glasgow	W 2–0
May 16	Italy	Turin	W 4–0

Season 1948–49

Date	Opponents	Venue	Result
Sept. 26	Denmark	Copenhagen	D 0–0
Oct. 9	Ireland	Belfast	W 6–2
Nov. 10	Wales	Villa Park	W 1–0
Dec. 2	Switzerland	Highbury	W 6–0
Apr. 9	Scotland	Wembley	L 1–3
May 13	Sweden	Stockholm	L 1–3
May 18	Norway	Oslo	W 4–1
May 22	France	Paris	W 3–1

Season 1949–50

Date	Opponents	Venue	Result
Sept. 21	Rep. Ireland	Everton	L 0–2
Oct. 15	Wales	Cardiff	W 4–1 WCQ
Nov. 16	Ireland	Manchester	W 9–2 WCQ
Nov. 30	Italy	Tottenham	W 2–0
Apr. 15	Scotland	Glasgow	W 1–0 WCQ
May 14	Portugal	Lisbon	W 5–3
May 18	Belgium	Brussels	W 4–1
June 25	Chile	Rio de Janeiro	W 2–0 WC
June 29	U.S.A.	Belo Horizonte	L 0–1 WC
July 2	Spain	Rio de Janeiro	L 0–1 WC

Season 1950–51

Date	Opponents	Venue	Result
Oct. 7	Ireland	Belfast	W 4–1
Nov. 15	Wales	Sunderland	W 4–2
Nov. 22	Yugoslavia	Highbury	D 2–2
Apr. 14	Scotland	Wembley	L 2–3
May 9	Argentina	Wembley	W 2–1
May 19	Portugal	Everton	W 5–2

Season 1951–52

Date	Opponents	Venue	Result
Oct. 3	France	Highbury	D 2–2
Oct. 20	Wales	Cardiff	D 1–1
Nov. 14	Ireland	Villa Park	W 2–0
Nov. 28	Austria	Wembley	D 2–2
Apr. 5	Scotland	Glasgow	W 2–1
May 18	Italy	Florence	D 1–1
May 25	Austria	Vienna	W 3–2
May 28	Switzerland	Zürich	W 3–0

Season 1952–53

Date	Opponents	Venue	Result
Oct. 4	Ireland	Belfast	D 2–2
Nov. 12	Wales	Wembley	W 5–2
Nov. 26	Belgium	Wembley	W 5–0
Apr. 18	Scotland	Wembley	D 2–2

Date	Opponents	Venue	Result
May 17	Argentina	Buenos Aires	0–0
	(Abandoned after 23 min.—rain)		
May 24	Chile	Santiago	W 2–1
May 31	Uruguay	Montevideo	L 1–2
June 8	U.S.A.	New York	W 6–3

Season 1953–54

Date	Opponents	Venue	Result
Oct. 10	Wales	Cardiff	W 4–1 WCQ
Oct. 21	F.I.F.A.	Wembley	D 4–4
Nov. 11	Ireland	Everton	W 3–1 WCQ
Nov. 25	Hungary	Wembley	L 3–6
Apr. 3	Scotland	Glasgow	W 4–2 WCQ
May 16	Yugoslavia	Belgrade	L 0–1
May 23	Hungary	Budapest	L 1–7
June 17	Belgium	Basle	D 4–4 WC
June 20	Switzerland	Berne	W 2–0 WC
June 26	Uruguay	Basle	L 2–4 WC

Season 1954–55

Date	Opponents	Venue	Result
Oct. 2	Ireland	Belfast	W 2–0
Nov. 10	Wales	Wembley	W 3–2
Dec. 1	Germany	Wembley	W 3–1
Apr. 2	Scotland	Wembley	W 7–2
May 15	France	Paris	L 0–1
May 18	Spain	Madrid	D 1–1
May 22	Portugal	Oporto	L 1–3

Season 1955–56

Date	Opponents	Venue	Result
Oct. 2	Denmark	Copenhagen	W 5–1
Oct. 22	Wales	Cardiff	L 1–2
Nov. 2	Ireland	Wembley	W 3–0
Nov. 30	Spain	Wembley	W 4–1
Apr. 14	Scotland	Glasgow	D 1–1
May 9	Brazil	Wembley	W 4–2
May 16	Sweden	Stockholm	D 0–0
May 20	Finland	Helsinki	W 5–1
May 26	Germany	Berlin	W 3–1

Season 1956–57

Date	Opponents	Venue	Result
Oct. 6	Ireland	Belfast	D 1–1
Nov. 14	Wales	Wembley	W 3–1
Nov. 28	Yugoslavia	Wembley	W 3–0
Dec. 5	Denmark	Wolverhampton	W 5–2 WCQ
Apr. 6	Scotland	Wembley	W 2–1
May 8	Rep. Ireland	Wembley	W 5–1 WCQ
May 15	Denmark	Copenhagen	W 4–1 WCQ
May 19	Rep. Ireland	Dublin	D 1–1 WCQ

Season 1957–58

Date	Opponents	Venue	Result
Oct. 19	Wales	Cardiff	W 4–0

Date	Opponents	Venue	Result
Nov. 6	Ireland	Wembley	L 2–3
Nov. 27	France	Wembley	W 4–0
Apr. 19	Scotland	Glasgow	W 4–0
May 7	Portugal	Wembley	W 2–1
May 11	Yugoslavia	Belgrade	L 0–5
May 18	Russia	Moscow	D 1–1
June 8	Russia	Gothenburg	D 2–2 WC
June 11	Brazil	Gothenburg	D 0–0 WC
June 15	Austria	Boras	D 2–2 WC
June 17	Russia	Gothenburg	L 0–1 WC

Season 1958–59

Date	Opponents	Venue	Result
Oct. 4	Ireland	Belfast	D 3–3
Oct. 22	Russia	Wembley	W 5–0
Nov. 26	Wales	Villa Park	D 2–2
Apr. 11	Scotland	Wembley	W 1–0
May 6	Italy	Wembley	D 2–2
May 13	Brazil	Rio de Janeiro	L 0–2
May 17	Peru	Lima	L 1–4
May 24	Mexico	Mexico City	L 1–2
May 28	U.S.A.	Los Angeles	W 8–1

Season 1959–60

Date	Opponents	Venue	Result
Oct. 17	Wales	Cardiff	D 1–1
Oct. 28	Sweden	Wembley	L 2–3
Nov. 18	Ireland	Wembley	W 2–1
Apr. 9	Scotland	Glasgow	D 1–1
May 11	Yugoslavia	Wembley	D 3–3
May 15	Spain	Madrid	L 0–3
May 22	Hungary	Budapest	L 0–2

Season 1960–61

Date	Opponents	Venue	Result
Oct. 8	Ireland	Belfast	W 5–2
Oct. 19	Luxembourg	Luxembourg	W 9–0 WCQ
Oct. 26	Spain	Wembley	W 4–2
Nov. 23	Wales	Wembley	W 5–1
Apr. 15	Scotland	Wembley	W 9–3
May 10	Mexico	Wembley	W 8–0
May 21	Portugal	Lisbon	D 1–1 WCQ
May 24	Italy	Rome	W 3–2
May 27	Austria	Vienna	L 1–3

Season 1961–62

Date	Opponents	Venue	Result
Sept. 28	Luxembourg	Highbury	W 4–1 WCQ
Oct. 14	Wales	Cardiff	D 1–1
Oct. 25	Portugal	Wembley	W 2–0 WCQ
Nov. 22	Ireland	Wembley	D 1–1
Apr. 4	Austria	Wembley	W 3–1
Apr. 14	Scotland	Glasgow	L 0–2
May 9	Switzerland	Wembley	W 3–1

Date	Opponents	Venue	Result
May 20	Peru	Lima	W 4–0
May 31	Hungary	Rancagua	L 1–2 WC
June 2	Argentina	Rancagua	W 3–1 WC
June 7	Bulgaria	Rancagua	D 0–0 WC
June 10	Brazil	Vina del Mar	L 1–3 WC

Season 1962–63

Date	Opponents	Venue	Result
Oct. 3	France	Sheffield	D 1–1 ECQ
Oct. 20	Ireland	Belfast	W 3–1
Nov. 21	Wales	Wembley	W 4–0
Feb. 27	France	Paris	L 2–5 ECQ
Apr. 6	Scotland	Wembley	L 1–2
May 8	Brazil	Wembley	D 1–1
May 29	Czechoslovakia	Bratislava	W 4–2
June 2	East Germany	Leipzig	W 2–1
June 5	Switzerland	Basle	W 8–1

Season 1963–64

Date	Opponents	Venue	Result
Oct. 12	Wales	Cardiff	W 4–0
Oct. 23	F.I.F.A.	Wembley	W 2–1
Nov. 20	Ireland	Wembley	W 8–3
Apr. 11	Scotland	Glasgow	L 0–1
May 6	Uruguay	Wembley	W 2–1
May 17	Portugal	Lisbon	W 4–3
May 24	Rep. Ireland	Dublin	W 3–1
May 27	U.S.A.	New York	W 10–0
May 30	Brazil	Rio de Janeiro	L 1–5
June 4	Portugal	Sao Paulo	D 1–1
June 6	Argentina	Rio de Janeiro	L 0–1

Season 1964–65

Date	Opponents	Venue	Result
Oct. 3	Ireland	Belfast	W 4–3
Oct. 21	Belgium	Wembley	D 2–2
Nov. 18	Wales	Wembley	W 2–1
Dec. 9	Holland	Amsterdam	D 1–1
Apr. 10	Scotland	Wembley	D 2–2
May 5	Hungary	Wembley	W 1–0
May 9	Yugoslavia	Belgrade	D 1–1
May 12	West Germany	Nuremberg	W 1–0
May 16	Sweden	Gothenburg	W 2–1

Season 1965–66

Date	Opponents	Venue	Result
Oct. 2	Wales	Cardiff	D 0–0
Oct. 20	Austria	Wembley	L 2–3
Nov. 10	Ireland	Wembley	W 2–1
Dec. 8	Spain	Madrid	W 2–0
Jan. 5	Poland	Everton	D 1–1
Feb. 23	West Germany	Wembley	W 1–0
Apr. 2	Scotland	Glasgow	W 4–3

Date	Opponents	Venue	Result
May 4	Yugoslavia	Wembley	W 2–0
June 26	Finland	Helsinki	W 3–0
June 29	Norway	Oslo	W 6–1
July 3	Denmark	Copenhagen	W 2–0
July 5	Poland	Chorzow	W 1–0
July 11	Uruguay	Wembley	D 0–0 WC
July 16	Mexico	Wembley	W 2–0 WC
July 20	France	Wembley	W 2–0 WC
July 23	Argentina	Wembley	W 1–0 WC
July 26	Portugal	Wembley	W 2–1 WC
July 30	West Germany	Wembley	W 4–2 WC

Season 1966–67

Date	Opponents	Venue	Result
Oct. 22	Ireland	Belfast	W 2–0 ECQ
Nov. 2	Czechoslovakia	Wembley	D 0–0
Nov. 16	Wales	Wembley	W 5–1 ECQ
Apr. 15	Scotland	Wembley	L 2–3 ECQ
May 24	Spain	Wembley	W 2–0
May 27	Austria	Vienna	W 1–0

Season 1967–68

Date	Opponents	Venue	Result
Oct. 21	Wales	Cardiff	W 3–0 ECQ
Nov. 22	Ireland	Wembley	W 2–0 ECQ
Dec. 6	Russia	Wembley	D 2–2
Feb. 24	Scotland	Glasgow	D 1–1 ECQ
Apr. 3	Spain	Wembley	W 1–0 EC
May 8	Spain	Madrid	W 2–1 EC
May 22	Sweden	Wembley	W 3–1
June 1	West Germany	Hanover	L 0–1
June 5	Yugoslavia	Florence	L 0–1 EC
June 8	Russia	Rome	W 2–0 EC

Season 1968–69

Date	Opponents	Venue	Result
Nov. 6	Rumania	Bucharest	D 0–0
Dec. 11	Bulgaria	Wembley	D 1–1
Jan. 15	Rumania	Wembley	D 1–1
Mar. 12	France	Wembley	W 5–0
May 3	Ireland	Belfast	W 3–1
May 7	Wales	Wembley	W 2–1
May 10	Scotland	Wembley	W 4–1
June 1	Mexico	Mexico City	D 0–0
June 8	Uruguay	Montevideo	W 2–1
June 12	Brazil	Rio de Janeiro	L 1–2

Season 1969–70

Date	Opponents	Venue	Result
Nov. 5	Holland	Amsterdam	W 1–0
Dec. 10	Portugal	Wembley	W 1–0
Jan. 14	Holland	Wembley	D 0–0
Feb. 25	Belgium	Brussels	W 3–1

Date	Opponents	Venue	Result
Apr. 18	Wales	Cardiff	D 1–1
Apr. 21	Ireland	Wembley	W 3–1
Apr. 25	Scotland	Glasgow	D 0–0
May 20	Colombia	Bogota	W 4–0
May 24	Ecuador	Quito	W 2–0
June 2	Rumania	Guadalajara	W 1–0 WC
June 7	Brazil	Guadalajara	L 0–1 WC
June 11	Czechoslovakia	Guadalajara	W 1–0 WC
June 14	West Germany	Leon	L 2–3 WC

Season 1970–71

Date	Opponents	Venue	Result
Nov. 25	East Germany	Wembley	W 3–1
Feb. 3	Malta	Valletta	W 1–0 ECQ
Apr. 21	Greece	Wembley	W 3–0 ECQ
May 12	Malta	Wembley	W 5–0 ECQ
May 15	Ireland	Belfast	W 1–0
May 19	Wales	Wembley	D 0–0
May 22	Scotland	Wembley	W 3–1

Season 1971–72

Date	Opponents	Venue	Result
Oct. 13	Switzerland	Basle	W 3–2 ECQ
Nov. 10	Switzerland	Wembley	D 1–1 ECQ
Dec. 1	Greece	Athens	W 2–0 ECQ
Apr. 29	West Germany	Wembley	L 1–3 EC
May 13	West Germany	Berlin	D 0–0 EC
May 20	Wales	Cardiff	W 3–0
May 23	Ireland	Wembley	L 0–1
May 27	Scotland	Glasgow	W 1–0

Season 1972–73

Date	Opponents	Venue	Result
Oct. 11	Yugoslavia	Wembley	D 1–1
Nov. 15	Wales	Cardiff	W 1–0 WCQ
Jan. 24	Wales	Wembley	D 1–1 WCQ
Feb. 14	Scotland	Glasgow	W 5–0
May 12	Ireland	Everton	W 2–1
May 15	Wales	Wembley	W 3–0
May 19	Scotland	Wembley	W 1–0
May 27	Czechoslovakia	Prague	D 1–1
June 6	Poland	Chorzow	L 0–2 WCQ
June 10	Russia	Moscow	W 2–1
June 14	Italy	Turin	L 0–2

Season 1973–74

Date	Opponents	Venue	Result
Sept. 26	Austria	Wembley	W 7–0
Oct. 17	Poland	Wembley	D 1–1 WCQ
Nov. 14	Italy	Wembley	L 0–1
Apr. 3	Portugal	Lisbon	D 0–0

FOOTBALL LEAGUE CHAMPIONS AND THEIR RECORDS

Season	Champions	P	W	D	L	F	A	Pts
1888–89	Preston N.E.	22	18	4	0	74	15	40
1889–90	Preston N.E	22	15	3	4	71	30	33
1890–91	Everton	22	14	1	7	63	29	29
1891–92	Sunderland	26	21	0	5	93	36	42
1892–93	Sunderland	30	22	4	4	100	36	48
1893–94	Aston Villa	30	19	6	5	84	42	44
1894–95	Sunderland	30	21	5	4	80	37	47
1895–96	Aston Villa	30	20	5	5	78	45	45
1896–97	Aston Villa	30	21	5	4	73	38	47
1897–98	Sheffield Utd.	30	17	8	5	56	31	42
1898–99	Aston Villa	34	19	7	8	76	40	45
1899–1900	Aston Villa	34	22	6	6	77	35	50
1900–01	Liverpool	34	19	7	8	59	35	45
1901–02	Sunderland	34	19	6	9	50	35	44
1902–03	Sheffield Wed.	34	19	4	11	54	36	42
1903–04	Sheffield Wed.	34	20	7	7	48	28	47
1904–05	Newcastle Utd.	34	23	2	9	72	33	48
1905–06	Liverpool	38	23	5	10	79	46	51
1906–07	Newcastle Utd.	38	22	7	9	74	46	51
1907–08	Manchester Utd.	38	23	6	9	81	48	52
1908–09	Newcastle Utd.	38	24	5	9	65	41	53
1909–10	Aston Villa	38	23	7	8	84	42	53
1910–11	Manchester Utd.	38	22	8	8	72	40	52
1911–12	Blackburn Rov.	38	20	9	9	60	43	49
1912–13	Sunderland	38	25	4	9	86	43	54
1913–14	Blackburn Rov.	38	20	11	7	78	42	51
1914–15	Everton	38	19	8	11	76	47	46
1915–19	No competition—First World War							
1919–20	West Brom. Albion	42	28	4	10	104	47	60
1920–21	Burnley	42	23	13	6	79	36	59
1921–22	Liverpool	42	22	13	7	63	36	57
1922–23	Liverpool	42	26	8	8	70	31	60
1923–24	Huddersfield Town	42	23	11	8	60	33	57
1924–25	Huddersfield Town	42	21	16	5	69	28	58
1925–26	Huddersfield Town	42	23	11	8	92	60	57
1926–27	Newcastle Utd.	42	25	6	11	96	58	56
1927–28	Everton	42	20	13	9	102	66	53
1928–29	Sheffield Wed.	42	21	10	11	86	62	52
1929–30	Sheffield Wed.	42	26	8	8	105	57	60
1930–31	Arsenal	42	28	10	4	127	59	66
1931–32	Everton	42	26	4	12	116	64	56
1932–33	Arsenal	42	25	8	9	118	61	58
1933–34	Arsenal	42	25	9	8	75	47	59
1934–35	Arsenal	42	23	12	7	115	46	58

Season	Champions	P	W	D	L	F	A	Pts
1935–36	Sunderland	42	25	6	11	109	74	56
1936–37	Manchester City	42	22	13	7	107	61	57
1937–38	Arsenal	42	21	10	11	77	44	52
1938–39	Everton	42	27	5	10	88	52	59
1939–46	No competition—Second World War							
1946–47	Liverpool	42	25	7	10	84	52	57
1947–48	Arsenal	42	23	13	6	81	32	59
1948–49	Portsmouth	42	25	8	9	84	42	58
1949–50	Portsmouth	42	22	9	11	74	38	53
1950–51	Tottenham Hotspur	42	25	10	7	82	44	60
1951–52	Manchester Utd.	42	23	11	8	95	52	57
1952–53	Arsenal	42	21	12	9	97	64	54
1953–54	Wolverhampton W.	42	25	7	10	96	56	57
1954–55	Chelsea	42	20	12	10	81	57	52
1955–56	Manchester Utd	42	25	10	7	83	51	60
1956–57	Manchester Utd	42	28	8	6	103	54	64
1957–58	Wolverhampton W.	42	28	8	6	103	47	64
1958–59	Wolverhampton W	42	28	5	9	110	49	61
1959–60	Burnley	42	24	7	11	85	61	55
1960–61	Tottenham Hotspur	42	31	4	7	115	55	66
1961–62	Ipswich Town	42	24	8	10	93	67	56
1962–63	Everton	42	25	11	6	84	42	61
1963–64	Liverpool	42	26	5	11	92	45	57
1964–65	Manchester Utd.	42	26	9	7	89	39	61
1965–66	Liverpool	42	26	9	7	79	34	61
1966–67	Manchester Utd.	42	24	12	6	84	45	60
1967–68	Manchester City	42	26	6	10	86	43	58
1968–69	Leeds United	42	27	13	2	66	26	67
1969–70	Everton	42	29	8	5	72	34	66
1970–71	Arsenal	42	29	7	6	71	29	65
1971–72	Derby County	42	24	10	8	69	33	58
1972–73	Liverpool	42	25	10	7	72	42	60
1973–74	Leeds United	42	24	14	4	66	31	62

Summary of Champions

Arsenal	8	Sheffield Wed.	4	Portsmouth	
Liverpool	8	Huddersfield	3	Preston	
Everton	7	Wolves	3	Tottenham	
Manchester Utd.	7	Blackburn	2	Chelsea	
Aston Villa	6	Burnley	2	Derby County	
Sunderland	6	Leeds	2	Ipswich	
Newcastle	4	Manchester City	2	Sheffield Utd.	
				West Bromwich	

F.A. CUP WINNERS

Cup Final venues:

1872–92	Kennington Oval (except 1873 — at Lillie Bridge, London)	1895–1914	Crystal Palace
		1915	Old Trafford, Manchester
1893	Fallowfield, Manchester	1920–22	Stamford Bridge
1894	Anfield, Liverpool	1923 to date	Wembley

* = Replay; † = After extra time

Season	Winners	Runners-up	Result	Attendance
1871–72	Wanderers	Royal Engineers	1–0	2,000
1872–73	Wanderers	Oxford University	2–0	3,000
1873–74	Oxford University	Royal Engineers	2–0	2,500
1874–75	Royal Engineers	Old Etonians	*2–0 (after 1–1 draw)	3,000
875–76	Wanderers	Old Etonians	*3–0 (after 0–0 draw)	4,000
1876–77	Wanderers	Oxford University	†2–0	3,000
1877–78	Wanderers	Royal Engineers	3–1	5,000
1878–79	Old Etonians	Clapham Rovers	1–0	5,000
1879–80	Clapham Rovers	Oxford University	1–0	6,000
1880–81	Old Carthusians	Old Etonians	3–0	4,000
1881–82	Old Etonians	Blackburn R	1–0	7,000
1882–83	Blackburn Olympic	Old Etonians	†2–1	8,000
1883–84	Blackburn R	Queen's Park, Glasgow	2–1	4,000
1884–85	Blackburn R.	Queen's Park Glasgow	2–0	12,500
1885–86	Blackburn R.	W.B.A.	*2–0	15,000
	(Replay at Derby — after 0–0 draw)			
1886–87	Aston Villa	W.B.A.	2–0	16,000
1887–88	W.B.A.	Preston N.E	2–1	19,000
1888–89	Preston N.E.	Wolves	3–0	22,000
1889–90	Blackburn R.	Sheffield Wed.	6–1	20,000
1890–91	Blackburn R.	Notts County	3–1	23,000
1891–92	W.B.A.	Aston Villa	3–0	25,000
1892–93	Wolves	Everton	1–0	45,000
1893–94	Notts County	Bolton W.	4–1	37,000
1894–95	Aston Villa	W.B.A.	1–0	42,500

Season	Winners	Runners-up	Result	Attendance
1895–96	Sheffield Wed.	Wolves	2–1	49,000
1896–97	Aston Villa	Everton	3–2	66,000
1897–98	Nott'm Forest	Derby County	3–1	62,000
1898–99	Sheffield Utd	Derby County	4–1	74,000
1899–1900	Bury	Southampton	4–0	69,000
1900–01	Tottenham H.	Sheffield Utd.	*3–1	30,000

(Replay at Bolton—after 2–2 draw, att: 110,820)

1901–02	Sheffield Utd.	Southampton	*2–1	33,000

(Replay at Crystal Palace—after 1–1 draw, att: 77,000)

1902–03	Bury	Derby County	6–0	63,000
1903–04	Manchester C.	Bolton W.	1–0	61,000
1904–05	Aston Villa	Newcastle U.	2–0	101,000
1905–06	Everton	Newcastle U.	1–0	76,000
1906–07	Sheffield Wed.	Everton	2–1	84,500
1907–08	Wolves	Newcastle U.	3–1	75,000
1908–09	Manchester U.	Bristol City	1–0	68,000
1909–10	Newcastle U.	Barnsley	*2–0	69,000

(Replay at Goodison Park, Everton—after 1–1 draw, att: 78,000)

1910–11	Bradford City	Newcastle U.	*1–0	58,000

(Replay at Old Trafford, Manchester—after 0–0 draw, att: 69,000)

1911–12	Barnsley	W.B.A.	*1–0	38,500

(Replay at Bramall Lane, Sheffield—after 0–0 draw, att: 54,500)

1912–13	Aston Villa	Sunderland	1–0	120,000
1913–14	Burnley	Liverpool	1–0	73,000
1914–15	Sheffield U	Chelsea	3–0	50,000
1915–19	No competition—First World War			
1919–20	Aston Villa	Huddersfield T.	†1–0	50,000
1920–21	Tottenham H.	Wolves	1–0	73,000
1921–22	Huddersfield T.	Preston N.E.	1–0	53,000

Results, with scorers, since the F.A. Cup Final has been played at Wembley

Season	Winners	Runners-up	Result	Attendance
1922–23	Bolton W *(Jack, J. R. Smith)*	West Ham U.	2–0	126,047
1923–24	Newcastle U *(Harris, Seymour)*	Aston Villa	2–0	92,000
1924–25	Sheffield Utd. *(Tunstall)*	Cardiff City	1–0	92,000
1925–26	Bolton W. *(Jack)*	Manchester C.	1–0	91,500
1926–27	Cardiff City *(Ferguson)*	Arsenal	1–0	91,000
1927–28	Blackburn R. *(Roscamp 2, McLean)*	Huddersfield T. *(Jackson)*	3–1	92,000

Season	Winners	Runners-up	Result	Attendance
1928–29	Bolton W (Butler, Blackmore)	Portsmouth	2–0	92,500
1929–30	Arsenal (James, Lambert)	Huddersfield T.	2–0	92,500
1930–31	W.B.A. (W. G. Richardson)	Birmingham (Bradford)	2–1	92,500
1931–32	Newcastle U. (Allen 2)	Arsenal (John)	2–1	92,000
1932–33	Everton (Stein, Dean, Dunn)	Manchester City	3–0	93,000
1933–34	Manchester C. (Tilson 2)	Portsmouth (Rutherford)	2–1	93,500
1934–35	Sheffield Wed. (Rimmer 2, Palethorpe, Hooper)	W.B.A. (Boyes, Sandford)	4–2	93,000
1935–36	Arsenal (Drake)	Sheffield Utd.	1–0	93,500
1936–37	Sunderland (Gurney, Carter, Burbanks)	Preston N.E. (F. O'Donnell)	3–1	93,500
1937–38	Preston N.E. (Mutch—pen.)	Huddersfield T.	†1–0	93,500
1938–39	Portsmouth (Parker 2, Barlow, Anderson)	Wolves (Dorsett)	4–1	99,000
1939–45	No competition—Second World War			
1945–46	Derby County (H. Turner own goal, Doherty, Stamps 2)	Charlton A. (H. Turner)	†4–1	98,000
1946–47	Charlton A. (Duffy)	Burnley	†1–0	98,000
1947–48	Manchester U. (Rowley 2, Pearson, Anderson)	Blackpool (Shimwell—pen., Mortensen)	4–2	99,000
1948–49	Wolves (Pye 2, Smyth)	Leicester City (Griffiths)	3–1	100,000

Season	Winners	Runners-up	Result	Attendance
1949–50	Arsenal *(Lewis 2)*	Liverpool	2–0	100,000
1950–51	Newcastle U. *(Milburn 2)*	Blackpool	2–0	100,000
1951–52	Newcastle U. *(G. Robledo)*	Arsenal	1–0	100,000
1952–53	Blackpool *(Mortensen 3, Perry)*	Bolton W. *(Lofthouse, Moir, Bell)*	4–3	100,000
1953–54	W.B.A. *(Allen 2—1 pen., Griffin)*	Preston N.E. *(Morrison, Wayman)*	3–2	100,000
1954–55	Newcastle U. *(Milburn, Mitchell, Hannah)*	Manchester C. *(Johnstone)*	3–1	100,000
1955–56	Manchester C. *(Hayes, Dyson, Johnstone)*	Birmingham C. *(Kinsey)*	3–1	100,000
1956–57	Aston Villa *(McParland 2)*	Manchester U. *(Taylor)*	2–1	100,000
1957–58	Bolton W. *(Lofthouse 2)*	Manchester U.	2–0	100,000
1958–59	Nott'm Forest *(Dwight, Wilson)*	Luton Town *(Pacey)*	2–1	100,000
1959–60	Wolves *(McGrath own goal, Deeley 2)*	Blackburn R.	3–0	100,000
1960–61	Tottenham H. *(Smith, Dyson)*	Leicester C.	2–0	100,000
1961–62	Tottenham *(Greaves, Smith, Blanchflower *pen.)*	Burnley *(Robson)*	3–1	100,000
1962–63	Manchester U. *(Law, Herd 2)*	Leicester C. *(Keyworth)*	3–1	100,000
1963–64	West Ham U. *(Sissons, Hurst, Boyce)*	Preston N.E. *(Holden, Dawson)*	3–2	100,000
1964–65	Liverpool *(Hunt, St. John)*	Leeds United *(Bremner)*	†2–1	100,000

Season	Winners	Runners-up	Result	Attendance
1965–66	Everton (Trebilcock 2, Temple)	Sheffield Wed. (McCalliog, Ford)	3–2	100,000
1966–67	Tottenham H. (Robertson, Saul)	Chelsea (Tambling)	2–1	100,000
1967–68	W.B.A. (Astle)	Everton	†1–0	100,000
1968–69	Manchester C. (Young)	Leicester City	1–0	100,000
1969–70	Chelsea	Leeds United	*†2–1	62,000

(Replay at Old Trafford, Manchester—after †2–2 draw at Wembley—att:—100,000)

Scorers at Wembley Chelsea: *Houseman, Hutchinson.* Leeds: *Charlton, Jones.*

Scorers in replay Chelsea: *Osgood, Webb.* Leeds: *Jones*

Season	Winners	Runners-up	Result	Attendance
1970–71	Arsenal (Kelly, George)	Liverpool (Heighway)	†2–1	100,000
1971–72	Leeds Utd. (Clarke)	Arsenal	1–0	100,000
1972–73	Sunderland (Porterfield)	Leeds United	1–0	100,000
1973–74	Liverpool (Keegan 2, Heighway)	Newcastle	3–0	100,000

Summary of F.A. Cup Winners

Aston Villa	7	Sheffield Wed.	3	Cardiff	1
Blackburn	6	Bury	2	Charlton	1
Newcastle	6	Liverpool	2	Chelsea	1
Tottenham	5	Nottingham F.	2	Clapham Rovers	1
Wanderers	5	Old Etonians	2	Derby	1
West Bromwich	5	Preston	2	Huddersfield	1
Arsenal	4	Sunderland	2	Leeds Utd.	1
Bolton	4	Barnsley	1	Notts Co.	1
Manchester City	4	Blackburn Olympic	1	Old Carthusians	1
Sheffield Utd.	4	Blackpool	1	Oxford	1
Wolves	4	Bradford C.	1	Portsmouth	1
Everton	3	Burnley	1	Royal Engineers	1
Manchester U.	3			West Ham Univ.	1

FOOTBALL LEAGUE CUP WINNERS

For the first six seasons, before the fixture was taken to Wembley, the Football League Cup Final was played on a home-and-away basis.

Season	Winners	Runners-up	Aggregate	Home	Away
1960–61	Aston Villa	Rotherham U	3–2	3–0	0–2
1961–62	Norwich City	Rochdale	4–0	1–0	3–0
1962–63	Birmingham	Aston Villa	3–1	3–1	0–0
1963–64	Leicester	Stoke City	4–3	3–2	1–1
1964–65	Chelsea	Leicester	3–2	3–2	0–0
1965–66	West Brom.	West Ham	5–3	4–1	1–2

Results, with scorers, of League Cup Finals at Wembley:

Season	Winners	Runners-up	Result	Attendance
1966–67	Q.P.R. *(R. Morgan, Marsh, Lazarus)*	W.B.A. *(Clark 2)*	3–2	97,952
1967–68	Leeds United *(Cooper)*	Arsenal	1–0	100,000
1968–69	Swindon *(Rogers 2, Smart)*	Arsenal *(Gould)*	†3–1	100,000
1969–70	Man. City *(Doyle, Pardoe)*	W.B.A. *(Astle)*	†2–1	100,000
1970–71	Tottenham *(Chivers 2)*	Aston Villa	2–0	100,000
1971–72	Stoke City *(Conroy, Eastham)*	Chelsea *(Osgood)*	2–1	100,000
1972–73	Tottenham *(Coates)*	Norwich City	1–0	100,000
1973–74	Wolves *(Hibbitt, Richards)*	Man. City *(Bell)*	2–1	100,000

(† = After extra time)

SCOTTISH LEAGUE CHAMPIONS

Season		Points	Season		Points
1890–91	Rangers / Dumbarton	29	1928–29	Rangers	67
			1929–30	Rangers	60
1891–92	Dumbarton	37	1930–31	Rangers	60
1892–93	Celtic	29	1931–32	Motherwell	66
1893–94	Celtic	29	1932–33	Rangers	62
1894–95	Hearts	31	1933–34	Rangers	66
1895–96	Celtic	30	1934–35	Rangers	55
1896–97	Hearts	28	1935–36	Celtic	66
1897–98	Celtic	33	1936–37	Rangers	61
1898–99	Rangers	36	1937–38	Celtic	61
1899–1900	Rangers	32	1938–39	Rangers	59
1900–01	Rangers	35	1939–46	*No competition*	
1901–02	Rangers	28	1946–47	Rangers	46
1902–03	Hibernian	37	1947–48	Hibernian	48
1903–04	Third Lanark	43	1948–49	Rangers	46
1904–05	Celtic	41	1949–50	Rangers	50
1905–06	Celtic	49	1950–51	Hibernian	48
1906–07	Celtic	55	1951–52	Hibernian	45
1907–08	Celtic	55	1952–53	Rangers	43
1908–09	Celtic	51	1953–54	Celtic	43
1909–10	Celtic	54	1954–55	Aberdeen	49
1910–11	Rangers	52	1955–56	Rangers	52
1911–12	Rangers	51	1956–57	Rangers	55
1912–13	Rangers	53	1957–58	Hearts	62
1913–14	Celtic	65	1958–59	Rangers	50
1914–15	Celtic	65	1959–60	Hearts	54
1915–16	Celtic	67	1960–61	Rangers	51
1916–17	Celtic	64	1961–62	Dundee	54
1917–18	Rangers	56	1962–63	Rangers	57
1918–19	Celtic	58	1963–64	Rangers	55
1919–20	Rangers	71	1964–65	Kilmarnock	50
1920–21	Rangers	76	1965–66	Celtic	57
1921–22	Celtic	67	1966–67	Celtic	58
1922–23	Rangers	55	1967–68	Celtic	63
1923–24	Rangers	59	1968–69	Celtic	54
1924–25	Rangers	60	1969–70	Celtic	57
1925–26	Celtic	58	1970–71	Celtic	56
1926–27	Rangers	56	1971–72	Celtic	60
1927–28	Rangers	60	1972–73	Celtic	57
			1973–74	Celtic	53

Summary of Scottish League Champions

Rangers	*34	Dumbarton	*2	Kilmarnock	1
Celtic	29	Aberdeen	1	Motherwell	1
Hearts	4	Dundee	1	Third Lanark	1
Hibernian	4				

(*Includes one shared title)

SCOTTISH F.A. CUP WINNERS

(* = Replay)

Season	Winners	Runners-up	Result
1873–74	Queen's Park	Clydesdale	2–0
1874–75	Queen's Park	Renton	3–0
1875–76	Queen's Park	Third Lanark	*2–0 (after 1–1 draw)
1876–77	Vale of Leven	Rangers	*3–2 (after 0–0, 1–1 draws)
1877–78	Vale of Leven	Third Lanark	1–0
1878–79	Vale of Leven	(Rangers did not appear for replay after 1–1 draw)	
1879–80	Queen's Park	Thornlibank	3–0
1880–81	Queen's Park	Dumbarton	3–1
1881–82	Queen's Park	Dumbarton	*4–1 (after 2–2 draw)
1882–83	Dumbarton	Vale of Leven	*2–1 (after 2–2 draw)
1883–84	Queen's Park	(Vale of Leven did not appear for Final)	
1884–85	Renton	Vale of Leven	*3–1 (after 0–0 draw)
1885–86	Queen's Park	Renton	3–1
1886–87	Hibernian	Dumbarton	2–1
1887–88	Renton	Cambuslang	6–1
1888–89	Third Lanark	Celtic	2–1
1889–90	Queen's Park	Vale of Leven	*2–1 (after 1–1 draw)
1890–91	Hearts	Dumbarton	1–0
1891–92	Celtic	Queen's Park	5–1
1892–93	Queen's Park	Celtic	2–1
1893–94	Rangers	Celtic	3–1
1894–95	St Bernard's	Renton	2–1
1895–96	Hearts	Hibernian	3–1
1896–97	Rangers	Dumbarton	5–1
1897–98	Rangers	Kilmarnock	2–0
1898–99	Celtic	Rangers	2–0
1899–1900	Celtic	Queen's Park	4–3
1900–01	Hearts	Celtic	4–3
1901–02	Hibernian	Celtic	1–0
1902–03	Rangers	Hearts	*2–0 (after 1–1, 0–0 draws)
1903–04	Celtic	Rangers	3–2
1904–05	Third Lanark	Rangers	*3–1 (after 0–0 draw)

Season	Winners	Runners-up	Result
1905–06	Hearts	Third Lanark	1–0
1906–07	Celtic	Hearts	3–0
1907–08	Celtic	St Mirren	5–1
1908–09	*Cup withheld because of riot following two drawn games (2–2, 1–1) between Celtic and Rangers.*		
1909–10	Dundee	Clyde	*2–1 (after 2–2, 0–0 draws)
1910–11	Celtic	Hamilton	*2–0 (after 0–0 draw)
1911–12	Celtic	Clyde	2–0
1912–13	Falkirk	Raith Rovers	2–0
1913–14	Celtic	Hibernian	*4–1 (after 0–0 draw)
1914–19	*No competition*		
1919–20	Kilmarnock	Albion Rovers	3–2
1920–21	Partick Thistle	Rangers	1–0
1921–22	Morton	Rangers	1–0
1922–23	Celtic	Hibernian	1–0
1923–24	Airdrieonians	Hibernian	2–0
1924–25	Celtic	Dundee	2–1
1925–26	St Mirren	Celtic	2–0
1926–27	Celtic	East Fife	3–1
1927–28	Rangers	Celtic	4–0
1928–29	Kilmarnock	Rangers	2–0
1929–30	Rangers	Partick Thistle	*2–1 (after 0–0 draw)
1930–31	Celtic	Motherwell	*4–2 (after 2–2 draw)
1931–32	Rangers	Kilmarnock	*3–0 (after 1–1 draw)
1932–33	Celtic	Motherwell	1–0
1933–34	Rangers	St Mirren	5–0
1934–35	Rangers	Hamilton	2–1
1935–36	Rangers	Third Lanark	1–0
1936–37	Celtic	Aberdeen	2–1
1937–38	East Fife	Kilmarnock	*4–2 (after 1–1 draw)
1938–39	Clyde	Motherwell	4–0
1939–46	*No competition*		
1946–47	Aberdeen	Hibernian	2–1
1947–48	Rangers	Morton	*1–0 (after 1–1 draw)
1948–49	Rangers	Clyde	4–1
1949–50	Rangers	East Fife	3–0
1950–51	Celtic	Motherwell	1–0
1951–52	Motherwell	Dundee	4–0

Season	Winners	Runners-up	Result
1952–53	Rangers	Aberdeen	*1–0
			(after 1–1 draw)
1953–54	Celtic	Aberdeen	2–1
1954–55	Clyde	Celtic	*1–0
			(after 1–1 draw)
1955–56	Hearts	Celtic	3–1
1956–57	Falkirk	Kilmarnock	*2–1
			(after 1–1 draw)
1957–58	Clyde	Hibernian	1–0
1958–59	St Mirren	Aberdeen	3–1
1959–60	Rangers	Kilmarnock	2–0
1960–61	Dunfermline	Celtic	*2–0
			(after 0–0 draw)
1961–62	Rangers	St Mirren	2–0
1962–63	Rangers	Celtic	*3–0
			(after 1–1 draw)
1963–64	Rangers	Dundee	3–1
1964–65	Celtic	Dunfermline	3–2
1965–66	Rangers	Celtic	*1–0
			(after 0–0 draw)
1966–67	Celtic	Aberdeen	2–0
1967–68	Dunfermline	Hearts	3–1
1968–69	Celtic	Rangers	4–0
1969–70	Aberdeen	Celtic	3–1
1970–71	Celtic	Rangers	*2–1
			(after 1–1 draw)
1971–72	Celtic	Hibernian	6–1
1972–73	Rangers	Celtic	3–2
1973–74	Celtic	Dundee United	3–0

Summary of Scottish F.A. Cup Winners

Celtic	23	Falkirk	2	Dumbarton	1
Rangers	20	Hibernian	2	Dundee	1
Queen's Park	10	Kilmarnock	2	East Fife	1
Hearts	5	Renton	2	Morton	1
Clyde	3	Third Lanark	2	Motherwell	1
Vale of Leven	3	St Mirren	2	Partick	1
Aberdeen	2	Airdrieonians	1	St Bernard's	1
Dunfermline	2				

SCOTTISH LEAGUE CUP WINNERS

(* = Replay)

Season	Winners	Runners-up	Result
1945–46	Aberdeen	Rangers	3–2
1946–47	Rangers	Aberdeen	4–0
1947–48	East Fife	Falkirk	*4–1
			(after 1–1 draw)
1948–49	Rangers	Raith Rovers	2–0
1949–50	East Fife	Dunfermline	3–0
1950–51	Motherwell	Hibernian	3–0
1951–52	Dundee	Rangers	3–2
1952–53	Dundee	Kilmarnock	2–0
1953–54	East Fife	Partick Thistle	3–2
1954–55	Hearts	Motherwell	4–2
1955–56	Aberdeen	St Mirren	2–1
1956–57	Celtic	Partick Thistle	*3–0
			(after 0–0 draw)
1957–58	Celtic	Rangers	7–1
1958–59	Hearts	Partick Thistle	5–1
1959–60	Hearts	Third Lanark	2–1
1960–61	Rangers	Kilmarnock	2–0
1961–62	Rangers	Hearts	*3–1
			(after 1–1 draw)
1962–63	Hearts	Kilmarnock	1–0
1963–64	Rangers	Morton	5–0
1964–65	Rangers	Celtic	2–1
1965–66	Celtic	Rangers	2–1
1966–67	Celtic	Rangers	1–0
1967–68	Celtic	Dundee	5–3
1968–69	Celtic	Hibernian	6–2
1969–70	Celtic	St Johnstone	1–0
1970–71	Rangers	Celtic	1–0
1971–72	Partick Thistle	Celtic	4–1
1972–73	Hibernian	Celtic	2–1
1973–74	Dundee	Celtic	1–0

Summary of Scottish League Cup Winners

Celtic	7	Dundee	3	Hibernian	1
Rangers	7	East Fife	3	Motherwell	1
Hearts	4	Aberdeen	2	Partick	1

The Field of Play

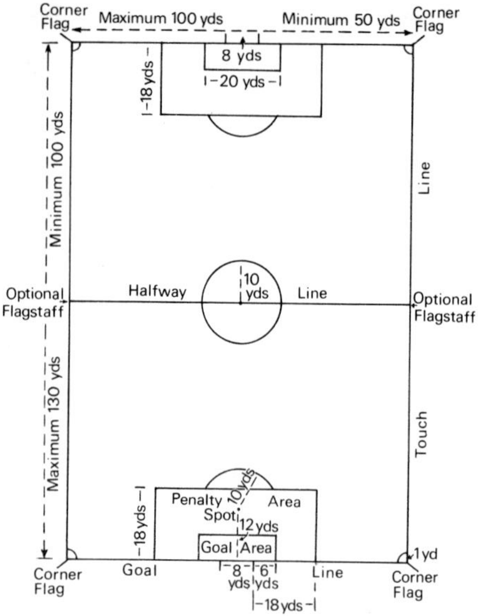

Diagram of a football field with the following labels:

- Corner Flag (at all four corners)
- Maximum 100 yds / Minimum 50 yds (goal line)
- 8 yds (goal)
- 18 yds, 20 yds (penalty area)
- Minimum 100 yds / Maximum 130 yds (touch line)
- Optional Flagstaff (both sides at halfway)
- Halfway Line
- 10 yds (centre circle)
- Touch Line
- Penalty Spot, Penalty Area, 10 yds
- 12 yds
- Goal Area, 8 yds, 6 yds
- 18 yds
- Goal Line
- 1 yd

The International Board has approved this table of measurements:

	metres		metres
130 yards	120	10 yards	9.15
120 yards	110	8 yards	7.32
110 yards	100	6 yards	5.50
100 yards	90	1 yard	1
80 yards	75	8 feet	2.44
70 yards	64	5 feet	1.50
50 yards	45	28 inches	0.71
18 yards	16.50	27 inches	0.68
12 yards	11	5 inches	0.12